Holy Land Mosaic

Holy Land Mosaic

Stories of Cooperation and Coexistence between Israelis and Palestinians

Daniel Gavron

ROWMAN & LITTLEFIELD PUBLISHERS, INC.
Lanham • Boulder • New York • Toronto • Plymouth, UK

ROWMAN & LITTLEFIELD PUBLISHERS, INC.

Published in the United States of America
by Rowman & Littlefield Publishers, Inc.
A wholly owned subsidary of The Rowman & Littlefield Publishing Group, Inc.
4501 Forbes Boulevard, Suite 200, Lanham, Maryland 20706
www.rowmanlittlefield.com

Estover Road
Plymouth PL6 7PY
United Kingdom

British Library Cataloguing in Publication Information Available

Library of Congress Cataloging-in-Publication Data
Gavron, Daniel.
  Stories of cooperation and coexistence between Israelis and Palestinians /
Daniel Gavron.
     p. cm.
  Includes bibliographical references and index.
  ISBN-13: 978-0-7425-4012-5 (cloth : alk. paper)
  ISBN-10: 0-7425-4012-X (cloth : alk. paper)
  ISBN-13: 978-0-7425-4013-2 (pbk. : alk. paper)
  ISBN-10: 0-7425-4013-8 (pbk. : alk. paper)
  1. Arab-Israeli conflict. 2. Arab-Israeli conflict—1993– —Peace. 3. Israel—
Ethnic relations. 4. Jews—Israel—Attitudes. 5. Palestinian Arabs—Attitudes.
I. Title.
DS113.6.G38 2008
956.9405'4--dc22
                                                                    2007033038

Printed in the United States of America

♾™ The paper used in this publication meets the minimum requirements of
American National Standard for Information Sciences—Permanence of Paper
for Printed Library Materials, ANSI/NISO Z39.48-1992.

I like to believe that people in the long run are going to do more to promote peace than our governments. Indeed, I think that people want peace so much that one of these days governments had better get out of the way and let them have it.

—Dwight D. Eisenhower

In the Israeli town of Ramle, a wall separates Jewish and Arab neighborhoods. On the Jewish side is a playground with swings, slides, and roundabouts. One day some Arab kindergarten children decided to burrow under the wall. They were soon joined by the children on the Jewish side, digging in the opposite direction. In due course, three tunnels were completed, and the five-year-old children crossed in both directions to play with each other. When the municipality discovered the tunnels, it blocked them up.

—reported in the Israeli media

Contents

Chronology   ix

Prologue   xv

1   Human Rights in the Shadow of Conflict   1

2   Courage to Listen   15

3   Refusing to Be Enemies   25

4   The Ultimate Symbol of Peace   35

5   Learning Together   47

6   Living Together   57

7   Island of Sanity   73

8   An Encounter That Spans the Centuries   87

9   Building Blocks of Equality   105

10   Creativity and Recreation   119

11   Donkey Garden of Eden   133

12   Academy for the Environment   139

13   Thinking Together   149

14   Joint Media Initiatives   157

15   The Veterans in the Field   165

16   Religious Faith: Problem or Solution?   177

17   First among Equals   187

Epilogue   195

Selected List of Organizations   199

Selected Bibliography   201

Index   203

Chronology

1000 BCE (approx.): An Israelite entity forms in the hills of Canaan. King David conquers Jerusalem; Solomon builds First Temple.

586: Temple destroyed by Babylonians; some Israelites exiled.

538: Israelites (Jews) return to Judaea; construction of Second Temple begins.

70 CE: Second Temple destroyed by Romans; most Jews exiled; start of Diaspora.

630: Muhammad conquers Mecca and establishes religion of Islam.

640: Muslims complete conquest of Middle East, including Jerusalem. Jews and Christians, tolerated as the "People of the Book," achieve positions of influence.

661: Ali, fourth Muslim caliph, assassinated; Islam splits into Shia and Sunni sects.

756: Muslims conquer most of Spain; Cordoba center of fruitful Muslim-Jewish-Christian coexistence, which Jews remember as the Golden Age.

1099: Crusaders conquer Jerusalem, indiscriminately massacring its Muslim, Jewish, and Christian inhabitants.

1187: Muslims under Saladin retake Jerusalem with minimal bloodshed.

1204: Death of Maimonides, greatest Jewish postbiblical philosopher.

1260: Muslim Mamluks turn back Mongol invasion of Middle East.

1453: Turks capture Constantinople; start of Ottoman Empire.

1492: Jews expelled from Spain; find new homes in Europe and Ottoman Empire.

1516: Palestine becomes province of Ottoman Empire; significant Jewish settlement.

1868: Ottoman land ordinances change, enabling foreigners to buy land in Palestine. European and American churches build extensively.

1881: Wide-scale pogroms (semiofficial violence) against Jews of Russia.

1882: Start of organized Jewish immigration to Palestine.

1896: Theodor Herzl publishes *The Jewish State*.

1897: First Zionist Congress establishes Zionist Organization.

1903: Zionist Congress confirms that Jewish state must be in Palestine.

1910: Tel Aviv, first modern Jewish town, founded; establishment of first kibbutz.

1914: Outbreak of World War I.

1915: Britain promises Hussein, the sharif of Mecca, "independence for the Arabs."

1917: British army invades Palestine and conquers Jerusalem. Balfour Declaration issued, promising the Jews a "national home" in Palestine.

1920: First serious attacks on Jews by Arabs of Palestine. The Jews establish the Haganah, the forerunner of the Israel Defense Forces (IDF).

1921: Britain awarded League of Nations Mandate for Palestine.

1929: Wide-scale Arab attacks on Jewish settlements in Palestine.

1933: Adolph Hitler becomes German chancellor; first concentration camps established; surge in Jewish immigration to Palestine.

1936: Arab General Strike leads to major rebellion against the British administration and the Zionist enterprise.

1937: British Peel Commission recommends partition of Palestine. Semiofficial and unofficial talks take place between Jewish and Palestinian Arab representatives.

1939: Outbreak of World War II.

1942: Wannsee Conference on "Final Solution" of Jewish problem. Rumors of mass murder of Jews start to leak out of Europe.

1945: End of war; horrific dimension of Holocaust becomes generally known.

1947: United Nations votes to partition Palestine into two states: Jewish and Arab. Clashes between Jews and Arabs escalate in Palestine.

1948: British Mandate ends; State of Israel declared; neighboring Arab states dispatch armies to assist Palestinian militias. Some seven hundred thousand Palestinian Arabs flee or are expelled and become refugees in West Bank, Gaza, Syria, and Lebanon.

1949: Armistice agreements between Israel and Arab states. Transjordan takes over West Bank and changes name to Jordan. Egypt administers Gaza Strip. Palestinian state as envisaged by the UN is stillborn. Some 120,000 Arabs remain in Israel as citizens under military administration.

1956: Palestinian armed infiltrations and Israeli counterattacks escalate into the Sinai Campaign. Israel captures Gaza and Sinai, but is forced to withdraw its forces.

1959: Fatah military force established in Kuwait.

1964: Palestine Liberation Organization (PLO) established by Egypt.

1965: Military administration for Israeli Arabs abolished.

1967: Six Day War: Israel captures West Bank, Gaza, Sinai, and Golan. Establishes military rule and initiates Jewish settlement in these territories. Fatah takes over the PLO, which attempts resistance operations in Israel, West Bank, and Gaza. PLO withdraws across the Jordan and organizes international campaign of hijackings and attacks on Jewish targets.

1970: "Black September": PLO expelled from Jordan, sets up bases in south Lebanon.

1973: Yom Kippur War: Israel repels attacks by Egypt and Syria.

1974: Arab summit recognizes PLO as representing Palestinians; PLO leader Yasser Arafat addresses UN General Assembly; Gush Emunim Jewish settlement movement founded, extends Jewish settlements in West Bank and Gaza.

1977: Right-wing Likud government elected in Israel. Egyptian President Sadat visits Jerusalem; PLO refuses to join his initiative.

1979: Egypt-Israel Peace Treaty signed. Jewish settlement stepped up in West Bank and Gaza. Israeli and Palestinian personalities pursue various channels of communication.

1982: Israel completes withdrawal from Sinai, but continues to occupy West Bank, Gaza, and Golan. IDF invades Lebanon to strike at PLO and reaches Beirut.

1985: Israel pulls back from most of Lebanon, retaining "security zone" in south. Fundamentalist Hezbollah movement becomes dominant among Lebanese Shiites.

1987: Palestinians in West Bank and Gaza launch uprising against Israeli rule, the Intifada. Clashes continue, as IDF is only partially successful in controlling situation. Despite this, contacts between Israeli peace groups and Palestinians intensify.

1991: The Gulf War: U.S.-led coalition expels Iraq from Kuwait, which deports some four hundred thousand Palestinians from its territory. Israel imposes closure, preventing Palestinians from entering Israel to work. The expulsion from Kuwait and the Israeli closure deprive Palestinians of half of their GDP. U.S. convenes Madrid peace conference with Israel, Syria, and a "Jordanian-Palestinian" delegation, which unofficially coordinates with the PLO.

1992: Israeli Labor party wins election; Yitzhak Rabin becomes prime minister; unofficial channel opened between Israel and the PLO.

1993: Israel and PLO sign Oslo Agreement, recognizing each other.

1994: Israel-Jordan Peace Treaty signed; Israel withdraws from Gaza and Jericho. Palestinian Authority is established with Arafat as chairman, resident in Gaza. Numerous NGOs are active in heyday of Israeli-Palestinian grassroots contacts.

1995: Israel hands over major Palestinian towns, except Hebron, to the Palestinian Authority; Palestinian dissidents launch wave of terror; Prime Minister Rabin assassinated.

1996: Benjamin Netanyahu of the right-wing Likud becomes Israeli prime minister. Israel withdraws from Hebron, but steps up settlement in other parts of West Bank.

1999: Labor's Ehud Barak wins election. Pledging to continue Rabin's path, he pulls IDF out of Lebanon and starts talks with Syria and Palestinians. Negotiations are unsuccessful.

2000: Israeli-Palestinian talks at Camp David collapse; second Intifada erupts; IDF responds harshly. Both sides fail to control escalating violence. Many Israeli-Palestinian coexistence and cooperation ventures are disrupted.

2001: Ariel Sharon wins election, forms "unity government" with Labor party, and escalates response to Palestinian violence. Unprecedented casualties on both sides as Palestinians carry out suicide bombings and Israel retaliates.

2002: In Operation Defensive Shield, Israel reoccupies most of West Bank, sets up roadblocks that effectively divide Palestinian territory. Arafat is besieged in his Ramallah government offices. Palestinian Authority is virtually abolished. Extreme poverty is rife in Palestinian territories and economic hardship is felt in Israel. Saudi Arabian initiative, offering Israel recognition and normal relations in return for withdrawal to 1967 borders, is adopted by Arab League. In the chaos prevailing at the time, this dramatic development is virtually unnoticed in Israel.

2003: U.S. and Britain launch second Gulf War, gaining an initial swift victory. Sharon is reelected as head of right-wing government; Mahmoud Abbas elected prime minister of Palestinian Authority under President

Arafat. President Bush convenes summit with Sharon and Abbas. Sharon pledges to dismantle "illegal settlements"; Abbas declares "end to armed Intifada," but the violence continues.

2004: Yasser Arafat dies. He is replaced as president by Mahmoud Abbas.

2005: Israel unilaterally disengages from Gaza, dismantles settlements, and pulls back IDF, but retains control of all crossing points. Palestinians fire short-range rockets into Israeli territory, causing damage and some casualties. Israeli incursions fail to stop rockets. Prime Minister Sharon splits from his Likud party over disengagement, forming a new party, Kadima. After initial U.S. victory in Iraq, violence escalates causing thousands of casualties, including American troops. President Bush loses popularity as support for war slumps. U.S. is too busy with Iraq to attend to Israeli-Palestinian matters.

2006: Israeli Prime Minister Sharon suffers massive stroke and goes into coma. Islamist Hamas movement, which does not recognize Israel, wins Palestinian election. Israel and international community boycott Hamas government. Palestinian rocket fire from Gaza intensifies. Ehud Olmert of Kadima wins Israeli election and becomes prime minister, forming coalition with Labor Party. Following the kidnapping of two IDF soldiers and the killing of eight by Lebanese Hezbollah militia, Israel launches air strikes on Lebanon followed by ground forces invasion. Northern Israel bombarded by Hezbollah rockets. The monthlong war, ended by a cease-fire, is perceived as failure in Israel; a government committee of inquiry is established. Olmert, Labor Defense Minister Amir Peretz, and the IDF Chief of Staff come under intense criticism.

2007: Israeli Chief of Staff and Defense Minister resign. PLO and Hamas form Palestinian unity government. Olmert and Abbas continue to hold meetings, and grassroots Israeli-Palestinian contacts continue. Saudi Arabia revives its 2002 initiative. Israeli leaders acknowledge that this initiative has "positive elements." Hamas takes over Gaza strip. Rockets into Israeli territory continue. PLO forms new government in West Bank. President Bush convenes Israeli-Palestinian-Arab summit in U.S.

Prologue

The last seven years have been enormously frustrating for those who believed in the possibility of peace between Israelis and Palestinians. Since the Oslo process of the 1990s blew apart in the fall of 2000 with a particularly savage outburst of violence, the deadlock between the sides appears to be unbreakable. The basic lack of trust between the two peoples has reached new levels. It is almost impossible to find anyone who is optimistic about the situation.

Even the Arab League initiative, which offers Israel peace and recognition in return for withdrawal from the West Bank and Gaza and which would seem to represent the ultimate success for the Zionist enterprise, has not elicited the sort of excitement that might have been expected. It has been met with apathy on both sides. While there is an international consensus in favor of the two-state solution—Israel and Palestine existing peacefully side by side—and this also has the support of a large majority of Israelis and Palestinians, progress toward its implementation is virtually nonexistent.

The devil is in the details, which admittedly are enormously complex. Security coordination, the Israeli settlements in the West Bank, the location of the border between the two states, the connection between the West Bank and Gaza, the Palestinian refugees, economic relations including a possible customs union, environmental matters (notably water and sewerage), and the multiple disputes concerning Jerusalem are only some of the major problems that have to be solved. Because of these fundamental questions, some people, myself included, have been thinking aloud about an alternative resolution of the dispute in the form of one multicultural state for Jews, Arabs, and others living between the Mediterranean and the river Jordan. In the current political climate, however, such a revolutionary concept appears somewhat utopian.

Meanwhile, the daily reality is grim: although the Israeli occupation of Gaza has been formally terminated, Israel remains in effective control of that territory; the occupation of the West Bank continues; and the separation barrier is nearing completion. At best, Israelis and Palestinians want to separate from each other. In a worst-case scenario, low-level armed confrontation is liable to persist intermittently for the foreseeable future.

Yet, despite this deplorable state of affairs, there are continuous contacts between Israelis and Palestinians on a wide range of topics in dozens of frameworks: official, semiofficial, and unofficial. Hundreds of Israelis and Palestinians continue to talk to each other, to create together, and to cooperate. Although the violence is extensively reported in the media, the ongoing dialogue and cooperation is less often mentioned.

While it is true that Jews and Arabs have been locked in an existential confrontation in the Holy Land for more than a hundred years, there have always been periods of peace and coexistence between the two peoples. The centuries-long encounter between Jews and Arabs, recounted in chapter 8 of this book, demonstrates that the narrative is not exclusively one of enmity and violence, even in modern times. Yet it must be admitted that the current situation is the result of the armed clashes between the two peoples.

Jews have lived in Palestine since the time of the Bible, and, in the two thousand years since their dispersion by the Romans, there was never a time without some Jewish immigration to the land. In Ottoman-ruled Palestine, Arab Muslims and Christians coexisted amicably with their Jewish neighbors. However, the migration that started at the end of the nineteenth century was of a different scale and character. Inspired by Zionism, the revival of Jewish nationhood, it resulted in the establishment of the State of Israel in 1948.

Zionism preceded the emergence of an Arab national movement, but only by a few years. Thus, a collision between the two movements was inevitable. Although there were some clashes between Arabs and Jewish immigrants in Ottoman Palestine, it was only after Britain was granted the Palestine Mandate by the League of Nations in 1921 that the conflict between Zionism and Arab nationalism fully manifested itself. During World War I, the British had made contradictory promises to the Jews and the Arabs, and they spent the next thirty years trying to balance the claims of the two sides.

In 1937, the British concluded that the only solution was to partition Palestine into two separate states. The plan was revived in a slightly different form by the United Nations in 1947. By then the holocaust of Europe's Jews in World War II had transformed the Jewish wish for sovereignty into an existential need. Consequently, they eagerly accepted the plan. For their part, the Arabs rejected partition, continued to demand independence, and insisted that they should not be made to pay the price for the crimes of others.

In 1948, the Jews declared statehood in their part of Palestine, but the local Arabs fought to prevent the establishment of Israel. They were joined in their battle by the armies of the neighboring Arab states, but the Jewish forces prevailed. In 1949, armistice agreements were signed between Israel, Egypt, Transjordan, Syria, and Lebanon, leaving the Jews in control of a larger area than that envisioned under the UN partition plan. After the agreements, Israel controlled 78 percent of the territory of Mandatory Palestine; the other 22 percent was taken over by Egypt and Transjordan, which changed its name to Jordan. The Palestinian state was stillborn. Some seven hundred thousand Arab refugees fled or were expelled from the territory of Israel.

For the next nineteen years, there was intermittent violence with cross-border raids by Palestinians and Israeli retaliations. These actions culminated in the Sinai Campaign of 1956, when the Israel Defense Forces (IDF) conquered Gaza and Sinai from Egypt, but were subsequently forced to withdraw to the armistice lines. A decade later, in the Six Day War of 1967, Israel recaptured Gaza and Sinai from the Egyptians, occupied Syria's Golan Heights, and took the West Bank from Jordan.

Sinai was returned to Egypt after a remarkable psychological breakthrough by Egyptian president Anwar Sadat, who came to Israel and addressed its parliament. Under the terms of the subsequent peace treaty, Sinai was returned to Egypt in 1982. The Golan was formally annexed by Israel that same year, but the area is still claimed by Syria. In the Palestinian territories of the West Bank and Gaza, the situation remained unresolved. Jewish settlement there started slowly, but gained momentum. In some cases, outposts were established by the government of Israel, but many of the settlements were initiated by religious zealots based on their belief that the entire land of the Bible belonged to the Jewish people. Most of these settlements eventually won official recognition. Although a right-wing Israeli government was elected in 1977, and it promoted extensive Jewish settlement in the occupied territories, it nevertheless forbore to annex Gaza and the West Bank.

In 1987, the Intifada, a Palestinian civil uprising, erupted. Starting out as a grassroots movement, it was subsequently taken over by the Palestine Liberation Organization (PLO), a military and political movement initially organized by Egypt, which had been carrying out armed actions against Israel since 1967. As a result of the Intifada, Israel and the PLO initiated contacts and in 1993 signed the Oslo Accords, agreeing to recognize each other and work toward a solution. The IDF was withdrawn from the major population centers in Gaza and the West Bank and the Palestinian Authority (PA) was established there.

During the 1990s, negotiations proceeded between Israel and the PA, and there was an upsurge in unofficial contacts between Israelis and Palestinians. An economic protocol was negotiated in Paris; the atmosphere improved; the casualty toll declined. Subsequently, both sides have bitterly criticized the Oslo Agreement. The Israelis maintain that the Palestinians continued with terror operations; the Palestinians contend that Jewish settlement in the West Bank and Gaza was stepped up. The Palestinians insist that the Israelis had no intention of returning enough territory for a viable state; the Israelis counter that the Palestinians have never been willing to live in peace with their Jewish neighbors.

Both sides make valid points: Oslo was an imperfect agreement, but it was working and it created both hope and relative tranquility. If it had continued, it would have led to a solution of the problem and the establishment of a Palestinian state alongside Israel. Sadly, the Oslo process collapsed following an abortive Israeli-Palestinian summit at Camp David in the summer of 2000. The subsequent violence resulted in thousands of deaths and injuries on both sides and led to a feeling that there was nobody to talk to and nothing to talk about.

This approach led to Israel's so-called disengagement from Gaza, a unilateral withdrawal of both Jewish settlements and the IDF implemented without consultation with the Palestinians. It was a sudden, impulsive, illogical move, carried out with manifest brutality, which left everyone the loser. The settlers lost, but the Palestinians did not gain. Israel continued to control the Gaza border, which was fenced off from Israeli territory, effectively making the densely populated region into a gigantic prison. For their part, the Palestinians started firing missiles over the fence at Israeli targets. It was not long before the IDF retaliated with raids into Gaza.

Whereas the Oslo Agreement was flawed, the Gaza disengagement was an unmitigated disaster. An examination of Oslo and Gaza inevitably leads to the conclusion that the unilateral approach is without merit, and that there is no alternative to negotiation.

In my view, the following pages prove that Israelis and Palestinians are capable of talking to each other, that there is plenty to talk about, and that they can even reach agreements—or at least agree to disagree. The Israelis and Palestinians who work together in scores of NGOs, movements, organizations, and projects, do not always see eye to eye about political matters. What they have in common is their refusal to be enemies, their determination to find ways of living together, their dedication to dialogue and mutual respect. In other ways, they make up a mosaic of different beliefs, cultures, opinions, and ethnic groups.

In pursuing their story, I have journeyed from the hills of Galilee to the valleys of the Negev desert and from the olive orchards of Samaria to the caves of the Hebron hills. Tulkarm and Tel Aviv, Bethlehem and Haifa, Jerusalem and Jaffa are only some of the places that I visited. This account is a personal one and makes no claim to being comprehensive. Rather I hope to share with the reader my experiences and feelings during my quest for this lesser-known story of the peaceful encounters between Israelis and Palestinians.

1

Human Rights in the Shadow of Conflict

On a recent spring evening, Muhammad Tanji, a twenty-six-year-old Palestinian school counselor, was arrested by Israeli security forces. Tanji, known to his friends as Aziz, was at the end of a long and annoying day spent trying to register for postgraduate studies at al-Kuds University in the eastern part of Jerusalem.

Aziz lives in the Tulkarm refugee camp in the northern West Bank, a neighborhood of makeshift homes where some twenty thousand people live crammed into less than two hundred acres. On the day of his arrest, he left home at 7:30 a.m., traveling by bus to Ramallah and from there by minibus to Abu Dis just outside Jerusalem. On the way, he and his companions were held up at numerous roadblocks by Israeli soldiers, causing him to arrive at his college just before midday. The 110-kilometer journey should have taken some ninety minutes, but the roadblocks and security checks tripled the time of the trip.

Aziz was accustomed to this. It had become routine for Palestinians in the West Bank in recent years, but it was not only the Israelis who caused him aggravation. At his Palestinian university, he was shuttled from the registration clerk to the dean of students to the head of the Science Department and later to the grants officer in the Office of Student Affairs. Aziz found himself in a typical catch-22 situation: he could not register at al-Kuds until he had his study grant, and he could not obtain his grant until he had registered. An appeal to the grants officer at Student Affairs failed to solve his problem.

All this became irrelevant, however, when the Israeli military authorities closed off the Abu Dis area. With soldiers in the streets, troop carriers roaring by, and helicopters clattering around in the skies, Aziz resolved to make for home. The first part of his trip back was "normal." He tried a number of different taxis and minibuses, he was held up at several roadblocks, and he sought alternative ways to reach his destination. At the next roadblock, however, according to his account, the soldiers took his ID card, threw him to the ground, and searched him several times. His briefcase was confiscated and he was handcuffed, blindfolded, and driven to an army camp. There he was set on and beaten by a number of soldiers. Some of the soldiers spoke Hebrew to him, calling him "Azizi" and pretending that they knew him. They told him he had long been a "target" and was "lucky to be alive." They also cursed him as a "son of a whore," adding that he would be "screwed up his ass." Later, a soldier told him he had been on a wanted list for over a year. As his ID had been examined countless times during the past year, and as he had even traveled abroad, Aziz doubted this.

He was then driven from the army camp to a military prison, where he was examined by a doctor who asked him whether he was suffering from any sickness. He told the doctor that he had an ulcer and inflammation of the urinary tract. He was subsequently questioned for some ninety minutes and asked about his contacts with one "Nidal." He admitted to having met Nidal and other members of his family in connection with plans to establish a cheese-making business in the Tulkarm area, which he hoped would give employment to Palestinian villagers. He further admitted that Nidal had warned him not to act against the Islamic Jihad.

The Israeli interrogator informed Aziz that he was in possession of secret documents that proved Nidal had asked him to "do something." Aziz replied that the only thing Nidal had asked him to do was to take some goat cheese to a local official in Italy, where he was due on a fund-raising mission.

The following day, Aziz was questioned by another interrogator, who advised him to admit that he was a member of the Islamic Jihad and that Nidal had ordered him to carry out military operations on behalf of that movement. The interrogator demanded to know why Aziz had traveled to Jerusalem, saying it was obvious that the reasons were "military." When he denied this, he was told he would be examined with a lie detector. Connected to the machine, Aziz was asked whether he possessed a weapon, whether he had ever used the weapon against Israelis, whether he had come to Jerusalem to carry out a military operation for Nidal, and what Nidal had ordered him to do.

After four hours of questioning, he was informed that he had failed the lie detector test with regard to two questions: his relationship with Nidal and his intention to carry out a military operation in Jerusalem. He was subsequently questioned by several other interrogators, including two women, who made fun of him and told him that he "stank." He was also warned that he would be interrogated until he confessed. During all the interrogations, he was handcuffed and shackled to a chair. His legs were bleeding from the shackles. Altogether, he was questioned for fourteen hours with short breaks.

At various stages during his interrogations, Aziz says that he was threatened several times that he would be exposed as a "phony peace activist" who was really a terrorist. In fact, Aziz was a genuine peace activist. A former student militant, arrested and imprisoned twice during the Intifada of 1987–1991, he had for the past three years been the Tulkarm coordinator of Windows—Channels for Communication, an Israeli-Palestinian non-profit association, striving for dialogue and conciliation between the two peoples. He was coeditor of *Windows*, the association's Hebrew-Arabic journal, written by junior high school students from Israel, Gaza, and the West Bank. When Aziz failed to return, his family turned to Windows for assistance, and his friends in Windows passed on the case to the Moked [Focus] for the Defense of the Individual, an Israeli human rights organization that specializes in assisting individual Palestinians.

There is often an overlap of membership between the various Israeli-Palestinian groups. Thus Yatom Ben-Hillel, the Moked's website supervisor, is also a Windows volunteer. When he heard about Aziz, he immediately spoke to Orly Barmak, the Moked's coordinator for missing persons, about locating him.

Orly swiftly went to work, using her contacts in the Israeli police and military. The Moked has these contacts because of the ambivalent relationship it has achieved with the various Israeli military and security authorities controlling life in the Palestinian territories: part adversarial, part cooperative. Starting out on the cooperative route, Orly's first phone call was to the IDF Control Unit, which supplies information on all categories of prisoners: those being held by the army, the police, or the Shin Bet internal security service. The unit had no information about Aziz, so she phoned each of the five Temporary Detention Centers (TCDs) in the West Bank. The Moked has learned from experience that most people detained in the territories are initially held at a TDC, but on this occasion, none of the calls turned up any information about Aziz. Even a special call to the office of the army's coordinator for the territories, often an effective follow-up procedure, failed to achieve results.

After two days of fruitless activity, a call came through to the Moked's emergency hotline, which operates twelve hours per day in the Jerusalem office to receive distress calls from Palestinians in trouble. The call gave the information that Aziz was being questioned by the Shin Bet security service. Although the IDF was not prepared to say where he was being held, this news at least indicated that Aziz was alive, which afforded his family and friends considerable relief. At the same time, interrogation by the security service was usually bad news for a Palestinian. Orly again contacted the office of the coordinator for the territories, the civilian administration which operates under IDF auspices. The official there confirmed that Aziz was with the Shin Bet, but he also could not disclose his whereabouts.

Used to searching for alternative channels, Orly placed a direct call to the Shatta jail, where the Prisons' Service has its main computer. There she learned that Aziz was being questioned in the Shin Bet facility at the Kishon jail in Haifa. He had apparently been sent straight there from the IDF's Nablus headquarters. This indicated to the experienced staff of the Moked what Aziz himself had already been told: he was on the wanted list of the security services.

The Moked's role was over. Once they knew where he was, Aziz's family hired an Israeli Arab attorney, who immediately got to work on the case. The attorney's first move was to enlist the Public Committee against Torture in Israel, which applied to the Supreme Court asking for an order to prevent further mistreatment. The court turned down the appeal, but after a month of imprisonment, during which he was interrogated every day, Aziz was brought before a military court judge who ruled that the classified evidence placed before him by the Shin Bet was inadequate. He ordered Aziz to be released on bail. The bail was paid by an Israeli Jewish friend.

Why was Aziz arrested, and what did the security services really have on him? Aziz thinks that the Israeli security services collaborate unofficially with the Islamic Jihad, the most extreme Palestinian group in the West Bank. It is in the Israeli interest, he argues, to foster Palestinian extremism, which gives the Israeli authorities an excuse to tighten their control of the Palestinians. They wanted to harass him because, as a popular peace activist, he is the main enemy of the Jihad in the Tulkarm area. "The Jihad is harmful to the Palestinians," he states forthrightly, "that is why the Israelis covertly support it. Tulkarm is the poorest town in the West Bank, which is why the Jihad is so strong here, but I am against them and the people support me."

There is no doubt that Aziz is a popular figure in the Tulkarm area. A rangy young man with penetrating gray eyes and a thin face framed by a short beard and mustache, he speaks in sharp bursts and punctuates his talk with jokes and anecdotes. He smiles frequently. A stroll with him around the town and the crowded refugee camp shows his close links with all sectors of the population. Every two paces, he is hailed by friends who embrace him and ask him how he is. In the market, he is approached both by people whom he has assisted and by others who would like his help.

Aziz is currently the local coordinator of Kufia, an Italian NGO that extends modest economic assistance to Palestinians. A stall run by a disabled young man sells cheap Chinese-manufactured shoes. Aziz arranged the Kufia grant that enabled the man to start the modest business, which today supports his family. Another youngster, also bankrolled by Kufia, is selling fruit from a rough wooden platform.

On our walk, Aziz draws my attention to a constant humming noise. It is made by an Israeli drone (pilotless spy plane), he informs me. Tulkarm is in Area A, which was classified under the Oslo Agreement of 1993 as being under full Palestinian control. The IDF returned to Tulkarm and the other cities in 2002 during the second Intifada, but following some months of comparative calm, the town has been handed back to the Palestinian Authority. Despite the army's withdrawal, suggests Aziz, the ever-present drone sends out a powerful message to the local citizens. A few months back, when the Israeli military was still in control, the noise of a drone was often followed by an attack from an Apache helicopter gunship. The plane identified a wanted Palestinian and the Apache attack followed. Now it is just for general surveillance. It tells Palestinians that the Israelis are watching them and that they can return any time.

After listening to a long plea for help from a plump woman in traditional *galabia* robe and kaffiyeh headscarf, we head for lunch at the home of Aziz's brother in the refugee camp. As opposed to the natives of the town of Tulkarm, the inhabitants of the refugee camp used to live in what is now Israel. Aziz's family lived in Tantura by the sea, some twenty miles south of Haifa, and Aziz has researched his ancestral village. He claims there was a massacre there in 1948, a claim vigorously disputed by surviving members of the relevant Israeli military unit who served in that war. His thesis was not accepted by Sweden's Göttingen University, where he studied for a master's degree. He proudly proclaims that he refused to agree to alternative compromise formulations of his work, insisting that the objections were "politically inspired."

Aziz works voluntarily for both Kufia and Windows. He makes his living as a counselor in several schools, employed by the Education Department of the Palestinian Authority. He finds the children traumatized by the violence, by the tanks in the streets, by the helicopters overhead, by the impotence of their parents whenever Israeli soldiers appear.

He allows that he himself needs psychological assistance following his recent ordeal, but there is nobody to treat him because all the potential counselors are themselves in need of help. He tells of a summer camp that he organized for Windows two years ago when Israeli soldiers shot the father of one of the participants. His bitterness does not prevent him from continuing to devote time and energy to Kufia and Windows. "Despite everything, we *can* help our people," he affirms.

He says that his Israeli Jewish friend Amir Sidi, who paid for his bail, "has helped me more than anyone else." He is aware that Windows did not abandon him in his ordeal, campaigning relentlessly—and eventually successfully—for his release. He recognizes the fact that when he disappeared, an Israeli organization, the Moked, located him, meaning that his family could hire an attorney to work on his case. Without the Moked, he might have remained in prison much longer.

Aziz was one of nearly five thousand prisoners found by the Moked in a given year, but locating missing persons is only part of its work. Altogether, it assists some nine thousand individual Palestinians annually, dealing with violence, damage to property, confiscation of personal belongings, home demolitions, unification of families, treatment for the sick and injured, prisoners' rights, freedom of movement, and a host of other matters.

The Moked developed from an initiative of Jerusalem city councilor Lotte Salzberger. The late Dr. Salzberger, a Holocaust survivor and sociology lecturer, was a dedicated campaigner for civil rights. In 1988, acting on behalf of Sovlanut [Tolerance], an advocacy group promoting political moderation and democracy, she asked Yossi Schwartz, a student activist whom she knew personally, to come up with a plan for improving the status of East Jerusalem Arabs to equalize their conditions with those of the Jews of West Jerusalem.

Schwartz, tall, pale, with steel-rimmed glasses and long black hair parted in the middle, was raised in a religious family with a strong nationalist bent. He grew up accepting his family's principles, but after military service in Lebanon, he changed his views and started participating in demonstrations against the continued occupation of the West Bank and Gaza.

Following Salzberger's approach, Schwartz went to work, but the outbreak of the first Intifada convinced him that her proposed project was now inadequate. It was the early days of the uprising and in response to the violent Palestinian demonstrations, Yitzhak Rabin, at that time defense minister, had made his infamous remark about "breaking their bones." Instinctively, Schwartz felt that something more radical was required. He visited the student dormitories, recruiting Jewish and Arab volunteers for his new project.

The Moked for the Defense of Victims of Violence from the Police and the IDF started with a hundred or so volunteers, operating out of a room in the American Colony Hotel on the seam between Jewish and Arab Jerusalem. Over the years, the American Colony has become more than a hotel. As one of the few places where Jews and Arabs meet on equal terms, it is an institution that symbolizes dialogue and conciliation between the communities of the Holy City. It was an appropriate location for launching the new movement.

In a matter of months, the Moked became an independent nonprofit association with Schwartz as its director. The New Israel Fund, an American organization that raises money for civil rights and social causes in Israel, gave the Moked its initial push, providing financial support and teaching Schwartz the basic facts about administration. "I didn't know anything about non-governmental organizations, NGOs," confesses Schwartz. "It was the New Israel Fund that taught me how to set up an association, with a structure, a work-plan, and a budget. The fund still grants us twenty thousand dollars a year, although today the Moked's annual budget has grown to some $2 million."

As the Intifada developed, the three major human rights groups operating in Israel discovered their appropriate roles. The veteran Association for Civil Rights in Israel (ACRI) was occupied with the overall situation. It initiated litigation, offered counseling, and worked in the fields of education and public opinion. Betzelem, founded around the same time as the Moked, took responsibility for documenting human rights abuses in the occupied territories, issuing reports, and maintaining contact with the media. The Moked, which changed its name to Moked for the Defense of the Individual, focused on the individual Palestinians, assisting them day by day with everything from offenses against their persons and property to violation of their elementary rights.

Finding the hotel inadequate, the Moked moved into a storefront office in East Jerusalem, opening fifteen hundred files in its first two years. The complaints ranged from police and army violence to damage to and theft of property, and from the confiscation of ID cards to random arrests. Early on, it became clear that one of the most important tasks was locating hundreds of Palestinians detained by Israeli troops and police. To handle the legal aspects, the association hired a professional attorney.

A big problem for Palestinians was the random seizure of their identity cards by police and soldiers. Walking around without identity papers often prevented them from performing routine tasks and made them liable to arrest. The Moked, acting together with ACRI, petitioned the High Court of Justice about the seizure of ID cards, and as a result, the security forces issued new regulations that reduced the number of confiscations.

A more serious issue was the violence, which had led to the Moked's establishment in the first place. Several cases of random violence against individual Palestinians were pursued by the Moked, and initially it seemed possible to convince the IDF and the Israel Police to proceed against offending soldiers and police officers. However, as time went by it became clear that the police were reluctant to take action, and the IDF was even less responsive.

Despite this, within two years the association had established reasonably correct relations with both the IDF and the Border Police. Several useful meetings were held with senior officers, and the Moked was granted access to the IDF central computer, which facilitated locating arrested Palestinians. This ambivalent relationship has continued over the years.

"We have had serious confrontations with the IDF," recalls Schwartz, "but we never gave up. We went to the courts, and then to the High Court of Justice, which made them take us seriously. We don't collaborate with them, but they know that we play by the rules. I think they respect us. A couple of years ago the IDF established its own unit, called 'Moked-109,' for dealing with 'humanitarian problems,' and they came to us for advice on how to operate it."

Less spectacular than violence or other blatant offenses were the daily irritations and humiliations suffered by ordinary Palestinians. One problem was the difficulty of traveling abroad. It was hard enough to secure permission to leave Israeli-controlled territory—and even more difficult to return—but even when permits were issued, their holders were delayed at the borders. Soldiers stationed at locations such as the Allenby Bridge across the river Jordan often refused travelers permission to cross without offering any explanation. The Moked staff and volunteers followed up such cases, often persisting in their efforts for several months.

In the field of family reunions, the Moked, while experiencing many failures, also chalked up successes. As a result of an application to the High Court of Justice, some 350 Palestinians who had not managed to secure official residency permits were allowed to carry on living with their families in the West Bank and Gaza. Husbands, wives, and children were granted renewable permits. It was a small victory, but it still left thousands of Palestinians who do not have such permits liable to arrest and expulsion at any time.

The Moked, which started out with unpaid volunteers, has been transformed into a smooth professional operation with a paid staff of thirty-five, including attorneys, officers, coordinators, computer experts, and hotline phone operators. The days when a group of enthusiastic do-gooders would spend hours searching through the dusty piles of documents in its untidy office in East Jerusalem and still not find the relevant file are long gone. Everything is computerized; everything is in order. The original volunteer effort with its naive enthusiasm has been replaced by a competent organization that gets results.

Presiding over this transformation, Dalia Kerstein, the chain-smoking, purposeful director, has succeeded in making the Moked more effective in assisting Palestinians in trouble with the Israeli military authorities. At the same time she stresses that its success is limited. Her first message to new employees is always be prepared for disappointment, get ready for frustration, anticipate failure. Even today, she points out, with so much experience and so many resources, the Moked fails more often than not.

Kerstein started working in the field comparatively late in life. In fact, she admits, she "discovered" human rights in the United States. As a student in Israel in the 1970s, she was totally self-absorbed. It was only after she went to live in America that she became aware of civil rights issues.

"I was waiting in the immigration office for a meeting about my residency permit," she recalls, "and these three enormous white men in suits and crew cuts came in, bringing with them three small black teenagers, who were handcuffed and manacled. They were also manifestly terrified. Nothing bad happened, but I sensed an atmosphere of fear and suppressed violence."

A friend who was involved in civil rights later told Dalia that the teenagers were almost certainly refugees from Haiti, and she started to take an interest. Before long, she found herself very involved in the American civil rights movement. When she returned to live in Israel in the late 1980s, she realized that the most pressing human rights agenda was that of the Palestinians. When the first Intifada erupted in 1987, she joined a women's group acting for political prisoners and started visiting Palestinian families in the West Bank.

"It was a new world for me," she recalls. "I heard about wrongful arrests, interrogations, torture. It was a complete eye-opener."

She joined the Moked in 1991 as codirector with Ala Khatib, an Israeli Arab biologist. When Ala returned to his village of Tira in 1994, she became the sole director of the association. With the Oslo Accords signed by Israel and the Palestinian Liberation Organization (PLO) in the fall of 1993 and the handing over of most of the large towns to the newly constituted "Palestinian Authority," some thought that the Moked would soon go out of business, but this proved overly optimistic. There was even an increase in files opened by the association. More Palestinians were arrested than before and their families were not informed of their whereabouts.

The Moked did not concern itself with human rights violations by the new Palestinian administration. This was the task of Palestinian NGOs. At the same time, Israel continued to exercise control over matters that affected the daily lives of many Palestinians. The Israeli authorities frequently violated the understandings reached with regard to family reunions and there was an increase in violence against individuals. Although the attacks were mostly carried out by Jewish settlers living in the territories, the Moked also continued to monitor the activities of the IDF and the Border Police.

In the spring of 1993, the Moked was the first Israeli organization to protest the closure of the West Bank and Gaza. The closing off of the occupied territories had started during the first Gulf War of 1991. After that conflict ended, closures continued as a means of preventing terrorist incursions. During the first Intifada, despite the violence, Palestinians had continued crossing over into Israel to work and conduct business. After the Gulf War, fewer workers were permitted to enter Israel and all of them had to pass through roadblocks, where they were often delayed and sometimes prevented from entering Israeli territory.

The Moked held a joint news conference with other human rights groups at one of the two main roadblocks preventing the entrance of Palestinians from the West Bank into Jerusalem. The roadblocks, also called checkpoints—*machsomim* in Hebrew—have since been established at hundreds of locations inside the West Bank, as well as at entry points to Israeli territory. They are one of the main reasons for the current anger and frustration felt by the Palestinian residents of the West Bank and Gaza.

Continuing its cooperation with Betzelem and ACRI, its fellow Israeli human rights groups, the Moked also developed a warm relationship with Al-Haq (Law in the Service of Man), a Palestinian human rights organization. Together they issued reports, organized protests, and initiated applications to the High Court of Justice. The individual, however, has remained the main focus of the Moked. This was what distinguished it from other organizations and associations working in the field of human rights.

Locating missing persons remains one of the major activities of the Moked. Kerstein worries that Israel is on the way to "a South American situation." She notes the recent Kafkaesque case of Ziad, a Jordanian citizen, who disappeared off the face of the earth. Cases involving Jordanians are more complicated because Jordanians do not possess Israeli identity cards. Ziad was married to a West Bank resident, but was not granted a permit to reside legally in the area. One day he simply went missing, and his family, as so many others have done, applied to the Moked. The case of Ziad was even more frustrating than others.

The first call, as always, was to the IDF Control Unit, which officially gives information about people arrested by any of the security forces. The unit disclosed that Ziad was being held in the Kishon jail in Haifa (the same prison where Aziz was held). Orly, the Moked's missing persons coordinator, informed Ziad's family of this, but a week later the family again asked her to find him. This was unusual, but Orly again called the Control Unit, which this time was unable to locate him. An attorney from the Moked contacted the IDF prosecution department, which reaffirmed that Ziad was being held in the Kishon jail, and the Moked attorney requested a meeting with him there.

After a number of phone calls to Kishon with contradictory answers as to whether Ziad was or was not there the attorney went there and demanded to see him. On arriving at Kishon, the attorney was again told that Ziad was not there. Refusing to accept this answer, the attorney continued to demand a meeting. After an hour's argument, Ziad made a "miraculous" appearance.

Ziad's case is now being dealt with, but Kerstein is worried by a new development that she regards as sinister: there was no record of Ziad. "Palestinians are arrested all the time," explains Dalia Kerstein, "but at least records are kept. In the case of Aziz, for example, everything was written down and filed. Ziad, on the other hand, was a 'non-person.' We are going to the High

Court on this one. We want the court order to the security authorities compelling them to keep records."

Since its establishment, one of the interesting features of the Moked has been the cooperation between its Jewish and Arab staff members and volunteers. Although established to deal directly with the problems faced by Palestinians, it is an Israeli association, registered in Israel, and its staff and volunteers have always been Israeli citizens. This way it is more effective in dealing with the IDF, the police, and other security organizations than a joint Israeli-Palestinian group would be.

Partly because of the need for Arabic speakers, and partly because of its aims and aspirations, Arab citizens of Israel have played a key role in the Moked. In the early years, the interaction between Israeli Jewish and Arab volunteers was one of the notable features of the association.

Early on, Schwartz invited Ala Khatib to be his codirector. Khatib, a student of biology at the Hebrew University, stayed on when Schwartz left for postgraduate studies abroad, eventually serving as codirector with Dalia Kerstein.

Khatib's mild, soft-spoken personality masks a remarkably determined character. Growing up in the Arab village of Tira, he was lucky to be taught Hebrew and English by a very able teacher, which equipped him for his encounter with the predominantly Jewish society of Israel. He relished the challenge of working at the Moked, where he quickly graduated from volunteer to employee, albeit at a token salary. "At university I had two Jewish friends," he recalls, "but at the Moked I had dozens. There was something special about it. You felt you were worth something and that Arabs and Jews really were equal. We were not all leftists, but we had a commitment to civil rights. It was a family of Jews and Arabs working together to change the situation."

Although he left voluntarily to take on the task of establishing a retirement home in Tira, the first of its kind in the Israeli Arab community, and has only praise for his former organization, Khatib regrets that Kerstein is now the sole director. Dual leadership is important, he thinks, both practically and symbolically, although it does create difficulties. He is currently coprincipal of a Jewish-Arab school in Jerusalem, and thinks the fact that there are two leaders—one Jewish and one Arab—is crucial in its success.

Khatib and Schwartz both make the point that Jews and Arabs make friends naturally when a group of people is performing a concrete task together. "When you meet just for the sake of meeting—to promote 'Jewish-Arab coexistence'—it doesn't last," says Khatib.

"In fact it tends to polarize people," suggests Schwartz, "because each group is forced into defining its own position. But when there is a specific job of work to be done, the differences in culture and background swiftly disappear."

Maha Abu-Salah, the coordinator for family unification at the Moked, goes even further. "I hate the term 'coexistence,'" she insists. "Most Israeli Jews don't want to live with us, and I am not going to ask them to accept me. I'm not going to prove that I am OK. When I talk in Arabic on my mobile phone in the bus, there is always surprise. Why? Don't the Jews know that there are Arabs in Israel?"

Maha grew up in a small Galilee village before studying at the Hebrew University. Coming to Jerusalem was like traveling to a foreign country, she recalls. She was far from home in an unfamiliar environment with a different language. Her Hebrew studies at school equipped her for reading the Hebrew Bible, but not for speaking with her fellow students. It took her some time to get used to the new social framework.

Studying for her second degree in philosophy, Maha wrote her paper on the philosophy of Muhammad Abdel Jabiri, a Morocco-based philosopher, seeking a balance between the Arab heritage and modern civilization. "It disturbed me that I was learning all about western philosophers, and I didn't know anything about my own Arab philosophy," she explains. "I hope my doctorate will deal with the same philosophical stream."

Initially the Moked was simply a job, she recalls. Even today, she does not view it as a "contribution" to her people. She notes that her success rate is small, and therefore she is not making much of a difference. Particularly since the outbreak of the second Intifada, the situation is frozen. So why does she continue?

"Even helping *one* person is worthwhile," she insists. "If a Jerusalem girl, who is now living in Gaza, visits her parents in Jerusalem, and then is not allowed back into Gaza, where she has a husband and a new life, you have to do what you can. It's not earth-shattering, but helping one couple to live a normal life is certainly worthwhile."

She is acutely aware of the fact that for every person she helps there are many more who are suffering. She also realizes that, at a certain level—working within the parameters permitted by the IDF and the other security forces—she is "recognizing the occupation." In trying to improve peoples' situations while acting legally, she is accepting the laws of the occupying power. She is uncomfortable with that, but she still thinks it is the best alternative.

Despite her scorn for the term "coexistence," Maha sees the Moked as an ideal work place, where there is real cooperation. She is full of admiration for the professionalism of the organization and notes that the Jewish and Arab employees, after working together, end up socializing naturally. It is not because they are Jews and Arabs, she stresses, but because they are a group of people doing a job.

Although Jews and Arabs do work together at the Moked every day of the year, it doesn't follow that there are no cultural clashes between the two groups. Recently, one of the new (Jewish) employees at the Moked found a puppy that she thought was neglected and handed it over to an animal shelter for adoption. It turned out that it belonged to son of the (Arab) owner of the building in which the Moked's office is situated. The boy burst into tears at the loss of his pet, and the landlord was incensed. The puppy was the cause of a major confrontation between the two groups, with the Arab employees of the Moked accusing their Jewish coworkers of "cultural imperialism."

Despite incidents such as these, cooperation between its Jewish and Arab employees remains an integral part of the Moked. About half of the association's employees are Jews and half Arabs, says Dalia Kerstein. She quickly writes down the names of all her workers on a pad to confirm this to herself. The interesting thing, she feels, is the way they work together so naturally. It is manifest as soon as a new employee starts work, she notes. "Most of the people who come to work here don't have a political background," she explains. "For many of the Jews it is their first real contact with Arabs and vice versa. It is an interesting dynamic: the work immediately buries the differences."

Schwartz reiterates that the special thing about the Moked is the fact that it deals with individuals. The organization is mostly reactive, responding to appeals and requests. One year the reunification of families is the dominant theme, another year it is the location of missing persons, then the rights of prisoners. Recently, freedom of movement has become the main problem. Reading the Moked's files tells the story of what is happening in the occupied territories.

"The Moked has changed," allows Schwartz. "It is no longer the effervescent enthusiasm of the volunteers that sets the tone. The professional attorneys, counselors, telephone operators, receptionists, and observers are performing gray, routine work, day by day. The important thing is that Palestinians from all over the occupied territories still turn to us. They call us because they know that we can and will help them."

2

Courage to Listen

When Aziz was arrested, interrogated, and threatened with exposure as a "phony peace activist," he realized that his reputation as a campaigner for coexistence was known to the security services. Apparently they were aware that he had served as Tulkarm director of Windows—Channels for Communication, an Israeli-Palestinian association promoting numerous joint projects between the two peoples.

With centers in Tel Aviv and Tulkarm, Windows is the epitome of a volunteer organization: enthusiastic, well-meaning, and a little chaotic. The first things a visitor notices, entering its shabby Tel Aviv center, are the cardboard boxes and the heaps of clothes, blankets, and household goods. Destined for needy Palestinians, they are spread out on and around the large table that almost blocks the entrance, on chairs and shelves, and form piles on the floor. Further into the room, he or she will find bottles of olive oil, the product of Palestinian villages, for sale. Only after struggling past these obstructions will the visitor discover the computers and telephones that are needed by any modern organization, but particularly by Windows, which is all about making contacts.

Established in 1991 as a nonprofit association to promote understanding between Israelis and Palestinians, it launched *Windows*, a bilingual Hebrew-Arabic youth magazine, and organized meetings between youngsters on both sides of the border. After the outbreak of the second Intifada in the fall of 2000, however, it found itself involved in many other fields. From a few dozen volunteers working with children, Windows has developed into an association of several hundred, carrying out a wide range of activities.

Unable to ignore distress or to turn down appeals from those in need, it has transported the sick to hospitals, sent supplies to hungry and impoverished

Palestinians, and organized youth groups for art, drama, sports, games, and language study. Members of Windows have joined other groups in picking olives with Palestinians farmers when nearby settlers threatened them, sponsored joint Israeli-Palestinian art exhibitions, and developed an educational program for use in schools. All the activities are carried out by Israelis and Palestinians working together, and they have continued throughout the years of bloodshed that followed the breakdown of the peace process in the fall of 2000.

Its founder and codirector, Ruti Atzmon, an easygoing, comfortably dressed woman in her forties, is liable to greet a visitor with a warm smile and a hug. Overflowing with emotion and enthusiasm, she personifies Windows. She may lack the ruthlessness necessary for efficiency, but she makes up for it with an energy that refuses to acknowledge limits. Her good will is manifest. Watch her with a group of twelve- to fourteen year-old Jewish and Arab children, who have come to an editorial board meeting of *Windows* magazine: switching easily from Hebrew to Arabic and back, she handles them with a relaxed authority, at once friendly and purposeful.

The situation in which the meeting is taking place is tense. The Intifada is still raging, and the mutual violence has taken its toll. No West Bank or Gaza Palestinians are present. The joint editorial meetings are a thing of the past. The only Arabic speakers are Israeli Arabs. Contact with their Palestinian opposite numbers is by phone, fax, and e-mail.

Hammad, a plump Arab twelve-year-old from Jaffa, has called his fellow reporter in the West Bank town of Nablus, Sa'id, who insists that the next edition of *Windows* should be all about the Palestinian uprising and the Israeli incursions into the territories. Sa'id is full of anger and does not want to talk to the Jewish kids. Hammad informs them that his conversation was "tough," and that Sa'id referred to [then Israeli Prime Minister Ariel] Sharon as "a dog."

The eight children—three Arab girls (two with traditional head scarves), three Jewish girls, and two Arab boys—break off to prepare a sandwich lunch together. They bicker good-naturedly over the chocolate.

Ruti inquires whether the coming edition should include interviews with religious Jews. She recalls that the Palestinian kids who visited Tel Aviv the previous year were more interested in meeting settler children than other Jewish children. Tina, a Jewish girl, tells of her frustration with a religious friend.

"There is no place for his views in our magazine!" she concludes.

"That's it?" asks Ruti, "we only publish opinions we agree with?"

"I don't mind interviewing a stranger with different ideas," explains Tina, "but when it's a friend I get annoyed."

"Lets ask Sa'id and others from Hebron and Gaza if they want to hear what Jewish religious kids are thinking these days," suggests Ruti.

The first editions of *Windows* in the early 1990s dealt with music, sports, computers, hiking, hobbies, and other youth activities. The peace process was in full swing then, and the editors felt that while the Israeli and Palestinian leaders were negotiating agreements the magazine should give the young people on both sides the chance to get to know each other. Not that the early issues lacked serious content: a comparison of children's rights in Israeli and Palestinian societies found that the Arab children were at a disadvantage. The structure of Arab society made it more difficult to report child abuse—and this applied both in Israel and the Palestinian territories. The Jewish children were far more aware of their rights. The Arab children didn't talk about the subject, and their teachers ignored it. These were indeed serious subjects, but the magazine also covered bungee jumping, fishing, pets, clothes, computer games, art, music, and recipes for ice cream.

Now, however, the violent confrontation of the past two years has created a new reality, and the magazine has to reflect this. The Palestinian children at the other end of the phone lines are bitter and angry. Their Jewish interlocutors are confused and full of fear. The Israeli Arabs are caught in the middle.

When edition number 19 of *Windows* comes out a few months later with the motto "Courage to Listen," it expresses these tensions clearly. Muhammad, an Israeli Arab from Jaffa, writes: "I have friends who like the Jews and others who are upset all the time and want to hit out at the Jews. Maybe, if we publish the magazine it will change opinions and there will be peace. I don't think peace will come from signing agreements, but only from the heart." Laila from Tulkarm: "Lives are destroyed. There are people being killed on both sides. With the help of the magazine, maybe we can learn to understand each other." Shai from Tel Aviv: "Some of the kids in my class think there should be a paper like this, but most of them don't. Many of them think we should speak to the other side, but they don't think that it will make any difference."

The emotional stress inherent in the situation is illustrated in an exchange between two thirteen-year-olds from opposite sides of the border. Ala from Ramallah: "Last night we heard breaking glass. When we looked outside we saw [Israeli] soldiers breaking car windows and stealing radio tape recorders. They broke our car window, but didn't steal the radio. In the morning, fifteen soldiers came into our house to arrest my father. I think they detained him because they found a Palestinian flag in our house. Now they are beating people before our very eyes. It is pure terror." Yael from Tel Aviv: "I never take the bus for fear it will blow up. I don't go shopping in malls any more. My parents have given me a cell phone and they are always calling me. I get very tense when I hear the sirens. I don't know why they are doing this to us."

As might be expected, the effect of television is crucial. Aliya from the Israeli town of Tivon: "I was saddened when I saw people being shot on television, people exactly like me. I became very depressed. I saw people crying, people being shot, people not caring about each other. I think lots of kids feel the way I do." Arij from Bethlehem: "I watch Al-Jazeera [the independent Arabic station broadcasting from Qatar] and we also watch Israeli TV, so we know what's going on in Israel. The Arabic stations show both sides: Jews who want peace, and those who don't. A lot of what I see causes me sorrow and pain."

Dreaming Peace, an Israeli-Palestinian art collection exhibited both locally and in several international locations, is featured. Pictures from Jaffa, Tulkarm, and Kfar Saba students are reproduced with the artists' comments. Ramzi from Tulkarm describes his picture of red-roofed houses surrounded by barbed wire as "a Jewish settlement established on confiscated Palestinian land." His picture is meant to demonstrate the illegality of the settlements, he explains, and he adds: "True peace will only come if they are dismantled." Ya'ara from Kfar Saba draws a Jewish child with a skullcap looking in a mirror, where he sees an Arab child with a kaffiyeh headscarf. "We are all the same," she writes. "The Jewish child is sort of seeing himself in the mirror."

Growing up in a socially aware home, Windows founder Ruti Atzmon had her first encounter with the Israeli-Arab situation when she joined the IDF as a young conscript in 1976. She served as a clerk in the Military Government offices at El Arish in Sinai. "Straight away I was amazed at the different attitudes toward the Arab residents," she explains. "Some soldiers behaved abominably, whereas others were manifestly trying to help the local people. I felt that education was the key—home, school, media, general environment—and even then I was determined to do something about it."

More than a decade later, when a friend showed her a trilingual South African youth magazine that aimed at conciliation between white and black children, Ruti determined to replicate the idea in Israel. It started out as an internal Israeli effort, with a group of Jews and Arabs from Tel Aviv and Jaffa. When they started, they found that it was difficult to interest anyone in the idea. Then the Oslo Agreement was signed, which improved the atmosphere, and the Israeli Ministry of Education granted them a budget for the first magazine. In the following years, after they managed to bring out several editions, interest grew among the Palestinians.

At the outset, although the children themselves produced, wrote, and edited *Windows*, adults were very involved in helping them. With the passing of time, the role of the adults has been reduced as much as possible. Following an approach from Palestinians in the territories, it was decided to register Windows—Channels for Communication as an Israeli-Palestinian

Association. People from both sides were in constant communication, and they frequently met face-to-face.

However, as the violence between Israelis and Palestinians escalated in 2000, it became increasingly difficult for both the adults and the children to hold meetings. The magazine's young reporters continued to communicate by phone, fax, and e-mail, and, as the violence continued into its second year, the Palestinian youngsters were invited to Israel for a workshop. Originally scheduled for August 2002, the workshop could not take place because of Israeli military activity in the Tulkarm area. It was finally held in October with the participation of twenty-five young journalists from both sides.

Some of the reactions to the workshop were published in the journal. Amira from Tulkarm: "The whole night before the meeting I kept thinking about what we were going to say to each other. Are they murderers? After all they have grown up in a racist environment." Gur from Israel: "I'm expecting to meet kids with opinions that differ from mine. I hope that they will dare to listen, and that I myself will be able to listen to different opinions also."

And these exchanges during the course of the get-together were also published:

"The suffering causes fear and hatred that makes [Palestinian] people decide to become martyrs."

"Israelis support the war out of fear of the bombings."

"My friends asked me: why are you going to meet Jews?"

"I was asked that too."

"If one Jew is killed in a suicide operation, dozens of Palestinians are killed."

"Lots of Israelis think we haven't done anything to the Palestinians and they are hurting us a lot."

The following year, the editorial workshop was taken to Italy. There, away from the atmosphere of conflict and confrontation, they met to discuss and plan future editions. Subsequently the young Israeli members of Windows invited their Palestinian counterparts for a "day of fun." Frequently delayed because of the difficulty of getting permission from the Israeli military authorities, the fun day eventually took place in Kalanswa, just on the Israeli side of the border.

The only time events were cancelled or postponed was when Palestinian participants in some program could not get through to the Israeli side of the border. In Tulkarm, there was no permanent friendship center during the years after the outbreak. Aziz operated improvised centers in private homes, offering youth activities, sports, art, theater, and English and Hebrew lessons, often with help from Israeli members of Windows. He continued to organize all this despite the almost impossible conditions of curfews, closures, occupation of homes, arrests, and searches.

Perpetually short of money for its activities, Windows has managed to establish support groups in Italy and Britain, which have enabled the organization to increase its activities significantly. Thanks to the money raised in those two countries, a permanent center has now been established in Tulkarm, with a lounge and television room, library, games room, lecture hall, a kitchen for preparing food, and rooms for sleeping over. The last two facilities are vital in the situation of continuing roadblocks and closures. Windows attracts children from as far away as Jenin and Nablus, and they and their leaders must have the option of eating supper and staying the night if the situation warrants it. The center is situated in a village on the outskirts of Tulkarm and some of the activities are held in the orchard adjoining the house.

After applying to the IDF for permission to enter Area A as a journalist, I am allowed through the roadblock. A reserve soldier with a heavy Russian accent, one of several manning the position, asks me why I am visiting Tulkarm. I explain that I am visiting the community center of Windows, an organization for Israeli-Palestinian coexistence. His thick eyebrows shoot up; his shrug of the shoulders is more eloquent than any comment.

Mahmoud Tanji, a stocky, curly-haired young man with a mustache and a ready smile who has taken over from his brother, Aziz, meets me on the Palestinian side in a bright yellow cab. He proudly shows me around the freshly painted center. His Hebrew is perfect, the result of many years working in Israel, some time in prison, and an Israeli Arab wife from the village of Fureidis near Haifa. He has established a regular program of activities, including games, art, drama, storytelling, video production, and classes for English and Hebrew. He has also organized training courses for youth leaders and discussion coordinators. Workshops for youngsters to prepare them for their encounters with Israeli children have already taken place in the new facility. "I wanted to organize a summer camp," states Mahmoud, "but unfortunately there are insufficient funds. These kids—particularly those from the refugee camp—have nowhere to go now that the summer vacation has started."

Mahmoud introduces me to Majdi, a slight young man who is preparing a group of children for a joint video workshop with Israeli Jewish and Arab youngsters at Tantur, a Christian college between Jerusalem and Bethlehem, which has agreed to host the Windows activity. The program there will consist of joint Israeli-Palestinian video workshops, financed by the Japanese government. Two groups of five teenagers will be attending the Tantur workshops. There are other leaders from Jenin and the village of Asira a-Shamaliya, as well as Tulkarm. Wafa and Fida, daughters of the landlord, assist Mahmoud with the secretarial and organizational work. They wear traditional head covers, but are dressed in jeans and sweatshirts.

Ahmad and Muhammad, two fourteen-year-olds in jeans and T-shirts, come by for their preparatory course for Tantur. Muhammad has a mobile phone and speaks better English than his companion. He is carrying a video camera, and the two boys explain that they plan to make films about themselves to show at Tantur. They plan to chronicle their village, their neighbors, their homes, the rooms where they sleep, their meals, school books, hobbies, their journey to Tantur (via Israeli roadblocks)—anything that will give their Israeli counterparts a picture of the reality of their lives. Some months after my visit, the two boys participated in a video workshop in Umbria, Italy, as part of a delegation that included other Palestinians along with Israeli Jews and Arabs.

People in Tulkarm and the area are much more positive about Windows than they used to be, maintains Mahmoud. There are always extremists opposed to any sort of coexistence, he allows, but the atmosphere has improved. Three years ago, when they started their activities in Tulkarm, the Palestinian Authority (PA) officials were suspicious of their contacts with Israelis.

"I told them that nothing is secret," recalls Mahmoud. "Aziz and I invited them to come to any of our activities whenever they wanted. Some of the PA officials are now learning Hebrew and English in our classes.

"They have come to realize that we at Windows are not traitors to the Palestinian cause. We explained to them that the Palestinian confrontation is with the Israelis, so we have to talk to them—not the French or the Americans. They seemed to understand."

The extra money raised in Britain and Italy has also facilitated the long-delayed publication of *Windows* number 20. The theme of this edition of the magazine is "Without Walls," reflecting the dominant concern among the Palestinian children today. The wall being built between the two peoples, called by the Israelis the "Separation Fence," is a controversial topic.

"We tried to find our way through the road blocks, the terror attacks, the demonstrations, and the walls," states the editorial committee. "In all of this, we have tried to maintain a positive approach." "Is it a security fence or a separation wall?" asks one article. Another reports a nonviolent protest by one Palestinian village against the wall that separates them from their olive trees. This is followed by a brief account of the life of Mahatma Gandhi, the Indian apostle of nonviolence. The magazine is full of angry letters and articles, but also contains declarations of a desire to meet, to discuss, to argue, to forge friendships.

An Arab youngster, Mahdi Manasra, aged eleven, writes that he lives on the "green line," the border before 1967. His father is always talking about peace, but he has only ever met settlers, or soldiers with guns. He would like to see the "other side" of his neighbors, decent people who understand his problems. "I would like to open my window and see people bearing olive branches," he concludes.

Ronni, an Israeli Jewish girl, who writes that she enjoyed the previous edition of the magazine, suggests that e-mail addresses be provided so that children from both sides can write to each other. She has become friends with an Arab girl from the Jerusalem suburb of Abu Dis, she recounts, and she likes hearing her opinions and tries to understand her feelings. In an attempt to humanize "the other," some of the exchanges are illustrated with photos of the children writing them.

Some ten pages are devoted to a dialogue between Israeli and Palestinian youngsters that took place in Italy. Although the participants returned to "the unchanged situation," they were somehow more hopeful after their Italian trip. No punches are pulled in the hard-hitting discussion about Palestinian suicide bombers and Israeli troops in the towns and refugee camps of the West Bank. "The trouble is that when five Israelis are killed, many Palestinians don't think of them as individual human beings with families," suggests one participant, "and the same applies when Palestinians are killed by Israeli soldiers."

Envisaged as a magazine that would come out five times a year (every two months with a break for the summer vacation) *Windows* has only managed twenty editions in nine years. Now it hopes to manage four to five editions every year. To celebrate ten years of (intermittent) publication, a workshop of all contributors over the years is planned in advance of a festive tenth anniversary edition.

A Windows team has created an educational program for schools in Israel and the Palestinian territories, aiming to instill the values of human rights, democracy, social justice, environmental matters, and understanding of the media. The program, which includes practical work on social projects, drama, art, and music, envisages contacts with peace groups, social justice movements, and organizations promoting change.

Ruti Atzmon explains that the association is aiming to increase its outreach by direct involvement in the schools. Palestinian schools in the territories and Israeli Arab schools are very receptive to the idea of the program, she says, but Jewish schools are more wary. "You have to understand that for Palestinians, *Windows* is 'good news,'" she explains. "They read the magazine and discover that not all Israelis are soldiers or settlers. On the other hand, the Israeli kids who read the magazine are liable to learn all sorts of unpleasant things for the first time."

Despite this, some Israeli schools have expressed interest in the educational program, which, for the time being, will be part of afternoon enrichment programs and not part of the formal curriculum. Two art exhibitions created by Windows, the aforementioned Dreaming of Peace and another called In the Shadow of War, continue to tour Europe and the United States.

All of which brings us back to the piles of clothes, foodstuffs, household goods, and other items collected from Israeli homes and stacked in the Tel

Aviv headquarters on their way to Tulkarm and other Palestinians communities. The humanitarian project continues unabated, with dozens of people providing assistance. Almost every week convoys of private cars have taken equipment, and on some occasions, a truck has been acquired to transport the goods. There is joint olive picking every season, and olive oil produced by the Palestinians continues to be on sale at the Tel Aviv center. Palestinians who receive permits to undergo treatment in Israel are transported by volunteers from the roadblocks to the various hospitals and returned the same day.

The Tulkarm center, which has pushed its outreach programs as far as Jenin and Nablus, hopes to extend it further. Editions of the magazine and video films will continue to be produced. A new video camera has been purchased and sent through to the Tulkarm branch. With the completion of the separation fence, it is going to become increasingly difficult for adults and youngsters of Windows to get together, but they will continue to try.

Recently Windows received a welcome grant from the European Community. This, together with its regular funds from Britain and Italy, will enable Ruti and Mahmoud to step up their activities. Possibly the Tulkarm center can be improved and extended. It is even possible that a larger office will be rented in Tel Aviv. After several years of struggling with limited funds, the members of Windows on both sides feel things are looking up.

Windows is part of an informal coalition of many different movements and groups of Israelis and Palestinians working to try to foster good relations. The various organizations cooperate on an ad hoc basis, supply volunteers for each other's projects, and pass on information. It was an e-mail on the Windows website that propelled me to the next stage of my journey into Israeli-Palestinian cooperation and dialogue.

3

Refusing to Be Enemies

The following e-mail appeared on my computer screen one morning in March:

> For the third year in a row, the Israeli Committee Against House Demolitions (ICAHD) is offering a summer work camp to foster learning, discussion, and friendship between Palestinians, Israelis, and internationals. Our cooperation will send a clear message to the world: we refuse to be enemies; together we resist the occupation. The program will center around rebuilding a Palestinian home that was demolished by the Israeli authorities for administrative reasons.

And here I am, four months later, on a desert hilltop to the east of Jerusalem, passing buckets of sand and aggregate in a chain gang of fellow Israelis and volunteers from the United States, Britain, France, Italy, the Netherlands, Germany, and Switzerland. To the north, we can see the buildings of Jerusalem's Hebrew University. To the east and south is the desert, its gray-brown emptiness broken by a large Israeli security headquarters and huge earth-moving tractors and bulldozers preparing the ground for the gray panels of the concrete wall that is remorselessly advancing over the barren hills, dividing Israelis from Palestinians.

The house that has been chosen for rebuilding is at the eastern edge of Anata, a village-suburb of Jerusalem that is partly in Jerusalem, partly in the West Bank. This side of the village presents a contrasting scene: on the one hand, relatively spacious houses, many of them handsomely faced in stone; on the other, the camp of the Jahaleen Bedouin, a sad jumble of tin shacks, canvas awnings, and traditional black tents. The Jahaleen, who used to live in the desert further south, eventually settled next to Anata and the nearby

Jerusalem neighborhood of Azariya. A year ago, twenty-five of their structures were bulldozed, and only an application to Israel's Supreme Court has postponed further demolitions. Abu Mussa, their *mukhtar* [headman], his white stubble glinting around his brown face, his red kaffiyeh head scarf contrasting with his black abaya robe, is a frequent visitor to our building site. He is fifty-three, but looks decades older.

A number of local children in their early teens enthusiastically help us with the work. They keep us continuously supplied with cold water and, from time to time, bring us a locally manufactured cola drink. Every few hours sweet tea is brewed and we sit down to drink and rest our sore limbs. The owner of the house being rebuilt, Arafat Hamdan, a clean-shaven, chain-smoking man in jeans and short-sleeved summer shirt with the looks of a Hollywood film star of the 1940s, hovers anxiously.

"Here, Danny, help me out please," he says in Hebrew. "These guys don't understand my English: explain to them where I need the fill—not here— over there, over there!"

A house painter by profession, Hamdan has worked in the Jewish neighborhoods of Jerusalem. Fluent in Hebrew, he speaks fondly of his Jewish partner from nearby Ma'ale Adumim, one of the biggest West Bank settlements, east of Jerusalem. They worked together for several years plastering and painting apartments and remain firm friends.

He claims ownership of the land where he built his house through his father, grandfather, and great-grandfather, the deeds dating to Ottoman times (pre-1917). He lived there with his wife, Fateh, and their five children for six years before it was demolished ten months ago while he was out at work. Gesticulating angrily, he describes how the demolition crew did not even give his family time to remove their possessions, but chased them out with the help of a police dog. He came home and found his house converted into a pile of rubble with pieces of furniture and children's toys sticking out of it.

Now, however, a new house is taking shape. The actual building operations—the pouring of the concrete, the bricklaying, the plastering inside and out, the electrical installations, the plumbing, the carpentry, and the floor tiling—are carried out by skilled Palestinian day laborers. We, a motley crew of young, middle-aged, and elderly volunteers, supply the muscle. We mix the concrete, pass along the sand and cinder blocks, unload the sacks of cement, place and tighten the props for the platform on which the concrete roof will be poured, sort the planks, extract the nails, level the ground, and do anything else needed.

Hamdan's house was demolished because it was built without a permit, which sounds reasonable enough until one considers the context. The part of Anata where the house was located is outside the municipal area of Jerusalem. It is therefore in the occupied West Bank, under the formal authority of the IDF Civil Administration. There is no master plan for Anata, but Arafat Hamdan paid an attorney for two years to obtain a building permit. He was unsuccessful. According to British Mandatory and Jordanian laws, the Hamdan house has been built in an "agricultural" zone, and that is what makes it illegal.

Assisted by more than twenty of us volunteers every day, the laborers were able to work fast. Documented by video and still photography, the new Hamdan home arose swiftly near the ruins of the old one. Day one saw the laying of the foundations, ground leveling, and the pouring of the concrete support pillars. The wooden and cinder block frame for the roof was erected on day two, and some of the walls started going up. On day three, the concrete roof was poured with the help of a machine. That same day an electricity pylon was inadvertently knocked over by a truck and an improvised repair was carried out. Walls continued going up on day four, plastering started, and grooves were hollowed in the walls for the electric wiring and plumbing installations.

Day five was mainly occupied with completing the outer walls and leveling the ground for laying the floor tiles, which we manually unloaded from the truck. The wooden plank roof supports were removed on day six—much too soon, according to some of the neighbors. Days seven, eight, and nine saw construction of the inner walls, tiling the floors, and near-completion of the plastering.

Ahmad, the electrician, was arrested during the night between days ten and eleven. A police patrol discovered live ammunition in his house. He was taken away for questioning, but the police accepted his claim that the three rifle bullets they found had been innocently collected by his children, who found them in the desert near his home, where they had apparently been dropped by members of an army or police patrol.

On day eleven the kitchen and bathroom fittings were installed, the floor was completed, and the windows fixed. On days twelve and thirteen, the painting, plumbing, carpentry, and electrical installations were finished. Soil was spread for a garden. The dedication ceremony took place on day fourteen, in the presence of several dozen Palestinians, Israelis, and internationals.

In rebuilding the Hamdan home, ICAHD is knowingly breaking the law. The Israeli and foreign volunteers knew that and were prepared to be cautioned and even arrested. We were a varied crew from a dozen different countries, with an age range from twentysomething to sixtysomething. Aaron, a young American from Texas, said he was there because he was Jewish. Middle-aged Kay from London, also Jewish, had visited Israel as a teenager and had found it racist. She now preferred to visit Palestine. John Hickox from North Carolina, one of the older volunteers, complained that as a self-declared Christian he was always typecast as "a right-wing evangelist." He was delighted to hear me describe myself as "a Zionist," and urged me to continue identifying myself in that way. "We mustn't let ourselves be forced into molds," he insisted. "The fact that you are sympathetic to the Palestinians doesn't mean that you can't be a Zionist, just as the reality of my Christian belief doesn't make me into a right-wing fanatic."

Pnina had come up from Sde Boker in the Negev desert to work at the camp. Like me, she often served as a translator between the local villagers and the volunteers, as the Anata Palestinians knew little English but were fluent in Hebrew. Michael, a slim, frizzy-haired Israeli volunteer, was pleased about the current refusal to serve in the IDF on the part of right-wing soldiers ordered to evacuate Jewish settlers from Gaza. He thought that the erosion of blind loyalty and patriotism was healthy, whichever direction it came from.

Mrijin from Holland, very tall and very blond, coordinated the volunteer effort. Larissa hitchhiked every day from the Dehaishe refugee camp near Bethlehem, where she was staying. A Palestinian Armenian from Berkeley, California, she spoke fluent Arabic. Lucy from Germany was making a television documentary and was eager to interview me, a veteran Israeli who had "lived through it all."

The camp headquarters was at the "Arabiya House." Salim Shawamreh, a construction engineer and formerly a resident of the Shuafat refugee camp near Anata, worked for nine years in Saudi Arabia to earn money. In 1987, he returned home with his wife, Arabiya, and bought a plot of land in Anata. After four years of fruitlessly applying for a permit, he built a house, which was eventually demolished. Despite well-publicized protests organized by ICAHD, Arabiya House has been destroyed and rebuilt five times, most recently in 2003.

The owner does not want to live there at the present time, as it is outside the Jerusalem municipal area and, if he lives there, he might lose his Jerusalem residency rights. Because of this, he has rented the house to ICAHD, which is using it for the summer construction camp. It is surrounded by a courtyard and garden, where some of the campers slept. The others were transported daily from their Old City hotel together with the Israeli volunteers.

All of us volunteers accepted the risk of clashes with the Israeli security forces. We were put through simulation games during intervals from our building activity, learning how to behave in a possible encounter with Israeli security forces. The simulations were conducted by a local branch of the Quakers, experienced in nonviolent resistance. In addition to any threats we might have faced from Israeli security forces, the building operations, carried out as they were by inexperienced people not wearing helmets, could have been dangerous, but in fact the only accident was entirely unpredictable.

ICAHD coordinator Jeff Halper was sitting listening to an evening lecture when his light plastic chair tilted sideways and slipped down an earthen slope toward the drainage channel around the Arabiya House. Losing his balance, Halper tumbled more than six feet into the concrete channel, banging his head and breaking his arm. Fortunately, the head injury was not serious, but his arm and wrist needed fairly complex surgery before being set in a plaster cast. The accident pretty well immobilized him for the remainder of the camp, although he insisted on making an appearance at the house dedication.

Halper, an energetic, stocky, bald man with a full graying beard, established ICAHD in 1997 together with a group of people who felt that the Israeli peace movement "existed in a bubble." There were numerous protest demonstrations about the occupation, he recalls, but when they were over, the participants simply went home. There was very little actual contact with Palestinians, and almost no understanding of the daily problems they faced. He and some others started to meet with Palestinians in an attempt to find out what the main problems were, and "the house demolitions came up all the time." Then one day they faced a specific practical problem: a Palestinian from Anata told them that he had been issued with a demolition order and asked for help.

"We didn't know how the system worked at all," recalls Halper. "We didn't know who issued the demolition orders, or why, or how they were carried out. A few of us got together and decided to establish a committee to look into the issue of house demolitions. The truth is that we didn't know what we were letting ourselves in for—we sort of backed into it."

Halper was born in 1946 "in the same small Minnesota town where Bob Dylan was born." He was a child of the 1960s, a member of the movement against the Vietnam War, who went to jail in Mississippi while campaigning for civil rights. Although his family was not at all religious, the 1960s atmosphere encouraged him to seek out his Jewish roots. For a time he even ran a weekend Hebrew school at the local synagogue. After his studies in anthropology, he decided to come to Israel. He never really liked America, he explains. He knew that he could live as an ex-pat anywhere, but he felt he had an authentic alternative identity as an Israeli. "I'm not sure how many of my Palestinian friends would endorse that," he adds with a smile.

Halper landed in the deprived Jerusalem neighborhood of Nahlaot, where he still lives, and conducted his doctoral research into the education of the local Jewish children of parents who had immigrated to Israel from North Africa, Iraq, and Yemen. He spent the next decade as a community worker for the Jerusalem municipality. In the mid 1970s, he briefly entered politics, running for the city council as an independent. He lost. In 1987, he became the director of the Middle East Center of the Friends World College, an educational institution without formal classes, where most of the work is based on projects. He subsequently spent two years in the United States as director of the college. Returning to Israel, he joined the staff of the Ben-Gurion University of the Negev, where he taught anthropology until recently.

"I leapfrogged over the Jewish-Zionist ideology straight into being an Israeli," he recounts, sitting in his cool living room in the Nahlaot, nursing the arm that is still in a plaster cast. "I came with a sort of left-wing pedigree from the U.S., and then married an Israeli from the left-wing Siah movement. I always felt identified as an Israeli national, rather than as a Jew. I was always in the peace movement, but it took me almost twenty years to 'discover' the Palestinians."

He emphasizes this point, recalling that although he published a book about Jerusalem, he never really knew the Arab part of the city. His book, *Between Redemption and Revival*, chronicles the Jewish community in nineteenth-century Jerusalem.

Halper and his fellow ICAHD members started finding out more about why Palestinian houses were being destroyed. Demolitions, they learned, were carried out by different authorities for different reasons. During the past five years of the second Intifada, most of the reported demolitions have been carried out by the IDF for "security reasons," either as punitive measures against the families of suicide bombers and convicted terrorists or to clear the houses from which fire was directed against military positions and Jewish settlements.

The demolition policy, however, goes back a long way. Since the Six Day War of 1967, some twelve thousand Palestinian homes have been demolished for various reasons. The IDF's civil administration, which rules the territories, can order demolitions of houses built without a permit as in the case of the Hamdan house. In Jerusalem, the municipality can order demolitions for the same reason. In some areas of Jerusalem, the Israeli Interior Ministry is the authority that orders a demolition.

ICAHD volunteers embarked on a course of direct action. When they knew in advance about an impending demolition, they tried to prevent it by sit-ins. When a home was demolished, they organized protest demonstrations. Early on, ICAHD resolved to rebuild at least some of the demolished houses. It has managed to rebuild three houses every year, one of them by means of the Israeli and international summer camp. So far, nineteen homes have been rebuilt—some of them several times. It isn't very much when set against the number destroyed, but ICAHD regards it as an important statement. Furthermore, all the rebuilding is done publicly and openly.

"We send out a press release when we decide to rebuild a house, and this reduces the potential numbers considerably," explains Halper. "Many Palestinians are only too happy to have their demolished homes reconstructed, but only very few are prepared to make the rebuilding a public gesture in defiance of the authorities."

Palestinian Land Defense Committees exist throughout the occupied territories and ICAHD works with them. Arabiya House owner Salim Shawamreh, now an ICAHD field worker, coordinates with the relevant local committees to decide which houses will be rebuilt. In the case of the Hamdan house, a letter of approval was also received from the Anata municipal council.

In 1998, ICAHD became a registered association with financial support from the European Community's Partnership for Peace Program. This funding enables ICAHD to run its office with a staff of seven, but some of their activities cannot be financed by the European Union (EU). The Europeans won't finance illegal operations, so ICAHD must look for special funding for its rebuilding activities. Much of the money for this is raised at parlor meetings in private houses organized by support groups in the United States and Britain.

Like the Moked, ICAHD is an Israeli organization. There is continuous cooperation with Palestinians and the organization employs one Palestinian field worker, but the public committee is solely Israeli. Halper points out that it is Israelis who are occupying Palestinian territory, and it is up to Israelis to deal with this reality. "Nevertheless, the Palestinians are not just our victims," he explains. "They are equal partners in everything we do, and I think that gives us credibility with them."

While focusing on house demolitions, Halper stresses that everything must be seen in the context of Israel's occupation of Palestinian territory. ICAHD's opposition to demolitions is part of a strategy aiming to bring this occupation to an end. Halper admits to "some tension" in ICAHD over policy. For example, he is firmly opposed to going to court to prevent demolitions. He thinks that, in taking legal action, ICAHD is recognizing the current state of affairs and by inference accepting the Israeli occupation of the Palestinian territories. "I think it is strategically wrong," he states emphatically. "I am becoming more and more in favor of international campaigning and lobbying."

On the other hand, ICAHD Field Coordinator Meir Margalit actively pursues the legal route whenever he can. He concedes that Halper disapproves, but feels free to pursue this policy "Let me tell you about yesterday," he says enthusiastically. "We received word from a source in the Housing Ministry that they were going to demolish three houses. We immediately informed the families, suggesting that they apply for a court injunction to stop the demolitions. Two families secured court orders, but the third one didn't. The only suitable attorney we could find for them was located in Nazareth in the north. Nevertheless, he faxed us an application to the court. We eventually secured an injunction against a guarantee of forty thousand shekels [$10,000]. We applied to a higher court and got the amount reduced to a quarter of that amount, which we borrowed from the Rabbis for Human Rights. For the time being, those three houses at least are saved."

We are sitting in the ICAHD office in the center of Jerusalem. On the wall someone has posted up an updated "Ten Commandments": Thou shalt not murder; thou shalt not destroy; thou shalt not torture; thou shalt not starve; thou shalt not close off; thou shalt not humiliate; thou shalt not delay ambulances; thou shalt not demolish houses; thou shalt not uproot trees; thou shalt not covet thy neighbor's field.

Like Halper, Meir Margalit wears a beard, but there the similarity ends. Small and wiry, his background is very different to that of his colleague. His accent in both Hebrew and English unmistakably Spanish; he was born in Buenos Aires to parents who had previously been active in the right-wing Betar Zionist movement in Poland. Visiting Israel as a teenager to study youth leadership, he returned in 1972 with a Betar settlement group, which helped to establish Netzarim, a Jewish settlement recently evacuated from the Gaza Strip. He was lightly wounded in Sinai in the 1973 Yom Kippur War and while recuperating started having second thoughts about his militant Zionist ideals.

He embarked on studies at the Hebrew University in Jewish History and Middle Eastern Studies, but when he started his doctorate on the formative phase of modern Jewish settlement in Palestine, he found himself fascinated by a neglected field. Most students of the subject have focused on the immigration of Jews from abroad, mainly eastern Europe. Immigration is termed aliya, ascending, and those who ascend are called olim. In research for his doctorate, Margalit decided to look into the story of those who went back to their countries of origin, the yordim, those who descended. He estimates that some eighty thousand Jews left Palestine during the thirty years of the British Mandate. His university supervisors thought he was "too sympathetic" to the yordim, so he presented his thesis at the more radical Haifa University, where it was accepted. Meanwhile, his political move toward the left continued, and he registered as a member of the dovish Meretz party.

In 1998, he was elected to the Jerusalem municipal council on the Meretz list, serving for four years. As a council member, he tried to prevent house demolitions, but felt that something more radical was required and joined Halper in establishing ICAHD. After leaving the council, he became field coordinator of the association. "Jeff and I disagree over the matter of applying to the courts," he admits, "but he lets me go ahead."

"Meir is the quintessential field worker," counters Halper, admiration manifest in his voice. "He is more interested in direct action than in long-term strategy." Halper's strategy is outlined in *Obstacles to Peace, a Re-Framing of the Palestinian-Israeli Conflict*. Lavishly illustrated with maps, it looks at what the author terms the "Matrix of Control," a complex system of administration, planning, law, and military regulations that Israel uses to maintain rule over the occupied territories. He seeks to "reframe" the conflict by "placing the occupation at the center of the debate."

After describing and analyzing the situation in a dozen chapters, Halper concludes that "a clear, compelling political vision accompanied by an aggressive strategy of advocacy" is required. Explaining that he supports Israel's right to exist as a normal nation and is therefore opposed to a comprehensive boycott, as in the case of South Africa, he nevertheless approves of "selective sanctions" aimed at ending the occupation. Halper sees his fellow citizens as mostly concerned with personal safety and willing to support anything that enhances this. Thus, most Israelis supported the disengagement from Gaza and support the separation wall because they think it affords them greater security.

As Israeli public opinion is a "lost cause," international society must be mobilized against the occupation. Halper intends to take advantage of ICAHD's excellent relations with U.S. State Department officials and officials of the EU and many foreign consulates.

This does not mean that the antidemolition campaign, which gives the association its identity and moral force, should be abandoned. ICAHD's latest e-mail makes this clear: the association has learned of a joint plan of the Israel government and the Jerusalem Municipality to build thirty housing units and a synagogue in the Muslim Quarter of the Old City, near Herod's Gate. Those receiving the e-mail are invited to protest to the ministers of the Interior and Construction, the mayor of Jerusalem, the director of Jerusalem District Planning, and others. ICAHD has come a long way from the days when it did not know how things worked. Today it understands where, how, and why policies are decided and implemented. It also knows which buttons to push to delay—or even prevent—their execution.

Returning to visit Arafat Hamdan in his rebuilt house, I find him very welcoming but worried about the future. He has planted three olive trees in the garden, and the light blue front door and window bars contrast pleasantly with the white walls inside and out. Sitting on a comfortable sofa in the well lighted, open-plan house, we drink tea as he relates that his youngest son has started waking up again at night since he returned to the scene of the demolition. The boy remains pathologically afraid of dogs.

Hamdan is also worried about the unemployment in Anata. He himself has not worked for several months and his neighbor has not worked for several years. The resulting poverty, he says, is a major cause of petty crime in the neighborhood. He also tells the sad story of another neighbor, who was killed last week in an accident in his workshop. The man, who supplied gas for air conditioners and refrigerators, somehow set off an explosion that blew his head off.

While rebuilding the Hamdan home, we met Abu Mussa, the mukhtar of the Jahaleen Bedouin, whose tents and shacks sprawl over the nearby hills. In the next chapter, we will start out by visiting the Jahaleen summer camp, organized by a small Israeli group called The Olive Tree Movement. As we shall see, the name has a symbolic significance.

4

The Ultimate Symbol of Peace

Within days of the completion of the Hamdan house, and only about half a mile away, a summer day camp for the children of the Jahaleen Bedouin tribe is in full swing. Ranging in age from four to fourteen, the kids are manifestly enjoying themselves. Dressed in special camp T-shirts and baseball-type caps, they rush around blowing up balloons; drawing pictures of trees, flowers, goats and chickens; and then sticking the drawings on their faces or on the balloons. Down the hillside, on a level piece of ground, some of the older boys are playing soccer.

The Jahaleen live under the threat of demolitions. In the winter of 2004, the bulldozers were advancing remorselessly on their encampment of tents and tin huts near Anata when tribal leaders and their Israeli sympathizers filed an application to the High Court of Justice. The court issued an injunction effectively halting further action by the authorities.

Not content with merely saving the homes, the tribe's Israeli friends determined to organize a summer day camp for the Jahaleen children, who have never experienced structured play, music, sports, and art. Abu Mussa, the mukhtar of the tribe—and a colorful presence during the ICAHD rebuilding activities—had his men put up a large tent and some other shaded areas; the Israelis supplied the teachers and counselors. Footballs, pens, pencils, paints, brushes, paper, cardboard, and balloons were purchased with contributions from a few private individuals.

Now Abu Mussa strides purposefully down the hill in his abaya robe and red kaffiyeh head scarf, a full partner with camp organizer Yaffit Biso, known to the Palestinians as Jamila. Tall and full-bodied, fluent in Arabic, the Syrian-born Jamila is a dominating presence. At night, she runs an emergency hotline for her fellow Jewish citizens in Rishon Lezion near Tel

Aviv, where she lives, but her days are devoted to the Olive Tree Movement, currently running this day camp for Palestinian children in the desert east of Jerusalem.

Not that everything is plain sailing: inside a ramshackle hut belonging to the tribe, some of the young boys are marching, stamping their feet to the rhythm of a drumbeat, led by a young man with a Palestinian flag. Jamila confronts Abu Mussa, who has organized the parade. "We said no flags," she shouts angrily. "If there is a Palestinian flag, there must be an Israeli flag also."

"If you produce an Israeli flag, I'll trample on it!" retorts the mukhtar.

Other leaders hurry to calm the two of them. The children finish their parade in the hut and emerge without a flag, but Jamila continues to grumble: "If he doesn't respect my flag, how can I respect his?" she asks. "I don't want any flags here. We are human beings—not Israelis and Palestinians. We are people who want to live together. If he wants to destroy my flag I won't come here."

Minutes later, she is belly dancing with a four-year-old Bedouin girl. She and her partner sway their bodies and flick their fingers as an Israeli youngster beats out the rhythm on an Arab drum. The whole crowd is in the large tent now, clapping in rhythm. Other youngsters join the dance, and soon dozens of them are dancing, swaying, flicking their fingers, and clapping. A teenager has a younger boy on his shoulders. The atmosphere is festive and jovial.

Israeli counselors distribute drinks and snacks to the eager children and, as they squat down in the dust eating and drinking, a Bedouin boy who can't be older than ten sets up a chant, which is answered with a roar by the whole assembly. Amazingly self-confident, he chants in a powerful voice, each time answered by his fellow tribesmen. At the end of the day, Jamila and Abu Mussa, apparently reconciled, thank all those who organized the camp.

Ezra Nawi has also been organizing a summer day camp for Palestinian children, but his field of operations lies in the Hebron hills, some fifty miles to the south. He tells me all about it as we rumble along the desert tracks in his four-wheel-drive pickup truck. The camp was for a week and the highlight was a trip to the Jericho water park.

"These kids had never seen a swimming pool," explains Nawi. "I would never take them to the sea, even if we could get permission. The sea would be so strange for them that there would be a real danger of kids drowning."

The Bedouin adopted by Nawi live in tents and caves in the desert south of Hebron near the old border between Israel and the West Bank. They are peaceful, even passive, he asserts, but they are subject to daily harassment by local Jewish settlers. Nawi insists that they have never shown hostility toward the settlers, who want to drive them far away from the region. The IDF is also keen to empty the area so that it can be used for training.

The fifty-three-year-old Nawi, his head shaved to complete baldness, looks like the villain of an early Chaplin movie. Born in Iraq, he speaks fluent Arabic and tends to immerse himself in the culture. The radio of his pickup is tuned to an Arab station, and as we travel, he sings along in a high nasal whine. A plumber by profession, he is said to charge exorbitant fees for his work, which he then donates to the south Hebron tribesmen.

Also along for the ride is Horesh, a young thin-faced Israeli in torn jeans and a T-shirt, who is recording our trip on videotape. Both Nawi and Horesh are associated with Ta'ayush, a Jewish-Arab group engaged in various forms of direct action. Ta'ayush is Arabic for living together, and its activities range from sit-down protests against the separation wall and the roadblocks to escorting Palestinian children to school and protecting them from the settlers.

The Bedouin children, aged from six to eleven, have suffered almost continuous harassment by settlers on their way to school. They can reach the regional school on foot in forty minutes by a route that takes them past the settlement of Carmel, but since the settlers effectively blocked off that route they started walking along meandering desert paths for two hours. Sympathizers from Ta'ayush and volunteers from abroad resolved to put an end to this infamy by escorting them along the shorter route. They were rewarded for their efforts by being beaten with iron bars by a group of masked men who came from the direction of a nearby settlement.

Fortunately, the matter came to the attention of the Committee for Child Welfare of the Knesset (Israel's parliament), which summoned the local IDF commander to testify. He was asked why the children of the southern Hebron region were being prevented from reasonable access to education. He had no reply, but, after being grilled by the committee members, the officer organized an IDF patrol to escort the children to school. Since then, every morning an armored personnel carrier with four soldiers aboard has driven slowly behind the walking children. The patrol was not, however, deployed for the summer day camp. A settler laughingly explained to Nawi that the Geneva Convention determined that children had a right to school—it did not, as far as he knew, say anything about the right to summer camps.

Nawi, Horesh, and other members of Ta'ayush aim to establish a presence in the area to protect the local Bedouin from the settlers. They spend days on end living in the area, sleeping in the Bedouin caves, tents, and houses. Nawi has rented a house in one of the villages. He shows it off proudly. A Bedouin boy who must be all of fourteen is backing up a truck with sand and bags of cement for repairing the walls. Next week, says Horesh, he is going to bring an Arabic language movie here and project it on the wall of the school building.

Scrambling up a steep incline to the entrance of a cave, we are warmly greeted by a Bedouin family. The scene is idyllic, even biblical. The bare desert hills, dotted with an occasional black tent, stretch into the distance. The intervening valleys are sown with wheat, which may or may not grow, according to the rainfall. "Nobody else would even try to grow anything in this place," snorts Nawi. "There is absolutely no reason to prevent these people from living here."

Sacks of grain and flour are stacked up in the cave, which is cool and pleasant. Mattresses, blankets, duvets, and cushions make up the furniture. One side is the "kitchen," with pots and pans. We are served very sweet tea. The children are extraordinarily beautiful. Their father, his face partly covered by a thick brown beard, has surprising blue eyes. A young deer is tied up in the cave. The children found it abandoned and it was suckled by one of the family's goats. Like most of the local caves and tent encampments, this one has electricity from a gasoline-powered generator, donated by a Palestinian sympathizer living abroad.

The Jewish settlers are relentless in their battle against the Palestinian residents of the territories. Apart from harassing their children, they steal their sheep and goats, plow up their crops, and cut down their olive trees. The assault on the olive trees is not confined to this Hebron hills location. It has become a plague throughout the West Bank, with settlers attacking the Palestinian harvesters, stealing their crops, and damaging, cutting down, uprooting, and burning trees. It is a campaign redolent with symbolism. It is not by chance that Jamila calls her group the Olive Tree Movement, because the tree, a symbol of peace, is central to the life of the Palestinian Arab. To counter the settlers, a number of Israeli Jewish organizations have joined forces, traveling to the countryside to help their Palestinian neighbors with the harvesting.

The Rabbis for Human Rights are one of the groups most active in this field, and soon after my trip with Ezra Nawi, I join one of their groups for olive picking in the northern West Bank between Nablus and Ramallah. Above us on the hilltop, the red-roofed houses of the Jewish settlement of Eli are visible; down in the valley, the Arab village of Sawiya blends with the gray and beige rocks of the countryside. It is a region of arid terraces where crops are wrested from the soil with difficulty. As usual, it is the hardy olive tree that best survives in such circumstances.

Sheets are spread under the trees and the Arab women beat the sheets with wooden rods. The olives that fall on the canvas are easily gathered, but some must be picked manually from the trees and others individually scavenged from the earth, a labor that is backbreaking. Olive trees experience alternating seasons: one with plentiful fruit and one with only a sparse crop. This year is the lean one, with relatively few olives on the trees, meaning that none must be wasted. Even the wrinkled and blemished fruit will be taken to the olive presses, explains Ziad Abu-Muhammad, a squat, round-faced man with a black topcoat over his abaya robe. Women and children from the village join us in our labors. Ziad has called some of the kids from school, taking advantage of our presence, which enables him to harvest his fruit without harassment. His oldest son, he tells us, is studying physical education at the nearby Birzeit University.

The call of the muezzin from the Sawiya mosque echoes over the valley as we sip sweet tea during a break. The silver-leaved trees with their gnarled trunks afford shade for Ziad's donkey, which munches steadily. The sky is clear blue above the gray stone terraces. The scene is so peaceful that it is difficult to conjure up the violence that is the reason for our presence here.

It has happened, though. Only last week, six sacks of painfully gathered fruit were slashed by teenage girls from a nearby settlement, who also attacked the old women who had harvested them, beating them with sticks. Nora, an Israeli volunteer, shows off the scars on her neck, which she says are the result of scratches inflicted by a woman settler during a previous harvesting operation. Born in Switzerland, she came to Israel through a pioneering Zionist youth movement, but says she is no longer a Zionist.

"I still believe in what we did then," I tell her, coming from a similar background in England. "Zionism was a great movement. I think that we have lost our way recently. We just have to find the right way back."

"I don't agree," she retorts. "I was taken in, but now I don't believe in it at all. It was always a lie, right from the start. Zionism was a false dream."

We agree to differ. Yannai, a former television soundman, is amused by this exchange between two western immigrants, which he terms "post-Zionist." He is between jobs and spends several days each week helping the Palestinians with their olive harvest. Another volunteer, Yair, has learned Arabic, but thinks he might return to Australia, where he has spent several years after his army service. "I'm not a fighter," he remarks. "I'm not sure I can live here, where every day is a constant fight."

Hannah, a flaming redhead, is tentatively courted by one of the local young men, whom she good-naturedly discourages. She is from an ultra-Orthodox family, but now wears trousers. Her parents would disapprove of the olive picking, she says, but not because she is helping Arabs. They would be distressed to see her in trousers, mixing with nonreligious people. She has a German boyfriend, she tells me. Her mother and father don't care about his being German, but they care a great deal about the fact that he isn't Jewish.

Reya, blond and blue-eyed, is from Finland. She met her Israeli husband on a peace march in the Netherlands protesting the Kosovo fighting. Now they live in Finland, but are spending some weeks in Tel Aviv with her husband's family. She heard about the harvesting and decided to come along. When somebody tells her that her orange head scarf is the color adopted by the Gaza settlers (who were just about to be removed from their homes in the "disengagement" operation) she is so appalled that she throws it away.

Anita, a Reconstructionist rabbi originally from the United States, relates how she saw an uprooted olive tree the previous week. "I've seen many destroyed trees this year," she notes, "but somehow this one isolated trunk with its roots in the air was very poignant. I was with a Palestinian guy when we found it, and we mourned the tree together."

Just sitting under a tree eating the same food with the Palestinian villagers is so important, she opines. The only Israelis they ever get to see are settlers, soldiers, and police officers. It is vital that they realize there are also other types of Israelis.

Contact between the groups of harvesters is maintained via cellular phone: how did we ever manage without them? Hillel, a white-bearded veteran of my own age, calls me to announce that their group is descending to the road to be picked up for the return to Tel Aviv and Jerusalem. He suggests that we wind up our picking and join them. When we meet, he tells me that they were asked by an armed person whether they had a permit. As the man refused to identify himself, they presumed he was a settler and not a policeman. Later a uniformed police officer told them they should not be harvesting so close to the settlement of Eli without an armed police escort. Nevertheless, it has been a peaceful day, a day free of the clashes that the volunteer harvesters often experience.

Nobody knows the origin of the olive, but it dates back thousands of years. India and Egypt have both been put forward as candidates for its first appearance. Olive stones have been found in Egyptian tombs from four millennia ago, and may have been cultivated on the island of Crete even earlier. Some of the trees growing on Jerusalem's Mount of Olives are reputed to be as much as two thousand years old.

The olive has a starring role in the Bible and in Greek mythology. In the biblical story of the flood, when the dove is released by Noah it returns with an olive branch to prove that the waters have subsided and that God has made His peace with humanity. Because of this, the olive branch has long been a symbol of peace. According to Greek legend, the gods competed as to which of them could produce the invention that would be most beneficial to mankind. The goddess Athena won the contest by planting the first olive tree on the Acropolis. Zeus judged it to be even more useful than the horse proposed by Poseidon. Subsequently, Greek athletes who triumphed in athletic contests were crowned with olive wreaths, a custom most recently seen at the 2004 Athens Olympic Games.

In the Bible, the olive is one of the seven species of the Holy Land. The biblical book of Deuteronomy recounts that wheat, barley, grapes, figs, dates, pomegranates, and olives flourish in Canaan, where the Children of Israel will eventually abide. The candelabra of the Temple of Jerusalem burned olive oil and the kings of ancient Israel were almost certainly anointed with it. Christians were baptized with olive oil. Muhammad, the founder of Islam, used the oil on his head and advised his followers to apply it to their bodies.

Lawrence Durrel has written: "What we mean when we use the word Mediterranean starts at that first vital point when Athens enthrones the olive as its reigning queen, and Greek husbandry draws its first breath." The writer goes on to suggest that the art of grafting was initiated with the olive. Today the tree in its multiple forms is cultivated in all the countries of the Mediterranean basin and as far off as California.

Mediterranean olives are harvested in the months of October and November, and in Israel every fall brings the Galilee Olive Festival, when thousands of visitors flock to the region touring the groves and villages to sample and buy olives and olive oil. It is two-week series of concerts, performances, singsongs, and food fairs.

Near the Hananya Farm in western Galilee, a former summer home of the British high commissioner for Palestine, hundreds of Jews, Muslim and Christian Arabs, Druze, and Circassians mill around in a grove of trees, buying, selling, tasting, eating, and drinking. Olives, olive oil, soap, perfumes, and a multitude of herbs spill over improvised tables. Jewish and Arab stallholders do a brisk trade in snacks of pita bread with *za'atar*, *labane*, hummus, tahini and falafel, as well as *knaffe*, baklava, and other sweetmeats. A record number of herb teas are available and the pungent smell of cardamom-flavored coffee is everywhere.

An elderly Arab woman in abaya tunic and kaffiyeh head scarf reclines on a traditionally woven carpet, contentedly smoking a nargileh. Jewish and Arab families sit around picnicking; others push strollers between the gnarled trees. A Druze is demonstrating cooking with olive oil. A special cookery workshop for children is in full swing. Jewish and Arab groups perform songs and dances.

Aside from those in traditional clothes and performing groups identifiable by their style and language, it is often impossible to tell who is Jewish, who Arab, or to distinguish a Russian immigrant from a Druze ex-serviceman. The atmosphere is festive. The participants are united by food and drink, song and dance.

Amin Salman Hassan, the director of the Israel Olives Council and a tall, lean, bespectacled Israeli Druze, presides proudly over the event. "The olive is a universal symbol," he declares. "You will see people of all religions and communities, sitting under the same tree. The olive symbolizes connection with the land, peace, hope, and light. It is a unifying force with which all of us can work together."

The festivities will close this evening at the mixed village of Maghar, where there has been a bitter dispute between Druze and Christian Arabs.

Tonight's ceremony, he hopes, will not only wind up the festival but will also bring reconciliation. "Believe me, it is only the minority that always foments disputes," he insists. "The majority of Druze and Christians in Maghar want live in peace and friendship, and they will prevail. Let us hope this will also happen in Israel and in the whole region."

Hassan served in the IDF, the Border Police, and the regular police before retiring to cultivate his olive grove in the Israeli Druze village of Sajur in Western Galilee. His father was one of those Druze who befriended the Jews before the establishment of Israel and was one of the first of that community to enlist in the Border Police.

He objects to the term "coexistence" because in Hebrew *du-kiyum* means cooperation between two entities. In Israel, he points out, there are many types of Jews: Moroccans, Russians, Poles, Egyptians, Indians, and Yemenites. Among the Arabs, there are Muslims, Christians, Druze, and Circassians. "Let's talk about shared lives," he suggests, "about *all* the different communities living together. All of us must feel that we belong equally."

Shortly after our conversation, Hassan went to the United States to raise money for his pet project: a national center for the olive, which will include an archaeological garden, a reconstructed ancient olive press, a museum, study rooms, and a lecture hall. It will be named after his daughter, who was killed in a terror attack. He hopes that young Jews and Arabs will come together to learn about the history of the olive, and he looks forward to possible international conferences on the subject.

Meanwhile, a start has been made on international cooperation, with a possible joint Israeli-Palestinian "peace brand" of oil that would be marketed in the United States, Europe, and Japan.

"We want to produce organic extra-virgin oil that will sell because of its excellence," explains Oded Salmon, one of the initiators of the idea. "Today the Palestinians sell their oil relatively cheaply to local customers, but they could get much higher prices if they exported their produce. They would have to improve the quality, of course, but they definitely have the requisite know-how."

Salmon, who studied geology and geomorphology at the Hebrew University, spent many years working for the Jewish National Fund in the field of land improvement and forestation. He also worked in Africa on various development projects. Today he is an independent businessman and consultant involved in olive cultivation, olive oil manufacture, and marketing.

It was after participating in a joint Jewish-Arab course for promising entrepreneurs that he conceived the idea of an Israeli-Palestinian olive oil project. The courses are organized in a Galilee industrial park by Zeev Hirsch, formerly the Dean of Tel Aviv University's business school and director of the Rishon Lezion College of Management. Professor Hirsch was approached by

Stef Wertheimer, one of Israel's leading businessmen, to set up a joint program for Jews and Arabs.

Wertheimer, a strong believer in utilizing business as a path to cooperation and peace in the Middle East, has established industrial parks in Israel, Jordan, and Turkey. A project for two parks on either side of the Israel-Gaza border was in an advanced stage when the second Intifada, which erupted in the fall of 2000, put a stop to it. As the violence continued and the prospects of the joint industrial parks receded, Wertheimer looked for other ways of fostering cooperation.

He resolved to assist the Arab citizens of Israel to improve their businesses by promoting entrepreneurship through joint courses for promising Arab and Jewish business people. Wertheimer put up the money and Hirsch constructed the program. Israel's top lecturers in administration and business management lecture at his courses, which are held for one week per month for three successive months. The aim is to ensure a fifty-fifty balance between Jews and Arabs, but it has proved difficult to recruit enough Arab candidates and the current course has twenty Jews and twelve Arabs

The participants, who pay the equivalent of eight hundred dollars for the three weeks, live at a nearby kibbutz and carry out practical projects under the supervision of the lecturers. The day I visited, they were working out strategies for raising capital for a new business. "Should you try for a large investment right off, or be content with a smaller one?" asks the lecturer. "Do you want a big investor, who will own half your business, or a smaller one, who will give you more freedom?"

The students learn about trade-offs; for example, accepting a smaller investment in order to get the money quickly. It may make sense to raise the money before you are ready for it, argues the lecturer. "You raise money when you can, rather than when you need it."

The courses are conducted in Hebrew, in which the Arab participants are fluent. The students crouch over their computers, typing away. Jews and Arabs sit next to each other. Except for the head scarf of one Arab woman, it is impossible to tell them apart. Frequently they stop typing to discuss the project. The students demonstrate great enthusiasm, often continuing their studies and exercises late into the night. "Our courses have nothing to do with olives as such," observes Hirsch, "but it quickly became clear that it was a topic that interested both the Jewish and Arab participants. They were always discussing olives."

Natural and organic produce is a growing field in the United States, Europe, and Japan, and both Jews and Arabs are involved in it, he points out. The Palestinians have more land under olive cultivation than Israel, but both are very small players on the world market, which is dominated by Spain and Italy with North Africa, Turkey, and Greece not so far behind. Despite the small scale of the Israeli industry, there is considerable expertise in the country. Professor Shimon Lavie of the Hebrew University's Agriculture Faculty, who serves as president of the International Olive Association, is an expert on adapting different types of olives for oil production, and there are other Israelis of international renown.

While discussing olives with his fellow Jewish and Arab students, Salmon had a feeling that a way should be found to involve West Bank residents, and came up with the idea of an Israeli-Palestinian joint project. He enlisted Japanese support through the Japanese International Cooperation Association (JIKA). The association maintains an office in Tel Aviv for giving assistance to Palestinian agricultural and industrial ventures.

"I originally had contact with JIKA when I was working for an Israeli company in Ethiopia," explains Salman. "The Japanese organization is second only to USAID in assisting developing countries. I know that their people do excellent work, so, when I thought about how to advance a cooperation project, I contacted JIKA's Tel Aviv office. Naruse Takeshi, the local director, turned out to be a really dynamic and enterprising person. When I put forward my idea, he immediately understood so I took him to see Israeli and Palestinian olive growers. He agreed that a joint project might be a good way to assist the Palestinians."

The Japan External Trade Organization (JETRO) also became involved and agreed to put up the money for a joint Israeli-Palestinian course on olive cultivation and olive oil manufacture. It was a complicated operation, as permits had to be acquired for Palestinian growers and manufacturers to come to Israel for the activity, but the difficulties were overcome and so far, two weeklong courses have taken place. Salmon mentions the difficulties casually, but Hirsch recalls that it was not easy. Salmon set up a stakeout at the crucial roadblock between Israel and the West Bank, waiting there to intercede with the military until the last Palestinian had passed through.

Salmon and his Palestinian colleagues have not yet come up with a name for their joint brand of olive oil, but they are sure it will include the word peace. They know that many on the Palestinian side are doubtful about cooperating openly, as it could be seen as "recognition of the Israeli occupation." In the current state of tension between Israel and the Palestinian Authority following the election victory of the Islamic Hamas movement, a joint project is even more problematic.

Apart from financing the courses, the Japanese are prepared to help with the marketing. They have agreed to arrange meetings in Tokyo between an Israeli-Palestinian delegation and representatives of the major Japanese supermarket chains. Wertheimer has agreed to pay the fares to Japan for the joint delegation.

Olive oil is a relatively new produce for the Japanese, who have been importing it for only twenty years, but recently demand has increased. At the same time, Japanese customers have become much more health conscious and have become very keen on organic produce. High quality olive oil is called "virgin" oil, and an even better grade is dubbed "extra-virgin." "The top grades are not necessarily organic," explains Salmon, "but there is no reason why they can't be both organic and extra virgin, particularly as the Arab growers, both in Israel and the Palestinian territories, don't use chemical fertilizers and pesticides anyway."

At a workshop organized by the Japanese embassy in Tel Aviv for graduates of the two courses, the participants discussed the benefits of olive oil, as healthy and cholesterol free. They heard lectures by experts and listened to a presentation by a Japanese representative, Sakuyoshi Mutsumi, who stated that her people were becoming increasingly interested in healthy food and explained her country's requirements regarding genuine organic produce. Olive oil was relatively new to Japan, she allowed, but more and more Japanese were consuming it.

The Israeli-Palestinian brand would have to compete with the products of Italy and Spain, which currently dominate the Japanese market, so it must be tasty, healthy, and organic. A brand name that included the word peace could be popular. In between sessions, Israelis and Palestinians, Jewish, Arab, and Druze growers compared notes and discussed future cooperation.

"We want to free the Palestinian producers from their dependence on Israeli and Palestinian middle men who don't give them a fair price," explains Salmon. "During the courses, the Palestinian growers made contacts with the Israeli participants. Today they can get to the Israeli outlets directly, and also export to Japan and other countries. The Japanese can help them to make top quality products: they are world champions when it comes to supervision and control. They want to help the Palestinians and they can."

Jerusalem's American Colony Hotel, that perennial meeting place for Israelis and Palestinians, is the scene for a planning session. Nadim Khoury of Taybeh (near Ramallah) is there with Moussa, a big olive grower from the Hebron area. Moussa, held up by Israeli army checkpoints, has traveled for three hours to reach Jerusalem, a journey that ought to be accomplished in less than an hour. Leaning forward, he sketches an olive tree and proposes the brand name Olive Oil for Peace.

Oded Salmon is there with a representative from Yad Mordechai-Elite, a partnership of a veteran kibbutz with Israel's largest food manufacturer. The four businessmen pore over Moussa's drawing, considering the brand name. They argue about whether their produce has to be extra-virgin or whether virgin is good enough. The oil, they say, must be a blend that contains both Israeli and Palestinian oil. It will be bottled both in Nadim Khoury's Taybeh factory near Ramallah and at Yad Mordechai in Israel. The product will be tested for quality in both Israeli and Palestinian laboratories. Perhaps they should contact a Japanese graphic artist to design a label that will appeal to the Japanese customer, suggests Salmon.

Sitting there in the hotel lobby watching and listening to the amicable and very practical discussion is an almost surreal experience. Only yesterday, the Israeli army has carried out a full-scale military operation in the Palestinian town of Jericho, seizing six prisoners. This was only the most recent in a series of daily armed clashes between Palestinian gunmen and the Israeli army, and yet here we are drinking coffee together and discussing cooperation in the production and export of a joint Israeli-Palestinian Olive Oil for Peace brand of oil.

The discussion moves on to the taste, color, consistency, and acidity of the product. At a recent meeting, one of the Japanese representatives found the Palestinian oil too pungent. A more delicate taste is required. Should they concentrate on Japan, which has shown interest and is providing financial assistance? Contacts are being made with a large British supermarket chain. Khoury notes that he exports several tons to France annually. The European market should not be neglected.

Initially, four companies, two Israeli and two Palestinian, will set up a framework to promote the joint project. Others can be invited to join later. The first task is to prepare samples, a label with the brand name, a Power-Point presentation, written material, and a two-man delegation to go to Japan. Each of the four companies will invest an equal sum to kick off the project. Stef Wertheimer has already promised an initial investment.

The four businessmen agree to communicate by e-mail and present each other with their ideas. They hope that the marketing of their Olive Oil for Peace brand in Japan and Europe can become a project that is worthwhile commercially as well as politically. It is only a small example of working together to promote something worthwhile, but the symbolic significance should not be underestimated. The olive branch that the dove brought to Noah can again bear fruit; the tree planted by the goddess Athena should extend and deepen its roots. Instead of confrontation and conflict, uprooting and cutting down, the way of patient cultivation must again become the norm in Israel and Palestine, extending around the Mediterranean and all the way to California and Japan.

5

Learning Together

The realm of Jewish-Arab cooperation in Israel and Palestine is an interlocked network of groups and organizations. We have come across several of these connections on our journey so far. Following the arrest of a Windows activist, we encountered the Moked's human rights work. A Windows e-mail informed us about ICAHD, and while rebuilding an Arab home in Anata we discovered the Jahaleen Bedouin tribe in the desert east of Jerusalem. This in turn led us to Ta'ayush and the destruction of Palestinian olive trees, which introduced us to the various Jewish-Arab partnerships for the protection, cultivation, and processing of this symbolic fruit. On the next stage on our voyage, we now double back to the Moked for the Defense of the Individual, where we met Ala Khatib, one of its first volunteers.

After eight years of activity at the Moked in Jerusalem, including several years as codirector, Khatib returned to his village of Tira to build a retirement home. The home, the first in an Arab community, was established by a joint Arab-Jewish team. Several Arab businessmen, including members of Khatib's own family, and a Jew who already owned a Jewish retirement home, invested in the new project.

"We had Jewish and Arab doctors, Jewish and Arab nurses, and a Jewish dietician," he recalls. "The very idea of a retirement home was revolutionary for our society. I like revolutions. I'm proud of them. I'm in favor of change."

Seven years later, changing course yet again, Khatib was back in Jerusalem to take up another challenging task as codirector of a bilingual school in Jerusalem where Jewish and Arab students study together. Each class has two teachers, a Jew and an Arab, and the children learn simultaneously in

Hebrew and Arabic. The school has maintained a balance between the numbers of Jewish and Arab students in each class. The "Arab" half of the student body in fact includes some twenty Christian Armenian students from the Old City of Jerusalem.

In the Israel of today, a visit to Jerusalem's bilingual school is a remarkable experience. You see the children, aged six to twelve, thronging the yard, shouting in Hebrew and Arabic, arguing, laughing, playing tag, kicking a ball, draping their arms affectionately around each other's necks, or—alternatively—putting each other in half-nelson holds, and you realize that half of them are Jews and half Arabs, and you rub your eyes in disbelief.

In the class, each teacher speaks her own language, and the children clearly understand. "We don't translate each other," says Ulfat Salman, an Arab teacher from nearby Beit Safafa. "The secret is working hard together to prepare the lessons. I have taught in an Arab school and I can tell you that this is much more difficult."

"Good preparation is the secret," agrees her Jewish colleague Etty Weiss. "I was very apprehensive at the start. My husband was worried that I would be spending all my time helping the Arab students with Hebrew. In fact it is the opposite: it is the Jewish students who find the Arabic difficult."

They both point out that Arabic is a harder language to learn than Hebrew. This combined with the fact of Hebrew dominance in the west Jerusalem environment tilts the balance toward Hebrew, but the school manages to maintain equality. There is no first language and second language—both languages are first languages. This equilibrium is also maintained on religious, cultural, historical, and political matters.

The teachers recall the story of Ilan Ramon, Israel's first astronaut, who died tragically along with the other crew members when an American spaceship exploded. At first, all the Jewish and Arab children were proud of the selection of Ramon, but after the accident, when it emerged that he was an Israel Air Force pilot who had bombed the Iraqi nuclear reactor in 1981, the atmosphere around the event changed. "Nothing was said out loud," notes Weiss, "but you felt the Arab kids found it difficult to mourn Ilan Ramon."

The school celebrates all the Jewish, Muslim and Christian festivals. The Jewish holiday of Purim, traditionally a costume party, is a notable hit with the Arab children. They enthusiastically join their Jewish friends in the dressing up. The school calendar differs from that of the other schools in Israel, being scheduled around Rosh Hashanah, Christmas, Eid al-Adha and the other holidays. For the most part it works well, but Israel's Independence Day, which is preceded by a memorial day for the fallen, presents a real problem. For Palestinians and other Arabs (including citizens of Israel), the 1948 war is the *Nakba*, the disaster. "I'm happy for the Jews that they found a homeland," says nine-year-old Moataz, "but it is a sad day for us."

· "The Arab kids remained in class," says his classmate, Shira. "No one forced them to celebrate."

Moataz, the son of an Arab lawyer, lives in a Jewish suburb where he has some Jewish friends, but says that "some neighbors don't like Arabs." No, he didn't hear that from his parents. "They never talk about it, but I know." He speaks fluent, confident Hebrew. Shira assures me that she is comfortable speaking Arabic, although she has some problems with the spelling.

Neither child makes friends on an ethnic basis. Shira's best friends are Suha and Hanin. When they play together, they talk Hebrew and Arabic without realizing which language they are talking. Suha and Hanin come to the Jewish suburb of Beit HaKerem to play with Shira, and she visits her friends in Beit Safafa. Moataz says his best friend is Jamie. He always makes sure that Jamie understands, explaining in Hebrew if necessary.

Standing in the corridor, outside one of the classrooms, Nathaniel, one of the teachers, a stocky man with a helmet of thick, wiry, black hair and a round, smiling face intercedes between two twelve-year-old boys. He slips from Hebrew into Arabic and back again. He seems to be speaking more Arabic to a sharp-faced boy with gelled hair in a bright green sweatshirt, apparently an Arab, and more Hebrew to a tow-haired youngster who looks Jewish to me.

Struggling with the Arabic part of the dialogue, I quickly understand that it is a quarrel about honor. The Arab boy demands to know why his family was brought into the argument.

"He started it," protests the other, "He said I preferred playing with girls, and anyway I didn't curse his family."

"Why bring my family into it at all?"

The dispute, patiently mediated by Nathaniel, continues for some five minutes and is concluded with a (slightly reluctant) hug of reconciliation. Later I discover that what I had taken for a riveting cross-cultural exchange was nothing of the sort: both students were Arabs. So why was Nathaniel speaking Hebrew some of the time?

"It was unconscious," he tells me. "My Arabic needs improving, so I sometimes find it easier to make a point in Hebrew. As you noticed, the kids understood perfectly well."

The Hand in Hand school was the brainchild of an Arab educator, Amin Khallaf, and a Jewish sociologist, Lee Gordon. Khallaf, who was born and raised in the small Galilee village of Mukeibila, came to Jerusalem to study Islam and Middle East History at the Hebrew University. He never had much contact with Jews at home and at university he was mainly active in the Arab Students Union. The turning point for him came in 1990 when he attended a workshop for "facilitators" at the Jewish-Arab village of Neve Shalom/Wahat al-Salam near Jerusalem. There he met both his wife and his future life's work.

He subsequently taught at the Neve Shalom village school and was active in other groups working for contacts between Jews and Arabs. When his son was four, he entered him at the YMCA kindergarten in Jerusalem, where Arab and Jewish children learned together, and began worrying about his children's future education.

"Israeli Arabs in Jerusalem can send their kids to east Jerusalem, where the curriculum was Jordanian and is now Palestinian," he explains, "or they can send them to a Jewish school, where they won't learn about their own language, history, and culture. I didn't want either."

A mutual friend introduced him to Lee Gordon, an Israeli Jew from the United States, who was thinking along the same lines. According to Khallaf, there was an immediate "chemistry" between them, and they began to lay their future plans in Gordon's kitchen. They set up a nonprofit association, Hand in Hand Center for Jewish-Arab Education, and started writing to local councils and local education authorities all over Israel, following up their letters with visits. The most enthusiastic response came from the director of education of Misgav Regional Council in western Galilee, who convened a meeting with representatives from three local Arab communities.

"We reached agreement on a plan for a bilingual school," recalls Khallaf, "but we had no idea whether there were any takers. We called a parents' meeting in the village of Kaukab Abu al-Hija for 8 p.m., and around quarter past they began trickling in. Before very long there were a hundred and fifty parents in the hall. Not all of them were ready to send their kids right away, but they were interested."

In Jerusalem, they were less successful. The Municipal Education Department told them that the time and place were "inappropriate." Fortunately, Yossi Sarid of the left-wing Meretz Party was education minister at the time, and he set up a meeting with his friend Ehud Olmert, then mayor of Jerusalem. As Olmert was at that time a member of the right-wing Likud party, Gordon and Khallaf were not sure of their reception, but the mayor promised them "a thousand percent support," and he subsequently kept his word.

With support in both Jerusalem and western Galilee, they decided to take the plunge: in 1998, the two projects were launched simultaneously. Jerusalem started out with a preschool kindergarten. Misgav established a kindergarten and first grade school class, which means that Misgav has remained one year ahead of Jerusalem.

In the fall of 2000, the second Palestinian Intifada broke out and there were parallel clashes inside Israel. Thirteen Arabs were killed by police fire. Parents from the Misgav met together in the Misgav school and resolved to take action. They advertised in all the local papers, urging moderation and self-control. Lauding their school as an example of living together, they set up intercommunal meetings. In Jerusalem, the Hand in Hand school set up a "peace tent" and invited the local residents to drink tea and coffee and participate in a dialogue.

In that same period residents of Kafr Kara, a small Arab town in the Wadi Ara region some thirty miles north of Tel Aviv, initiated meetings with people from the neighboring Jewish towns and villages to discuss how to counter the deterioration in relations between the two communities. After many discussions, they resolved to establish a Jewish-Arab school, The Bridge over the Wadi, and they asked Hand in Hand for help. In 2004, the third bilingual school was founded in Kafr Kara. This time, four classes started simultaneously: preschool and the first three grades.

All three schools serve mixed population areas, but whereas in Jerusalem and Misgav, the Arab students come to Jewish locations in Kfar Kara it is the turn of the Jewish children to attend school in an Arab community. It says a great deal about Jewish-Arab relations in Israel that for quite a few of the Jewish parents the journey to enroll their child in the Bridge over the Wadi school was their first ever visit to an Arab community. Many see the daily trip of Jewish children into an Arab town as a more revolutionary development than the existence of the bilingual schools as such.

All of those involved with the schools—the founders, the directors, the teachers, the parents, and the students—agree that the problems are far more serious for the parents than they are for the children. "Trust the children," says Ala Khatib, codirector of the Jerusalem school, when a parent who is planning to move to Jerusalem from Galilee asks him anxiously about the integration of her daughter in the school the following year.

"Should I bring my daughter to visit the school?"

"She is welcome," replies Khatib, "but don't worry. I promise you that the children know far better than us how to ensure that she fits in with the other kids."

His codirector, Dalia Peretz, admits that they are operating largely on a basis of trial and error. "If something works, we continue with it," she explains. "If not, we go on to other projects."

Peretz was born in the southern town of Sderot to a family of immigrants from Morocco. After serving in the army as a teacher, she studied anthropology and sociology at Tel Aviv University. While teaching exclusively in poor neighborhoods, she became attracted to the idea of multiculturalism, which eventually brought her to the bilingual school.

"It is a potential minefield," she says, "a terribly sensitive environment. You ask yourself all sorts of questions: how do you reconcile all the different traditions? How do you maintain your own traditions while entering into another culture? At the same time you can be too careful. The kids so often manage to sort things out for themselves."

Hand in Hand founder Khallaf is convinced that a child's exposure to other identities serves to strengthen his own. Some people are worried that the child will become confused, but in his experience, the opposite is the case. A Jewish child face to face with an Arab classmate is forced to define his own identity even as he learns to know and respect the Arab personality. The reverse is also true.

Codirectors Peretz and Khatib add another point: children who are already bilingual cope better with a third language. They have found that Jewish students who speak Russian or English as well as Hebrew at home learn Arabic more easily than children from purely Hebrew-speaking homes. The same, of course, applies to Arab children who know English.

Open Day provides an opportunity for parents to get together with the codirectors and teachers. Avigdor, a burly Jewish father, says that his twins "live" the school. He suggests that, whereas most of the Jewish parents are interested in cultural activities and character building, the Arab parents are more focused on academic excellence. "I think there is too much homework, but I know that some of the Arab parents feel there is too little."

No, says Shafik, elegantly dressed with rimless glasses, one of the school's founders, who has three children at the school. He is not only interested in academic achievement. He is also interested in personality development as well as a good environment. He had first met Jews when he was eighteen, and he wanted his children to have the encounter earlier. "We used to talk of tolerance," he lectures his fellow parents. "Then we talked about coexistence. Today the way to go is multiculturalism. There is a good atmosphere in this school. My children really feel at home."

Nevertheless, the school is no Garden of Eden. On the main notice board is an announcement about a discussion in the school assembly regarding playground violence. There is no serious abuse, we learn, but fights do break out. After a long discussion, the assembly comes up with a proposal for the older children to assist the younger ones in minor disputes. Thus, first-grade quarrels will by adjudicated by second-grade students, second graders will bring their problems to third graders, and so on.

However, when Hadass and Aliya, who have been the class representatives at the school assembly, report back to the sixth grade, there is a storm of protest. Many of the children say they won't tell the seventh graders about their problems.

"Anyway," demands Hanan, "who's supposed to solve the problems of the seventh grade?"

"The first grade!" shouts Mustafa, earning a hearty laugh.

Other sixth graders want to know why the counselors, whom the school pays to sort out such matters, can't do the work. The teachers try in vain to explain that the counselors will continue to deal with major problems, but surely everyday squabbles can be dealt with by the kids themselves.

"Exactly," agrees Dalia, "we can sort it out ourselves. We don't need some lout from the seventh grade to help us."

In the end, a majority votes for trying out the proposed system, but without enthusiasm.

Following a suicide bombing in Jerusalem, eight-year-old children discuss their feelings. First, the Jewish teacher tells how she heard the explosion in the staff room and immediately thought it must be an attack. Then the Arab teacher shares her fears. One of the children explains that the Jews and the Arabs cannot agree how to divide the land.

"So what should be done?" asks the Jewish teacher.

"I was thinking about that on the way here in the car," replies the child. "They should sit down and discuss it."

"And what would you tell them?"

"I would tell them that, if they can't agree, the land will belong to nobody, but if they can agree, it belongs to everybody."

"I used to think the Arabs were strange," chimes in a freckled carrot-top irrelevantly. "Now I've been at the school, I know they are the same as Jews, but a little bit different."

The three schools have close to seven hundred students altogether and look forward to a future in which all of them will have high school classes up to matriculation. At present they are housed in temporary improvised accommodations: the Jerusalem school has been given part of the city's Denmark School, the western Galilee school has its own section of the Misgav Regional School, and the Kafr Kara school is utilizing a former Khan.

All three schools are building permanent campuses. The Jerusalem Foundation has given a large grant for a new campus to be constructed between the Arab village of Beit Safafa and the Jewish Patt neighborhood. The Misgav school is scheduled to move to new buildings near the Arab town of Sakhnin, and a new school is under construction in Kafr Kara.

Lee Gordon, who established Hand in Hand with Amin Khallaf, now runs the Friends of Hand in Hand in Portland, Oregon. In Jerusalem, Khallaf's new codirector is South African–born Josie Mendelson. Mendelson was the teacher who first brought Arab children to the YMCA Jewish kindergarten. After serving as director of early education in the Jerusalem Municipality, she moved to Hand in Hand. "I've always been interested in Jewish-Arab relations," she remarks. "I think it was my experience in South Africa, as a member of the Jewish minority inside the white minority, which made me identify with Israeli Arabs."

Having been involved in several Jewish-Arab cooperation initiatives, Mendelson is able to say that what distinguishes Hand in Hand from the others is its "enforced continuity." When the Intifada erupted in 2000, many intercommunal organizations and movements stopped—or at least postponed—their activities. "You can't do that with a school," she says. "You simply have to go on."

She also points out that in the Hand in Hand schools the Arabs are not in a minority, as they are in Israeli society as a whole. In the association, everything is based on strict equality: two directors, two principals in each school, two teachers in each class.

"There are no unilateral decisions," she says with feeling. "It is the most difficult thing I've ever done. I cannot make a decision without Amin's approval and he can't decide anything before he's checked with me."

Her hope for the future is that the schools' graduates will grow up to be leaders in their communities, but she has no illusions about the difficulties that lie ahead for them. "We are creating a tapestry—not a melting pot," she suggests. "We can't hope to agree, but just to show the children who they are and also understand the other's point of view."

Codirector Khallaf hands me a copy of that day's *Haaretz* newspaper, with a report that the Carmel Heights School in Haifa is to become bilingual in the coming academic year. The school, which already has nearly 40 percent Muslim Arab, Christian Arab, and Druze students, will change from being a Hebrew-Jewish school with many non-Jewish students to the Hand in Hand model. The paper quotes Carmel Heights director Miri Solomon as saying: "The idea has energized the teaching staff."

"We have that request from Haifa," notes Khallaf, "and another from Upper Galilee, and one from Jaffa. So we are looking at six bilingual schools in the not-so-distant future."

At the present time, Hand in Hand is a purely Israeli enterprise. In the current situation, it is not realistic to envision a joint Israeli-Palestinian school, although a few Arab students come from East Jerusalem, including the Armenians from the Old City to the Jerusalem school. Today the separation wall is being built in Jerusalem and it is already difficult for some of the students to reach the school. "As for the future, if one day there is an independent Palestinian state living side by side with Israel in peace," suggests Khallaf, "a joint school could be a marvelous project."

As we have seen, Amin Khallaf's first experience of dialogue between Jews and Arabs began when he visited Neve Shalom/Wahat al-Salam. The Jewish-Arab village, situated half way between Jerusalem and Tel Aviv, has been the location of a joint school since 1984. Close ties between Neve Shalom and Hand in Hand would seem to be axiomatic, but contacts are limited and cooperation is minimal. Both sides express cautious regret that there is not a closer partnership, coupled with the hope that relations will improve in the future.

"In Neve Shalom the kids don't learn together all the time, and they often study separately in their own language," explains Khallaf carefully. "With us the kids are together all day and speak both languages continuously, so we have a slightly different approach. Look, don't get me wrong. I am not criticizing them. If not for Neve Shalom, I would not be where I am today." The joint village of Neve Shalom/Wahat al-Salam is the subject of our next chapter.

6

Living Together

Following the outbreak of violence in the fall of 2000, there was an immediate widening of the rift between Jews and Arabs in Israel. The Arab community was appalled by the fatal shooting of thirteen of their people, which was accompanied by renewed violence between the IDF and the Palestinians of the territories. The Jews were shocked by the violence of the demonstrations, both in Israel and in the territories, and frightened by the manifest alienation of the Arab fellow citizens. Contacts between the two communities, such as they were, sharply declined as Jews stopped visiting Arab towns and villages and Arabs cut their meetings with Jews to a minimum.

The reaction of many Jewish-Arab groups was to intensify contacts in an attempt—unsuccessful at first—to bridge the gap that had suddenly opened up. The Arabs of Kafr Kara initiated the contacts that led to the establishment of another bilingual school. The Jerusalem bilingual school pitched a peace tent for open discussion between Jews and Arabs. Other groups also tried to step up their activities.

At Neve Shalom/Wahat al-Salam, on the other hand, the School for Peace closed down in a monthlong strike of protest and mourning and the school's encounter program was significantly reduced. As violence escalated in the Palestinian territories, the school concentrated its efforts on organizing welfare activity for the Palestinians. Neve Shalom, the most comprehensive and long-term experiment in coexistence between Jews and Arabs in the modern era, was in a state of shock.

In this community, Jewish and Arab citizens of Israel live side by side, govern themselves jointly, educate their children together, and reach out both to the surrounding Arab and Jewish communities and to the Palestinians from across the border. The village runs a bilingual school, maintains an interfaith spiritual center, and manages the above-mentioned School for Peace, where thousands of Jews and Arabs have met each other in structured encounters. The villagers of Neve Shalom probably know more about relations between Arabs and Jews than anyone else. Perhaps it was because of this that their reaction to October 2000 was so severe.

Neve Shalom/Wahat al-Salam—"Oasis of Peace" in both Hebrew and Arabic—was founded in the early 1970s near Latrun, halfway between Jerusalem and Tel Aviv. Today there are fifty families living in the pleasantly landscaped village, half of them Arab and half of them Jewish. Plans have been approved for a further ninety homes and there is a long waiting list for admission to membership, so Neve Shalom must be counted as a success, but the road has not been an easy one, and even today the villagers are still striving to find a successful formula for living together.

It began with a vision: after the Six Day War of 1967, Father Bruno Hussar, a Dominican priest of Jewish origin, conceived the idea of a mixed community of Israeli Jews and Arabs. In a memoir published two decades later, Hussar wrote: "We had in mind a small village composed of inhabitants from different communities in the country. Jews, Christians, and Muslims would live there in peace, each one faithful to his own faith and traditions, while respecting those of others. Each would find in this diversity a source of personal enrichment. The aim of the village: to be the setting for a school for peace."

Hussar was born to Jewish parents in Cairo. After attending an Italian high school, he moved to Paris, where he studied engineering. At the age of twenty-four, he was received into the Roman Catholic Church. Although he remained a devout Catholic all his life, his experiences in Vichy France during World War II made him strongly aware of his Jewish origins. After the war, he joined the Dominican Order and in 1950 was ordained as a priest. In 1953, his church sent him to Jerusalem to establish a Center for Jewish Studies. His arrival in Israel increased his feeling of Jewish identity without weakening his Christian faith.

Hussar founded a center for Jewish-Christian reconciliation in Jerusalem, calling it Isaiah House. An interfaith activist, he participated in the Ecumenical Council of Vatican II in Rome. Later, as an Israeli citizen, he served as an adviser on relations with the church to his nation's delegation at the United Nations in New York.

He started to work on the Neve Shalom project in 1970, and that same year he was offered a lease on one hundred acres of land by the Trappist monastery of Latrun. On the border between Israel and the Kingdom of Jordan, the property, which was privately owned by the monastery, had been classified as no-man's-land after the 1948 war. Following the Six Day War of 1967, it came under Israeli control on the seam between Israel and the occupied West Bank.

Hussar divided his time between Isaiah House in Jerusalem and a primitive hut on the treeless, stony hillside, which was covered with brambles and thorns. Initially he was joined by people from abroad, many of whom lived in tents. Most of them did not remain for more than a few months, but a French Christian, Anne LeMeignen, took up permanent residence in another hut. Although he was encouraged by these supporters from abroad, Hussar was determined that Jewish and Arab Israelis would be the ones to flesh out his vision.

In 1977, he organized a summer camp for Jewish and Arab students, mostly from the Hebrew University. They were to become the first members of his new community. Some of them took up residence on the hillside together with a kibbutz couple and a family from the nearby Ben Shemen Agriculture College. Two of these founder families are still active members of the community today.

Abdel-Salam Najjar, who attended the camp, was born in Arrabe near Nazareth to a devout Muslim family. His father was the imam, religious leader, of the Galilee village. In 1972, he enrolled in the Agriculture Faculty of the Hebrew University of Jerusalem. In the aftermath of the Six Day War, the student body had become radicalized: right-wing Jewish students confronted their Arab counterparts, who were increasingly identifying with the Palestinians of the newly occupied territories. As a result, there were frequent brawls. Najjar, who had had little contact with Jews while he was growing up, now came face to face with the Arab-Jewish confrontation in Israel, and he found it traumatic.

Fortunately, as student of agriculture, his second year was in Rehovot, where the atmosphere was more relaxed and he was able to take stock and start thinking seriously about his relations with his Jewish fellow citizens. He and some other students started discussing the idea of a school where Jews and Arabs could learn together. In 1976, they visited Neve Shalom, where Father Hussar embraced the project with enthusiasm. Urging them to establish the school on his hillside, he also raised the practical problems of establishing a village. "We don't know anything about building a new settlement," the priest told Najjar. "The kibbutzniks have the experience, so go and learn from them."

With Bruno's encouragement, Najjar spent two months as a volunteer at Kibbutz Kerem Shalom on the Sinai border. There he met Ilan Frisch and his wife Tamar. The Frisches grew up in the left-wing Kibbutz Artzi movement, which once espoused the creation of a binational state and has always favored peace and compromise with the Palestinians and other Arabs. Kerem Shalom aspired to be a new type of kibbutz, revolutionary and politically active for peace, but the Frisches did not remain there. They tried to establish an urban commune and, when that didn't work out, it was natural for them to think of Neve Shalom. In 1978, they and their six-year-old daughter joined Hussar and Anne LeMeignen on their hillside. Only a few months later Najjar moved in with his wife, Ayesha. The Jewish-Arab village of Neve Shalom/Wahat al-Salam was on its way.

From the outset, Frisch was involved in planning and development at Neve Shalom, an activity he continues to this day. With his white hair and beard, his jeans and his blue work shirt, he is very much the Israeli kibbutznik. After welcoming me to the village, he points to a map of the settlement and explains the location of the thirty plots, which represent the next stage of the community's growth. Some years ago, the Latrun Monastery wound up its leasing arrangement with Neve Shalom and made the village an outright gift of half the land. Today the association owns fifty acres, enough for ninety more building plots, of which the thirty are the first stage. Later we walk around the village as he explains the future plans.

Following the walk, I meet up with Najjar, who wears rimless glasses and a neatly trimmed black chin beard. He has held a number of positions over the years, including four terms as village administrator, but has been chiefly involved in education. Ayesha, his wife, became a nursery school teacher almost accidentally when the first children were born. She enlisted the help of a Jewish fellow villager and established a bilingual nursery. Later both women took appropriate courses, but they started out simply using their instincts and motherhood skills. Today she is again in charge of the large, airy, well-equipped nursery school. Her husband, after teaching in Jerusalem for several years, became the first headmaster of the village school.

A believing Muslim who has been on the hajj pilgrimage to Mecca, Najjar concedes that it was not a religious motivation that brought him to Neve Shalom. His motivation was political and social, but recently he has found himself focusing on the religious aspects of living together. There are enough mosques and synagogues in other communities, he feels, but the interfaith center being constructed at Neve Shalom excites his enthusiasm.

Despite his fervent faith, Hussar realized from the outset that his Jewish and Arab villagers were not religious and he was unapologetic about it. When he argued with fellow priests, he used to maintain forcefully that the inhabitants of Neve Shalom, although not believers, were "doing God's work." Nevertheless, he and LeMeignen wanted to nourish the spiritual approach and they proposed a "Corner of Silence" for meditation and prayer. The "corner" was eventually built as a spherical structure. On one side, five round windows are set high up in the curved wall. Opposite them, a wide panoramic window looks out on the nearby Latrun Monastery.

When Bruno Hussar died, LeMeignen proposed that, in addition to the Corner of Silence, a spiritual center should be erected in his memory.

Alongside the sphere, a handsome new building faced with Jerusalem stone is almost complete, with a library, lecture hall, kitchen, and prayer hall. It is hoped that it will hold seminars and workshops on religious issues and hold both interfaith prayers and regular services of all religions.

Although the original settlers were mainly secular in their approach, religion in its various forms has become increasingly important to some of them. Yoga teacher Dorit Shipin is currently developing the spiritual center together with Anne LeMeignen and Najjar.

Born in the Tel Aviv suburb of Givatayim, Dorit had a typical Israeli upbringing, school, youth movement, and service in the Nahal agriculture unit of the army before studying at the Tel Aviv Yoga Center, where she met her English husband. Searching for a pluralistic community that would be receptive to their ideas, the young couple arrived in Neve Shalom in 1982. Dorit worked in the kindergarten and then the guesthouse, but she was seeking a way to combine her yoga philosophy with the village ideology of peace and coexistence. It was natural for her to link up with Hussar and LeMeignen.

"The Spiritual Center complements the Corner of Silence," explains Dorit. "It will be the location of Friday prayers for Muslims, Jewish services on the Sabbath, and Christian worship every Sunday." Although a specific program is still to be worked out, interfaith meetings, seminars on spiritual matters, workshops on interfaith topics, lectures on philosophy, debates, and discussions are on the agenda. The center hopes to inject some religion and tradition into the secular atmosphere of Neve Shalom. Jewish, Muslim, and Christian human rights movements will be encouraged to attend meetings at the center. Dorit Shipin adds her personal conviction that peace between people is connected to the inner peace of the individual. "At Neve Shalom it is not just that we don't fight," she declares, "We aspire to live together in harmony."

Some villagers think the center is irrelevant, she concedes, but others see it as an integral part of the village's activities. A few of them believe that it can be an opening for new ventures.

Although the committees running Neve Shalom and its institutions are carefully balanced between Jews and Arabs, there is no rule concerning rotation. The last Jewish administrator ended his term in 1995. Since then the top official of the village has always been an Arab. "We don't vote on ethnic lines," explains Rayek Rizek, the current administrator. "The person is voted in on the basis of suitability and availability."

Rizek, a Christian Arab from Nazareth, has been living in Neve Shalom with his wife and children since 1984. Because of his good English, Rizek has long been involved in the village's public relations efforts. He is writing a thesis at Britain's Coventry University titled "Neve Shalom/Wahat al-Salam, an

Experiment in Bi-national Coexistence," which he has suspended for the time being because of pressure of work.

Neve Shalom, he notes, does not encourage ideological uniformity. It is a community of two peoples and three religions that aims to live together in mutual respect, but there is no agreed political line. Some of the villagers see the village as a model for how Israel and Palestine should exist as a unitary state, but many still accept the principle of two states, Israel and Palestine, living side by side.

"Personally, I think we have to find something in the middle," says Rizek. "I don't believe in one ordinary state—or in two ordinary states for that matter. We have to create something new, a framework that will enable us to live together in peace and security. At Neve Shalom we have proved that this is possible."

Over the years, the village has afforded Israeli Jews and Arabs a window into a different reality. Sari, a young kibbutz volunteer who spent a year there in 1985, looks back on it as a fascinating period. It was a completely new experience, she recalls, the first time she had any real contact with Arabs. The volunteer team consisted of two Jewish girls, two Jewish boys, and four Arab boys. "It was a formative process in my life," she states. "It has stayed with me for the past two decades, and set my political views, which have remained liberal."

She remembers Neve Shalom of that time as "very fragile." There could not have been more than a dozen families. The general meetings were stormy, with the members shouting at each other and disputing fiercely. "You had the feeling that their arguments could blow up the entire enterprise," she recalls.

Ilan Frisch talks about the mid 1990s with fondness. In the post-Oslo years, when there was real progress toward peace between Israel and the Palestinians, Neve Shalom was on a roll. The atmosphere of peace was in the air, and people came to visit and experience the village experiment. "We had this wonderful feeling that we were riding the wave of the future," he relates. "But since the new outbreak of violence in 2000 it has been more difficult. Once again, we are swimming against the stream."

Najjar describes life in Neve Shalom as a "continuous dialogue." They are always striving to find a correct balance between compromise and principle. It is one of those things that are easy to say, but difficult to achieve. The most important thing about Neve Shalom/Wahat al-Salam is that it exists. It meets many challenges and the more the villagers have learned, the more they understand the difficulties. Arabs and Jews who live inside their own communities are not aware of the problems, but in Neve Shalom, they cannot be avoided.

"Most peace organizations are based on goodwill and values," suggests Najjar, "but they lack the understanding that comes from experience. We sometimes argue with each other—we even shout at each other—but it is still a dialogue."

Najjar's daughter, Laila, and Frisch's daughter, Adi, have grown up together on Neve Shalom and their companionship has continued into adulthood. At the age of twenty-three, they are still best friends. "I have other companions in the village and outside," says Adi, "but not at the level of Laila."

We sit in the Najjar family living room on satin-covered sofas. Glass shelves in an alcove contain iron and glass abstract sculptures, some of them designed by Laila, who works in a jewelry store in Tel Aviv, one of a well-known Jewish owned chain.

"I'm the only Arab there, and I'm the best saleswoman," she tells me proudly. She is petite and dark-complexioned with loose, medium length hair, a bracelet, and an almost invisible nose jewel. She wears scuffed jeans and a long-sleeved sweater. Adi, also wearing jeans and sweater, her hair drawn back from a pale face, sits next to her friend. Her tiny nose jewel is also barely visible.

Laila studied jewelry design at the Betzalel School of Arts and Crafts in Jerusalem. She has designed jewelry with Islamic themes and also one piece in the form of a ring with a box inside and the symbols of three religions, but doesn't yet feel ready to take up design full time. "I definitely want to design jewelry eventually," she asserts, "but three years of study is not enough. I've a lot more to learn."

Adi is in charge of client services at a health club in the nearby town of Modiin. Both girls have busy schedules, and it took two weeks to set up a meeting, but they manage to get together from time to time. Although they talk mostly about everyday matters—clothes, shoes, entertainment, and boyfriends—politics is not off the agenda. "We don't live in a bubble," insists Adi. "Things are always happening in this country and we discuss them very intensely. I guess we do try to avoid hurting each other's feelings."

Adi's first memory is of the nursery school, where it was entirely natural to talk in both Hebrew and Arabic. It was only when she went to high school in Jerusalem that she realized how unusual her schooling had been. Laila says she remembers school more than kindergarten, particularly preparing to celebrate the festivals of the three religions.

"Today Laila's Hebrew is much better than my Arabic," admits Adi sadly. "I spoke Arabic fluently when I was younger, but, unfortunately, I don't get to use it much at work and outside the village." She smiles at Laila, and adds: "It's marvelous having an additional language. When we are in Jewish company, and we don't want the others to understand, we speak to each other in Arabic."

The girls have been abroad together representing the village. They have toured Europe several times and made one visit to the United States. "Not just

Jewish communities," stresses Laila. "We appeared in churches and mosques, as well as synagogues. The Americans got very excited and quite often cried with emotion."

"We did sometimes feel like strange objects," adds Adi, "almost like animals in a zoo!"

Laila admits that she felt ambivalent when Adi served in the army. The appearance of her friend's IDF uniform was difficult for her. At the same time, she understood that this was a part of Adi's life, and when her friend phoned her from the army to tell her about her problems, she didn't think of her as a soldier.

"In basic training in the army it is very tough," explains Adi. "You always come to a crisis that seems overwhelming. When I reached that point, it was natural to phone my best friend. I talked to her for hours and I cried and cried. I couldn't stop crying, and she comforted me."

The girls look at each other and smile at the memory.

"Do you never have rows?" I ask.

"Of course we do!" They reply together, interrupting each other. "But it is never political or ethnic. We quarrel about stupid nonsense."

Adi already has an apartment in her parents' house and has every intention of staying in the village. She lives at Neve Shalom out of choice, she emphasizes. She can live wherever she chooses. Laila, on the other hand, knows that she won't stay. She loves the village and would be very happy to remain there, but next month she is becoming engaged, and her future husband, who lives in the Galilee town of Majd al-Krum, has his business there. They met while they were students in Jerusalem.

I ask them about marriages between Jews and Arabs in the community and the two girls differ about whether there is one couple or two. It doesn't happen very often, they say. It is not Neve Shalom policy to encourage intermarriage between Jews and Arabs. They want the two communities to live side by side, each preserving its identity. At the same time, while they don't promote assimilation, they don't disapprove of intermarriage. They both insist that it is an entirely personal matter.

Can Neve Shalom be replicated?

"Why not?" asks Adi. "There are several towns where both Jews and Arabs live, and there should be more joint activities, such as combined community centers. Maybe the young people can change things. On a national scale the best thing would be one state for Israelis and Palestinians, where both peoples can live in peace and without violence."

"That is our unrealistic dream," chimes in Laila.

"But maybe the best we can hope for is each people having its own state, with freedom of choice where they want to live," concludes Adi.

Laila identifies with the Palestinians, and is active in supporting humanitarian assistance. She has been to several demonstrations against the separation wall. Adi recalls the days when both of them attended peace rallies, but today they have less time for this kind of activity.

While neither girl has anything negative to say about Neve Shalom, Laila concedes that many members of her family in Arrabe and Nazareth are indifferent, or even hostile. "They are traditional Muslim Arabs," she states. "As far as they are concerned we have gone to live with the Jews. I don't accept this. Neve Shalom/Wahat al-Salam is an Arab village just as much as a Jewish one. I think that living here has opened up all sorts of options for me. My family doesn't really understand, but I still feel attached to them. I remain a traditional Muslim, and I fast during the month of Ramadan."

"I don't fast on Yom Kippur," says Adi. "It is a special day for me, but I don't fast."

This has nothing to do with the fact that Laila is a Muslim and Adi is Jewish. It is simply a function of their upbringing. The Najjars are observant Muslims; the Judaism of the Frish family is deep, but not religious.

Laila and Adi are products of the Neve Shalom primary school, the first Jewish-Arab school in Israel. Today more than two hundred students, aged from a few months old to fifteen, learn in the pleasant modern buildings surrounded by lawns, trees, and shrubs. Headmaster Fayez Mansur, fifty-six, a Christian Arab from nearby Ramle, proudly shows me as we walk around the campus the tomatoes, squash, cucumbers, and corn grown by the children in agriculture class.

"I grew up in a mixed neighborhood," he explains. "My first friend was a Jewish kid. I learned then that we were different, but that we can live together, so let's do it the best way possible, with knowledge, understanding, and respect for each other's history, culture, and religion."

"There should be more bilingual schools," adds Dalia Lugassi, his codirector, who commutes daily from Tel Aviv.

Both are adamant that the bilingual school is working well. Mansur has been a teacher all his life, working mainly in Arab schools, most recently as a headmaster. Lugassi, whose parents emigrated from Morocco, also worked in Arab schools before a sense of idealism brought her to the Neve Shalom school.

In recent years, they admit, a number of Jewish children have left the school for various reasons, which means about 60 percent of the students are Arabs, but they are striving to restore the fifty-fifty balance in the admission class. Lugassi notes that they are running Arabic classes for the Jewish teachers to try to remedy the dominance of Hebrew. The Arab teachers all speak, read, and write fluent Hebrew, but the Jewish teachers are less competent in Arabic. Each class has a Jewish and an Arab teacher, they note, but not each subject.

"We think that math is a difficult enough subject in itself," explains Mansur. "We don't have to add bilingualism to that. The classes have dividing partitions, so we divide the class for math with the Arab children learning in Arabic and the Jewish children in Hebrew."

The atmosphere in the classrooms is friendly and relaxed. In the third grade, the children are creating "my home," out of cardboard, colors, and other materials. Yasmin, one of the teachers, tells Muhammad not to hoard the mosaic stones. There are enough for everyone, she tells him. In the music class, the teacher is integrating western and eastern music as the children bang their drums, play their recorders, and clash their cymbals. On one of the lawns, a nature class is in progress, using a kitten as an illustration. In sixth grade, two Arab children try to lecture their fellow students about marine biology in Hebrew. They are not finding it too easy. "Later the Jewish kids will have to talk to the class in Arabic," explains Mansur.

Every year the school tries to find new methods of dealing with Israeli Independence Day and the Palestinian Nakba, says Lugassi. They have separate assemblies, but also get together for a joint discussion of the different narratives. This year they invited a group of veterans from an Arab retirement home to talk about their experiences. Both Jewish and Arab students quizzed the old timers, some of whom remained in Israel in 1948, some of whom fled or were expelled but managed to return. "It was difficult for the old people to talk about their experiences," recalls Lugassi, "but the children asked questions and they gradually opened up."

Regarding their contacts with the Hand in Hand schools, Mansur is sure that relations are improving.

"We participated together at a workshop in Haifa about establishing a new bilingual school there," points out Lugassi.

As we have seen, Bruno Hussar was determined from the outset that Neve Shalom/Wahat al-Salam would be the site of a School for Peace, where Israelis and Palestinians; Jews, Muslims, and Christians from outside the village would attend encounter groups, workshops, and seminars on coexistence and conciliation. Since it began functioning in 1979, an estimated thirty-five thousand people have participated in the school's programs in Neve Shalom and other locations in Israel and Palestine.

The encounters, organized in mixed groups of sixteen to twenty people, are run by Jewish and Arab facilitators. In order to become a facilitator, a candidate has to undergo a course of 160 hours spread over five weekends, after which they experience an encounter for themselves. The assumption is that only someone who has experienced an encounter personally can work through the experience and assist others in the process. Subsequently, the trainee facilitators observe an encounter and conduct one under supervision.

It is assumed that the facilitator's insights and awareness is his or her most important resource. Consequently, the emphasis is on personality development rather than technique. Rabah Halabi, editor of *Israeli and Palestinian Identities in Dialogue*, a book published by the School for Peace, describes the development of two facilitators, one Jewish, one Arab, showing that the encounter actually drove them further apart.

"I still haven't come to a coherent place inside myself about who I am," concludes the Arab. "I'm confused. I don't exactly have answers to all the questions I have."

"My worldview on the one hand says peace and on the other hand a Jewish state," resolves the Jew, "and I see that these don't go together. It's just a place that's hard to be in."

The goal is not to bring Jews and Arabs closer together, writes Halabi, but rather to raise participants' awareness of the conflict and foster development of their national and political identity. Despite or perhaps because of the not entirely positive changes in their opinions, the two currently work as facilitators at the School for Peace.

"I assure you," insists Halabi, "those facilitators do not come to blows!"

"When we started out, we wanted to establish friendships at a personal level," explains Wafa Zreik-Srour, the current director of the school, who has worked as a facilitator for fifteen years. "We achieved this relatively easily, but we soon realized that it didn't mean very much."

They aimed to abolish stereotypes of both Israeli Jews and Palestinian citizens of Israel, but they came to understand that they had to meet the stereotypes head on and to deal with them. Removing them only solved the problems in the short term and at a superficial level. The concept began to change soon after the school began operating, and today the facilitators relate to the participants not merely as individuals but essentially as members of national groups.

This idea is developed in Halabi's book by social psychologist Arie Nadler. Individual friendships, he notes, can lead to the conclusion that "Muhammad is a nice guy, but he's not a typical Arab." It is only when the confronting groups identify themselves for what they are that a change in perception of one group for another can occur. While it is true that ignorance of the other is a key reason for hostility, writes Nadler, it should be emphasized that there is a genuine conflict between Jews and Arabs in Israel and Palestine and we have to face this. Jews and Arabs do not resolve the problem simply by getting to know each other better.

Although the Arab community in Israel is a minority, strict equality is maintained in the encounter groups run by the School for Peace. This enables the groups to move toward conciliation even though the participants return to the outside, where the imbalance persists. Furthermore, the dialogue concentrates on striving for social change that can improve the status of Israeli Arabs rather than encouraging upward mobility for the individual.

In his contribution to the book, Ramzi Suleiman, a Haifa University psychologist, observes that the Jewish participants often want to avoid politics and keep the encounters personal because their social and political situation is superior. It is always Arab participants who bring up topics such as discrimination, inequality of opportunity, and confiscation of Arab land. It is up to the facilitators to ensure that political topics are discussed. Suleiman also notes the importance of sessions conducted within each group to consolidate feelings of national identity.

Developing this idea further in one of the chapters, Halabi himself and Nava Sonnenschein point out that the school's approach has changed from emphasis on human relations, which left the Arab participants frustrated, to conflict resolution, in which the problems are directly addressed. In the encounters, they now seek to instill in the participants awareness of the conflict and of their role in it as well as exploring of their national identities.

The Arabs have to face the fact that in Israeli society they are controlled and the Jews have to understand that they are the controllers. Both must find ways of escaping these roles. The encounters cannot, of course, change reality, only the perceptions of this reality. Typically, this means that the Jewish participants emerge proud of the changes in their attitudes, while the Arabs end up frustrated, aware that they have to return to an unsatisfactory reality.

The central program of the School for Peace is the youth project, which brings together Jewish and Arab eleventh-grade schoolchildren for four days of meetings. The assumption is that the sixteen- and seventeen-year-olds are at a stage of developing their social and political identity. Unlike the technique with adults, where free discussion is encouraged, the youth encounters are more structured.

The first day is devoted to getting acquainted. The second day sees a return to separate groups, as the children realize the genuine differences that exist. The third day is devoted to negotiations for a modus vivendi between the two nationalities, and the fourth day sums up the experiences and endeavors to prepare the children for going home. The mood develops from a sort of euphoria at the start as the Jewish and Arab kids find that they can meet and talk, through anger and frustration as they discover their differences, and ultimately to a sort of friendship that is more cautious than it was at the outset, but deeper and more genuine.

The School for Peace also organizes a yearlong university program, combining encounters with theoretical lectures. The course was initiated at Tel Aviv University, but it is now offered also at the Ben-Gurion, Haifa, and Hebrew universities. Given within the framework of the MA in psychology, it includes a two-day summing up in Neve Shalom. Tel Aviv began offering the program in 1991, and Halabi's book includes a description of the university's 1996–1997 course.

The first phase was one of mutual exploration as each side probed the intentions of the other. In general, the Jewish students pressed for interpersonal contacts, while the Arabs demanded political discussions. A number of social and political issues were raised, but in a superficial manner.

In the second phase, the Arab group became stronger, consolidating around a few leaders. The Arabs talked about the problems of living in a "Jewish State." "In Arab villages in Israel you see streets from the previous century," observed one participant. Another brought up the question of the occupied territories, and a third demanded to know why an Ethiopian Jew had the right to immigrate, "whereas an Arab who was born here does not have the right of return." The Jews, finding themselves labeled as "oppressors," were upset. In an internal discussion, the Arabs wondered whether they had gone too far.

In the next stage, the Jewish group took back control. "I am uncomfortable with the conflict and with discrimination," maintained a Jewish participant, "but we are not totally unethical rulers."

"With you the Jews are either good or bad," another told the Arabs, "but the situation is more complicated."

The Jewish group tried to portray the Arabs as insensitive, and one student even raised the matter of "family honor killings" to show that the Jews are more humane. This taking of the moral high ground by the Jews lead to an impasse, and many of the Arabs wondered aloud whether there was any point in continuing with the discussions.

At this point there was a breakthrough, as members of the Jewish group conceded that they had changed many of their opinions. They admitted that there was inequality between Arabs and Jews in Israeli society and took responsibility for it. The argument continued, but with a feeling of greater equality.

"I think we behave toward them [the Arabs] in a power-oriented way," conceded a Jewish student.

"I want to exist and belong," remarked an Arab, "but I walk around with a terrible feeling of lack or honor, fear, and inferiority."

Toward the end of the year, many of the Jewish students were prepared to accept the idea of a "state of all its citizens" instead of a Jewish state, but by then some of the Arabs were demanding autonomy within Israel. An Arab woman said that "she could not express herself within the Israeli collective."

In general, the Jews ended up satisfied with the yearlong university encounter. They were proud of the changes they had undergone. The Arabs, very aware that they were returning every day to the unsatisfactory reality of life in Israel, were far more ambivalent.

The facilitators concluded that both sides increased their awareness of each other and of the problems. It is hardly likely that a similar understanding can be extended beyond the sixteen participants in the encounter to a significant proportion of the population of Israel, they write. If it could, it would undoubtedly lead to significant changes.

In the youth workshops, the student programs, and the other activities of the School for Peace, language is of prime importance. There is basic inequality because Hebrew is the dominant language in Israel. Most Israeli Arabs know Hebrew, whereas few Israeli Jews know Arabic,

The programs of the School for Peace deliberately reverse this situation, starting all workshops with an announcement in Arabic, which is then translated into Hebrew. In many of the encounters, language became a subject of conflict, with the Jews resenting Arabic and even claiming that their Hebrew was not being translated correctly by the facilitator. The Arab children, who started out speaking Hebrew, increased their use of Arabic.

In one of the encounters, the Jewish children changed their attitude during the course of the four days. In contrast to their hostile—even patronizing—attitude toward Arabic during some of the discussions, they readily agreed that the final communiqué be read out in both languages, with Arabic first. They then resolved that they should wind up the meeting by singing two anthems, first singing Israel's national anthem, "Hatikva" [the Hope] in Hebrew, and then standing respectfully while their Arab counterparts sang the Arabic "Biladi, Biladi" [My Country].

During the adult encounters, it was found that Hebrew was even more dominant. In general, the Arab participants prefer to use Hebrew, which they speak well, in the interests of better communication.

School for Peace director Wafa Zreik-Srour is deeply troubled by the language issue. She sees it as symbolic of the situation, not only in Israel generally, but also at Neve Shalom. Although Arabs currently hold the posts of village administrator, school director, and hotel manager, she still feels the Jews are in control. She insists that she constantly has to remind herself that she is the director of the school. She wonders whether "deep down" the former Jewish director has accepted the reality of her appointment. "If I want to be understood, I have to speak Hebrew," she points out. "At Neve Shalom, there are Jewish families who still don't know Arabic, although they have lived here for twenty years."

"If you come to live in Neve Shalom, it is ridiculous not to know Arabic," she declares. "Everything is in Hebrew. It's bad enough that the minutes are recorded in Hebrew—by an Arab woman incidentally—but it is much worse that I have to speak Hebrew if I want to be understood. What sort of partnership is that?"

She is more outspoken about service in the IDF than other villagers to whom I talked. She has twin demands to her Jewish fellow villagers: no military service—at least not in a combat unit—and learn Arabic. If they cannot learn to speak the language, at least they should be able to understand her when she speaks it.

"Why do so many of the Arab members fail to attend village meetings?" she asks rhetorically. "I can tell you why *I* often don't show up. It's because I don't want to repeat what I have already said so many times before."

One of her Jewish fellow villagers told her that he didn't have the strength to learn Arabic at the age of forty. Subsequently she found out that the man was learning Sanskrit! She admires people who undertake new initiatives, such as the Spiritual Center, but wonders aloud whether finding "inner peace" can solve the problems of Neve Shalom

"I would rather someone learned Arabic than search for some internal peace," she asserts. "Living at Neve Shalom I am achieving a great deal. I have consolidated my own identity. The school is doing important work, but sometimes I wonder what I'm doing here."

This is startling and disturbing coming from the current director of the School for Peace. It suggests that, for all its enormous achievements, Neve Shalom is still to some extent a microcosm of Israel rather than a new phenomenon.

Maybe Wafa is expecting too much. Perhaps Neve Shalom is aiming too high. In the next chapter, we will view an example of functional coexistence where Israelis and Palestinians; Muslims, Jews, Christians, and others live and work together because they have to. Unlike Neve Shalom, it does not aim to transform the current reality in Israel. It merely endeavors to get the job done, and it manages pretty well.

7

Island of Sanity

Palestinian terror suspects share rooms with nationalist Israelis; ultra-Orthodox Jews and devout Muslims lie in adjoining beds; Israeli doctors heal Palestinian militants; Arab doctors treat Jewish settlers; Armenian nurses care for Palestinian and Israeli patients. Arab and Jewish children—and their parents—laugh uproariously at the antics of a Jewish medical clown. A blond nurse, whose thick accent indicates that she is a new immigrant from Russia, hands out pills to an Arab patient wearing a traditional head scarf. In the kitchens, an Arab chef prepares strictly kosher food for observant Jewish patients. A grateful Palestinian mother knits a skullcap for the religious Jewish doctor who diagnosed her son's appendicitis.

Welcome to Hadassah Hospital on Jerusalem's Mount Scopus. Hadassah is not an official coexistence project, but within its walls the peoples of Israel and Palestine live together, work together, eat together, gossip together, joke together, suffer together, recover together, and sometimes (sadly) die together. In the explosive hostility of Israel and Palestine today the hospital is, in the words of its director, an "island of sanity."

Hadassah Mount Scopus was opened in 1939 on the eve of World War II. Designed by world-famous architect Erich Mendelsohn, it was, in its time, the biggest and most modern hospital in the Middle East. Professor Zvi Stein, the current hospital director, and his wife were both born there shortly before the 1948 war forced its nineteen-year-long closure. After that war, Jerusalem was divided between Israel and Jordan and Hadassah found itself in the Jordanian part of the city.

Under the Israeli-Jordanian armistice agreement, a small IDF garrison was stationed there, but the hospital was left to decay. Following the Six Day War of 1967, Israel took control of Jerusalem and the isolation of the building was ended. In 1976, after extensive reconstruction, the facility was reopened. Stein became director in 2001, "completing a circle," as he puts it.

During the violence that raged after October 2000, things were tough for everyone working at the hospital, but Stein insists that there was little tension among the personnel. "The staff, Jewish and Arab, Israeli and Palestinian, worked together as a single team," he asserts. "We organized special workshops to deal with inter-communal hostility, but they were to defuse the strain between staff and patients, not tension within the team."

Since then the frequency of suicide bombings and other incidents has declined considerably, but while I was visiting the hospital to talk to the doctors, nurses, and patients I witnessed the aftermath of a riot in which several hundred angry Palestinian villagers from nearby Issawiya surrounded the hospital, vandalizing and torching cars.

It was nothing to do with Hadassah as such, explains Stein. A resident of Issawiya had been shot by a border policeman during a disturbance. His body was brought to the hospital and his family objected to a postmortem. Supported by their fellow villagers, they sought to take away the corpse for burial, but eventually the family agreed to an autopsy, which was conducted at the Abu Kabir pathology center near Tel Aviv. Although the incident ended quickly and without death or serious injury, it illustrates the fragility of the hospital's situation.

The distance between Issawiya and Hadassah can be measured in yards and the village regards it as its local hospital. Fifteen villagers work there, but despite this troublemakers have lobbed gasoline bombs from the village into the hospital area. Not long ago, Stein called the mukhtar of Issawiya and demanded that he put a stop to it. An announcement condemning the attacks was made from the minaret of the village mosque, and for a time, there were no more bombs.

The hospital's administrative manager, Nahum Gedalia, took an even stronger line. He summoned the Issawiya employees and told them they would be dismissed—if there were any more attacks. "I can't take action against the patients," he explains, "but I can fire the employees. They claim it was outsiders who threw the bombs, but that is piffle. We all know that it was their fellow villagers. My threat had nothing to do with their being Arabs; I would do the same if Jewish fanatics threw bombs."

"I am really sorry that Nahum said this," declares Ahmad Obeid, the son of the Issawiya mukhtar, who works at the hospital as a nursing assistant. "It is only three or four fanatics out of our population of eight thousand who are responsible. Nahum's secretary asked me to bring my father and some representatives to talk about it. I told her I would bring the entire village if she wanted, because we are all against the bombers. My father and the headmaster of the village school and some other leading villagers came.

We are really trying to stop it. We've denounced the attacks in the mosque, the school, the club house, and in the streets."

A well-built young man in a smart sweatshirt and tight jeans, sports watch, and bracelet, the thirty-three-year-old Obeid is fluent in Hebrew and English. He is married with three sons. He was attending the business school at Bethlehem University when his studies were interrupted by the second Intifada. He is determined to ensure that his children's studies won't suffer the same fate. He would have liked to study in the U.S., but failed to obtain a visa. He has a brother who studied in America and is now in business there.

He defines himself as an "Arab Muslim with Israeli citizenship," and intends to remain in Issawiya, although he has no intention of succeeding his father in the "thankless task" of village mukhtar. Obeid maintains that the Jerusalem Municipality has neglected the village shamefully. It hasn't issued a single building license for years, although the population is bursting at the seams. "We pay our taxes, and get nothing in return," he says, "but Hadassah is different. Here everyone is equal."

His fellow villager Abed Ayash emphasizes that Hadassah is the best place he has ever worked. Less polished in appearance and speech than Obeid, the stocky mustached Ayash is a sanitation worker. He is married with five children. "Believe me, there is no question of Arab and Jew here," he insists. "We are all in this together. If there is a problem, Nahum Gedalia's door is always open."

Ayash remarks with a smile that he doesn't regard himself as either Israeli or Palestinian, but "maybe something in between." Both Obeid and Ayash missed the Issawiya riot as they were on a hospital outing at a spa on the coast. The mixed group of Jewish and Arab employees had experienced an enjoyable day, including good food, a sauna, hot baths, and swimming in the pools. It was only when they got back that they heard about the riot.

Eyad Abu-Sara, a slim young man with close-cropped hair and rimless glasses, is the chief nurse in the pediatrics department. Born in East Jerusalem's Silwan neighborhood (thought to be the site of King David's city), he studied the Jordanian curriculum. He only learned Hebrew later at a preparatory course for the Hebrew University. His employment at Hadassah started in the third year of his BA nursing studies. After working at the hospital for ten years, he won the tender for the post of chief nurse three months ago. He administers a team of twenty-three nurses, including one Christian Arab and twenty-two Jews. Do the others accept him as their boss?

"Of course they do," he states. "After all they were my fellow workers until three months ago." He recalls working in the emergency ward during the period of suicide bombs, saying that his fellow workers never gave him the impression that it was anything to do with him. His supervisor, a Moroccan

Jewish woman, told him that she understood how he felt as she had been a member of a minority once. He appreciated the way she showed understanding. Outbursts by patients were very rare: a wounded person wants treatment and the doctors and nurses want to treat him.

"They are patients rather than Jews or Arabs," he suggests. "I found it difficult, particularly treating children with missing limbs and terrible burns. I remember we worked on a little boy for two hours and he died. It was awful. Suicide bombers harm everyone without discrimination. I assure you though: if a wounded Israeli soldier and a wounded Palestinian terror suspect are brought in at the same time, we treat the most urgent case first."

Not all the Arab employees are nurses, nursing assistants, cooks, or maintenance workers. Dr. Eitan Kerem, head of the pediatrics department, feels it is vital to have Arab doctors on the wards. He maintains that it creates a different atmosphere when Arab patients see one of their own doctors treating Jewish patients.

Dr. Mohanad Da'ana studied at Christian schools in Jerusalem and Aqaba in Jordan, where his father was a doctor. He studied medicine at Jordan's Amman University, carried out his practical work at East Jerusalem's Mukassid Hospital, and is now specializing in pediatrics at Mount Scopus.

With a round, smiling face, Da'ana looks much younger than his thirty years. He admits that during the period of tension, he was apprehensive as an Arab working in a Jewish hospital, but he immediately realized that none of the staff was behaving differently toward him. He feels very good as "part of the Hadassah family." In a crisis people behave unexpectedly because of the shock, he observes. Sometimes they smile at an inappropriate moment, or they laugh and cry at the same time. This applies to both Jewish and Arab victims of an attack.

"I deeply regret the situation," he declares. "I have treated Jewish and Arab kids who were blown up by bombs, some burnt horribly, some without limbs, but on TV I see that Palestinians are also killed and wounded. Any sensitive human being hates to see blood being spilt."

Manifestly on good terms with his fellow doctors and nurses, Da'ana makes a particular point of introducing me to a colleague wearing a skullcap. Dr. Michael Cohen is his "brother," he insists. All the doctors, led by Kerem, are encouraging and supportive. Department secretary Tzippi is "fantastic." He calls her "Bird" (a play on her name).

The secretary tells me that I could not be in better hands than those of Dr. Da'ana. The pediatrics ward is an extraordinarily pleasant environment, with multicolored walls and pictures of Donald Duck, Mickey Mouse, Pluto, tractors, dragons, monsters, bears, and rabbits. Mobiles dangle above the reception desk. There is a kindergarten with toys, computers, and a large selection of games. Arab and Jewish parents and children play there all the time. A notice on the wall reads, as if written by a patient: "Don't wear a white coat, don't wake me up too often, smile please, and ask my permission before you touch me."

Eitan Kerem presides benevolently over this relaxed environment. Jerusalem-born and -educated, he spent seven years undergoing specialist training in Toronto before returning to Israel. He has headed the department for three and a half years. The children come from different locations and include many Arabs, ultra-Orthodox Jews, and settlers, he informs me.

"We really do work as a team, with a large amount of friendship and mutual respect," he maintains. "You have met Eyad, our head nurse, and Da'ana. We have other Palestinian doctors and nurses. With the patients it is more problematic. During the violence we sometimes heard the older Arab kids applauding when a suicide bombing was shown on television. On the other hand, some of the Jewish patients were all smiles after a targeted assassination. We cannot shut out what is going on outside the hospital."

Kerem hands me a paper he and two other doctors have written for the *Lancet* on treatment of sick children during low intensity conflict:

> The stress placed on the staff is intense. The difficulties associated with the care of a multilingual, multi-ethnic population are exaggerated in time of war. Xenophobia is at a maximum and there is rampant distrust between Arab and Jewish families . . .
>
> Despite the difficult situation, the doctors and nurses—both Jews and Arabs—have maintained the highest degree of professionalism; keeping the war out of the hospital as much as possible. There is a near universally shared perception that children are innocent
>
> Physical contact is encouraged. A female doctor who embraces an anxious mother, or a male nurse gripping the hands of a distraught father, can do wonders to allay fear and distrust . . .
>
> There should be an appropriate representation of Palestinian and Israeli Arab doctors with direct patient responsibility. Our department has actively recruited Arab residents . . .
>
> For children we stress the importance of both verbal and non-verbal methods of communication. Medical clowns, fluent in the universal language of humor, have succeeded in breaking down the invisible barriers that divide ethnic groups.

Watching a medical clown in action is extraordinarily moving. With a red nose, a pair of children's pants on his head, wearing baggy jacket and trousers, and with odd socks, "Max" (real name Nimrod Eisenberg) proceeds down the corridor with a jerky Groucho Marx–style walk.

A tiny baby cries and Max rushes up to her blowing his whistle, playing his harmonica, shaking a rattle, and gesticulating until the crying stops. Nadine, a beautiful black-eyed Palestinian girl aged thirteen, is eating a *shawarma* (meat in pita bread.) Max grabs the sandwich and pretends to sprinkle it with sugar, telling Nadine in Arabic that it is "good for your teeth." Nadine and her mother burst out laughing. In the next bed is a Jewish girl, and Max switches to Hebrew. He sticks a fake tap on the wall and pretends to wash down a yellow rubber chicken. He clucks loudly. The girl roars with laughter.

A nurse comes in and asks for his help. Before leaving the two girls, he pulls a showerhead from his gladstone bag (the type doctors used to carry) and pretends to use it as a telephone, eliciting further chuckles. The nurse has called him to a young Arab couple with a toddler. The girl favors Max with a cautious smile. He hops on one foot and does the chicken routine. The little girl continues to smile and allows her mother to give her medicine. Later, while she is hooked up to some very frightening-looking machinery, Max continues to distract her, this time blowing soap bubbles at her that she punctures with her finger.

We go downstairs to the day care ward where we meet Binyamin, a twelve-year-old Russian immigrant who has come for an EEG. Max sits beside him on the bench and pretends to fall asleep, resting his head on the boy's shoulder and snoring loudly. The boy laughs and speaks Russian. Max throws in some Russian words. A doctor walks past with his white coat and stethoscope. Max salutes him with grave formality and an Arab couple in traditional dress burst out laughing.

In a side room, an eight-year-old boy from an ultra-Orthodox Jewish family lies on a bed recovering from a biopsy. His mother wears a long skirt and head covering. An Arab woman in abaya robe and head scarf joins the family around his bedside with her young daughter. The Jewish boy's sister brings out a recorder and plays a well-known Israeli folk tune. Max accompanies on his harmonica and everyone claps in rhythm.

"Today was a good day," Max/Nimrod tells me afterwards. "There was no tension, but I have to play by the rules. If a nurse or doctor tells me not to approach a patient I must obey." He studied clowning in Padua, Italy and in Paris. He is a street performer and part of a performing troupe, but working in the hospital takes up a large part of his time. Three of his colleagues have also trained as medical clowns. They have been working at Hadassah and other hospitals for three years.

"When we started, people didn't understand why we were here," he admits. "We also got told off by the nurses for making too much noise, but today we are an accepted part of the treatment. You have to understand the situation. Both parents and children are nervous and worried. You have to reach out to them."

Nimrod knows some Arabic and continues to study the language. He loves working with Arab families, whom he finds very warm and responsive. The same is true of ultra-Orthodox Jews. There are no Arab clowns as such, but Arab performers do occasionally entertain the children.

His father was a head of department at the hospital and his brothers are a doctor and an engineer. His mother would prefer him to learn a "sensible profession," but he is happy doing his thing.

One of the most famous wards at Hadassah Mount Scopus is the rehabilitation department, headed by Professor Mara Shochina, who immigrated to Israel from Moscow in 1974. She has been specializing in rehabilitation for thirty years. In that time there have always been Arabs in her team, including doctors, nurses, and physical therapists.

"Only recently we had an Arab patient with a head injury, undergoing rehabilitation next to a Border Police officer, who had been stabbed," she observes. "It does happen that Jewish patients don't want to be in the same room as Arabs, and vice-versa, but only very rarely."

The rehabilitation department is known all over the Middle East, and recently several Greek Cypriot patients were admitted. Noemzar "Nomi" Nalbandian, the deputy chief nurse, is an Armenian born in Haifa. She studied nursing in her hometown but married an Armenian from Jerusalem and has been in the rehabilitation department for eleven years. A state registered nurse, she also has a BA in administration. She speaks Armenian, Turkish, Hebrew, Arabic, English, and French. Now she is learning Spanish. She finds that her languages help her in her work.

"We have been treating Muslims and Jews for years," she notes. "Recently we have been rehabilitating some Christians from Cyprus, but it doesn't matter where they come from. It is our business to teach them to function again after their injuries."

She is adamant that all the members of her team internalize any feelings they have. The attitude is the same toward an Israeli Ethiopian soldier, a Druze border policeman, an Arab, or a Jewish settler. Her hardest case was a terror attack victim, a girl, who was suffering from burns all over her body. Every contact was excruciatingly painful, but the most difficult part was winning her trust. "She needed many operations and years of physical therapy," she explains, "but she is wonderfully strong. Today she comes and helps others to get through their crises, and they all love her—both Jewish and Arab patients."

Eliezer is a Jewish settler from Bat Ayin, south of Jerusalem. Wearing a knitted skullcap, his beard neatly trimmed, he was originally wounded in the 1982 Lebanon war. He was successfully rehabilitated from his head wound in that war, but six months ago he became infected with a virus that causes paralysis. Resident again in the ward that he describes as "the best in

Israel," he is undergoing daily physical and occupational therapy for all his limbs. He sits outside in the yard smoking intently, unaffected by the multiethnic reality around him.

"Call me a racist, if you want to. I would rather not be around Arabs. In my opinion, they should all be expelled across the Jordan. I do not look for contact with Arabs. If an Arab comes and sits beside me, I won't leave the table, but I won't deliberately sit at a table where there are Arabs. Yes, I know that Arab nurses look after me, but they get paid for it, don't they?"

Down in the occupational therapy room, two old men sit side by side, one Arab and one Jewish. An old Arab woman in traditional dress in a wheelchair is on the other side of the room. Jewish and Arab occupational therapists assist them gently but firmly.

Racheli approaches Mussa, who is slumped forward in his wheelchair. She pushes him forward so that he is seated at the desk. His paralyzed left arm rests on a board, which is on wheels. He moves the board with the help of his right arm. Racheli tells him he must do it with his left arm only, and he manages, but it takes a huge effort. He tells Racheli that it hurts. She smiles and tells him that it will get better. On the other side of the room the Arab woman, whose left arm is in a sling, tugs on a pulley with her right arm, raising a heavy-looking weight. The Jewish man on Mussa's right plays a board game, fitting wooden pieces into a box. The therapists project a warmth that is almost tangible.

The Department of Social Work, "on the seam between medical and social problems," has a large role to play in rehabilitation, but not only there. Department head Noah Shemesh, born on a kibbutz in the Jordan valley, has worked at the hospital since studying at the Hebrew University. She outlines the tasks of her department: communication between patient and family, patient and doctor, doctor and family. Then there are legal problems, including those of children, who might be neglected or abused. There is a social worker on each ward, and they are also on call for the emergency ward.

A recent dramatic example of her work was dealing with a single Arab woman, referred to Hadassah because of pregnancy. Drawing money from a special emergency fund, the department arranged to have her rushed from her West Bank village through the military roadblocks to have her termination in Jerusalem. The department ensured that she was returned home without her situation becoming known. Had she been found out, her father or one of her brothers would almost certainly have killed her for "dishonoring the family."

Other cases concern senior citizens who may be living in unsuitable conditions. Recently, an old man brought in with pneumonia was assessed by a hospital social worker, who determined he was suffering from neglect. The department members are currently debating whether to transfer him to a retirement home or to try to provide him with better services delivered to his home, such as nursing care, help around the house, and meals.

One of the most successful social workers is Lamis Sheikh-Suleiman, an Israeli Arab from Yafia near Nazareth. During the violent period following October 2000, Lamis was relieved from dealing with traumatized victims of suicide bombs and other attacks. "Lamis is one of us, and it's more important to look after her than to insist on some principle," asserts Noa Shemesh. "She speaks perfect Hebrew and probably nobody realized she was an Arab, but I did not want her exposed to some of the abuse that was flying around in the wake of the bombs. So for a few weeks, she manned the phones and did not have direct contact with patients."

Lamis comes from an impressive family. Her father was a building worker and her mother a housewife, but every one of their children acquired a profession. One brother is a social worker, another an electrical engineer, a third is a senior bank employee, and a twin sister is a nurse. Lamis herself has two degrees, the first in social work; the second in NGO management. Engaged to a doctor in the pediatric department, she used to run a community center in Issawiya in addition to her hospital work, but decided to concentrate on the latter.

"Look, I was at the front," she says, recalling the difficult period. "The emergency ward was a tough place to be. The atmosphere was hysterical. Although there were Arab victims as well as Jews, some of the families of victims tried to attack me.

"When there was a bomb, I only wanted to come and help people, but people said things to me that I found hard to listen to, like 'let all the Arabs die,' things like that. It only happened in extreme circumstances and Noa and the other members of the team always defended me. I never ever felt any hostility from a member of the hospital staff!"

When people know each other and work together, it is different, she notes. The members of the team are all rational people who like working together. In fact, she is confident that most people on both sides want to live together in peace. Only a few are troublemakers.

Growing up in Galilee, she was not conscious of any conflict. Her mother and father hated politics and were sure that education would afford a good life for their children. When she arrived in Jerusalem in 1998, during the Oslo years, the atmosphere was friendly. The second Intifada came as a great shock to Lamis.

She has been active in two organizations promoting Jewish-Arab coexistence, including meetings between Israelis and Palestinians. She also organized encounters between Israelis and Palestinians when she worked in Issawiya. At a certain point, though, she felt she had to make a choice, and she doesn't regret her decision to concentrate on her work at the hospital.

"I love children and want to work with them," she declares. "I want to study psychotherapy also. Even the Jewish community here has only recently started dealing with problems such as sexual abuse in the family, and we Arabs are not as advanced as the Jews in this. I see myself working in the field of family therapy."

Apart from treating patients of all nationalities and maintaining an effective multiethnic medical team, Hadassah makes additional contributions to coexistence and cooperation. Both Hadassah Mount Scopus and its sister hospital in West Jerusalem are actively engaged in extending assistance to Palestinian hospitals in Jerusalem and all over the occupied territories. Medical teams meet regularly with Palestinian doctors to improve and coordinate medical services. Many heads of hospital departments in the territories received their specialist training at the Hadassah hospitals. Funds for these programs are provided by the Peres Center for Peace and other foundations.

More than twenty Palestinian doctors attended a gathering with Patricia Kahane, director of the Karl Kahane Foundation of Vienna, which has given them training scholarships at Hadassah. The doctors presented Professor Shlomo Mor-Yosef, director of the West Jerusalem hospital, with an olive wood carving of Moses with the Tablets of the Law and Patricia Kahane with an inlaid box.

After lunch, some thirty of them took turns thanking Hadassah and the foundation for their assistance. Gynecologist Sa'id Zarchan, the director of Hebron Hospital, pointed out that the expertise gained by the Palestinian doctors at Hadassah had enabled them to promote improvements in their own hospitals all over the West Bank. "I thank all the Hadassah staff who made us feel comfortable and happy here," he concluded.

Dr. Nasri Muallem recounted how, after specializing in surgery at Hadassah, he had established the first neurosurgical department in the West Bank at his Ramallah Hospital. Both Muallem and Zarchan appealed for increased coordination and cooperation between Palestinian and Israeli hospitals.

Dr. Ali Ramadan, a specialist in ophthalmology who is now teaching in East Jerusalem's Al-Kuds University, related how Dr. Ben-Ezra of Hadassah took him to the United States with him and argued with airline officials until they agreed that both of them would travel business class. "It's only a small matter," he remarked, "but it shows the sort of relations we enjoy with our Jewish colleagues."

Dr. Hussein Hammad finished his dermatology specialization at Hadassah and is now chief consultant for the West Bank. He still comes to Hadassah twice a month to discuss difficult cases. Dr. Tayshir Milhem, who specialized in pediatric surgery, was later head of pediatrics at the Hebron

Hospital and has now left to found a private unit. Dr. George Baklin described himself as "the Ambassador of Hadassah in East Jerusalem and the Ambassador of East Jerusalem at Hadassah."

Dr. Rawan Matrud, a woman doctor who specialized in anesthesia, worked in her specialty in Nablus, and is now back in Hadassah for further training, proclaimed with some emotion: "It's not just the knowledge I acquired, but my personality and my attitude to work have been profoundly affected. I want to return to Nablus to the really fine team of doctors that we have there, many of them Hadassah-trained."

Dr. Ariz al-Khatib noted that in the West Bank there were only five pathologists for three million people—pathetically inadequate—but he lauded the training that he had received and thanked his Israeli colleagues, who have started providing biopsies to West Bank residents free of charge.

"Here I met for the first time Jews who are not soldiers," declared Jamil Kunsia from Bethlehem. "I learned a lot about the Jewish people that I did not know before. The quality of your medicine is high and I am proud of my relations with you."

Dr. Khaled Majabiya, a plastic surgeon from Bethlehem, added: "All of us are the sons of Abraham. Hadassah is the bridge of peace between the two nations that are really one nation."

"My contacts with Israeli doctors taught me to speak *tachless*," said Dr. Rahd Kiti (*tachless* is a Yiddish word meaning to talk straight). "We have difficulties in coming to Jerusalem because of the Israeli roadblocks, but this is nothing compared to the difficulties of our patients! Can you create a service to answer phones and faxes in Arabic? I waste at least an hour every day on technical arrangements. And then, when our patients finally arrive, they can't find their way around. Please set up an office which will direct them to the appropriate departments."

A lively discussion ensues, which discloses the horror of the general situation—endless roadblocks and the separation wall currently going up in the middle of Jerusalem—in contrast to the excellent work being performed by Hadassah and the other Israeli hospitals.

Mor-Yosef points out that he can't do anything about the political situation and praises Dalia Besser, the representative of the Israeli Ministry of Health, who struggles daily with the military authorities to persuade them to allow doctors and patients to pass from the West Bank to Jerusalem. Dalia, a slim blond woman, receives thunderous applause from the assembled Palestinian doctors and takes an embarrassed bow.

It is clear that the building of the separation wall between Israel and the West Bank—and in particular the so-called Jerusalem Envelope—sabotages the great efforts of Hadassah to cooperate with the Palestinian medical personnel to improve medical services for all. The wall, which in theory divides

Palestinian territory from Israeli Jerusalem to prevent terror attacks, in fact creates endless frustration for the inhabitants of the Palestinian suburbs of the city and the nearby Palestinian villages.

In striving to provide medical services for all, Hadassah is continuing the tradition of the founders, in particular that of a remarkable American woman, Henrietta Szold. The daughter of a rabbi, Szold was born in Baltimore in 1860. She was a creative biology teacher and later a dedicated social worker.

An early supporter of Zionism, she paid her first visit to the Holy Land in 1909 and was horrified at the misery and disease, particularly in the towns of Jerusalem, Haifa, Jaffa, and Tiberias. One of the first things she noticed were the scrawny legs and sick eyes of the Arab children, which she contrasted with the healthy children at the Jewish Girls' School in Jaffa, who enjoyed regular visits from a physician and a nurse.

Szold had already been among the founders of the Hadassah Study Circle, which she quickly transformed into a large organization of women Zionists with herself as president. Keeping the name Hadassah [Esther], the new organization took as its motto a Biblical passage: "Is there no balm in Gilead; is there no physician there? Why then is not the health of the daughter of my people recovered?" (Jeremiah 8:22).

At its third convention in 1916, Hadassah, with a membership of less than two thousand, resolved to take responsibility for sending a team of doctors and nurses to be called the American Zionist Medical Unit to Palestine. In the following two years, the size of the initial unit increased considerably and by 1918, when it set sail for Palestine, it consisted of twenty doctors, twenty nurses, and five administrative personnel. The unit arrived in Palestine just in time to deal with an outbreak of cholera in Tiberias. Within two years, the Hadassah Medical Organization had established numerous infant welfare stations, malaria control units, and a school for nursing. It also organized the provision of school lunches, school hygiene services, and distribution of pasteurized milk.

Szold herself settled permanently in Palestine in 1920, and the following year she awarded certificates to the first graduates of the newly established Hadassah Nursing School. The organization took over the administration of the Rothschild Hospital, refurbishing and equipping it until it reopened as the Rothschild-Hadassah Hospital. Following the establishment of the Hebrew University on Mount Scopus, Hadassah was a full partner in establishing the university hospital, which opened in 1939 with 215 beds.

Szold, a passionate Zionist, was always conscious of the situation of the Palestinian Arabs. Together with Judah Magnes, the president of the Hebrew University, she worked actively for Jewish-Arab conciliation, for a time even espousing the idea of a binational state instead of a purely Jewish nation.

A woman of action rather than a theoretician, she always stressed the importance of getting the practical job done. Szold never had any doubts that the medical services she established would be for the benefit of all the inhabitants of the Holy Land. Thus, from the outset, Hadassah Mount Scopus was a hospital for Jews, Arabs, and everybody else who needed it.

Despite this, in Israel the name Hadassah is associated with one of the most tragic incidents in a century of Jewish-Arab confrontation: the 1948 ambush of a medical convoy, in which seventy-six doctors and nurses were killed by Arab attackers. Hadassah director Haim Yassky was among the victims. "Yassky believed in and provided medical services for the Arab population," wrote a colleague at the time. "During his tenure Hadassah brought medical relief to thousands of Arabs of all classes."

Hadassah, then, represents both the positive and the negative side of the engagement between Jews and Arabs, a centuries-old encounter. In the next chapter, we will take a look at the history of this relationship. Frequently it has been a saga of savage confrontation and conflict, but for the most part—albeit less dramatically—it is a narrative of shared lives.

8

An Encounter That Spans the Centuries

The centuries-long confrontation between Jews and Muslims can be traced to the start of Islam in Arabia in 632 CE, when Muhammad, the founder of the new religion, looked to the local tribes of Jews for support. In view of the fact that his holy book, the Koran, recognized many of the biblical prophets and contained material similar to that of the Bible and other sacred Jewish texts, Muhammad was confident that the Jews living in Arabia would flock to his cause. When they rejected him, he was deeply insulted and took action accordingly. His fighters killed several hundred members of the leading Jewish tribe and expelled the others from Mecca and the surrounding area. A decade later, however, Muhammad signed an agreement with the Jewish and Christian tribes, taking them under his protection. Thus, from the earliest years of Islam, we see contradictory attitudes toward the Jews.

The Koran illustrates this ambivalence, stating that Allah (God) chose the Jews, but also that He punished them for disobeying His commandments. The Koran agrees with the biblical account that the Jews, who left Egypt under Mussa (Moses), were afraid to enter the land of Canaan, but, whereas the Bible makes it clear that their divine punishment for this lack of faith was merely a postponement of their taking possession of the land, the Koran indicates that the Jews were forever banned from it.

Today these differing interpretations in the two sacred books may have symbolic importance, but they are not grounded in history. According to the latest theories, which are based on archaeological evidence and textual analysis of the Bible and other documents, the exodus from Egypt is a myth. The Israelite entity was established by exiles from the Canaanite city-states, pushed to the borders of the desert by invading forces, probably from

Egypt. These Canaanites returned to the hill regions and settled there around 1200 BCE. This version of history views the Israelites and Canaanites as different branches of the same people.

Some modern Palestinian historians argue that the Palestinians were the original Canaanite inhabitants of the land, who were conquered by the Israelite invaders. Conversely, many early Jewish immigrants viewed the Palestinians as the descendents of Jews who were converted to Islam in the seventh-century Muslim invasion. In view of the fact, however, that most Palestinians identify themselves as Muslim Arabs rather than as ancient Canaanites, there is nothing to be gained by pursuing these various historical claims and counterclaims. It makes more sense to return to Arabia, where the Jewish-Muslim confrontation was also a Jewish-Arab encounter.

It should be stressed that, after the death of Muhammad, the relationship between the two peoples and their faiths was for the most part friendly. In the following centuries, Jews played a vital role in the Islamic empire, which permitted some of them to return to Jerusalem. In the twelfth century CE, Muslims and Jews were united there and in other places against the Crusaders, who aimed to save the Holy Land from both Muslim and Jewish "infidels."

In Mesopotamia, the Jews flourished under Islam. Although as non-Muslims they were in many ways second-class citizens, they were revered as the "People of the Book." Jews were prominent in Arabic literature and in science, particularly medicine, and played an important role in the consolidation of the Muslim civilization. Many important Jewish personalities thrived under Islam, notably Maimonides, the greatest Jewish thinker of the postbiblical age, who was born in Muslim-ruled Spain. He lived much of his life in Tunisia and Egypt, where he became personal physician to Saladin, who conquered Palestine from the Crusaders.

For some two centuries, Jews prospered in Spain and other Muslim nations to the extent that the period is known in Jewish history as the Golden Age. When the Christians regained control of Spain in the fifteenth century and expelled all those Jews who refused to convert to Christianity, it was in the Muslim Ottoman Empire that the Jews found a hospitable home.

During the following centuries, Jews lived under both Islam and Christianity and although they suffered discrimination in both societies, there is no doubt that they fared better under the Muslims than they did under the Christians. It is not by chance that *pogrom* is a Russian word. Meaning devastation, it was coined to describe the anti-Jewish atrocities that were frequent in Russia and Eastern Europe toward the end of the nineteenth century.

The pogroms undoubtedly stimulated the movement for a Jewish return to Palestine, the land of Israel, although they were not its primary cause. The movement for Jewish national renewal, which became known as Zionism, a term coined from one of the biblical names of Jerusalem, was an authentic expression of Jewish group identity. Although the Jews were for the most part exiled from their land by the Romans in the second century CE, a small Jewish community continued to exist there. Moreover, the Jews scattered all over the world prayed daily for a return to their land, celebrated their festivals according to its seasons, and maintained a constant trickle of immigration throughout the centuries.

It was natural that the increased Jewish influx into Palestine in the late nineteenth century provoked a number of clashes. The local Arabs had been living side by side with the Sephardi, Arabic-speaking Jewish communities in the Palestinian towns of Jerusalem, Tiberias, Safed, and Hebron, building, trading, and socializing in the cafes and Turkish baths. The European Ashkenazi Jews lived in their own neighborhoods, hardly making any contact with the Arabs, but they were accepted as part of the patchwork of Ottoman Palestine.

However, the immigrants, who established new villages and suburbs, sometimes clashed with the local Arabs, often because of a lack of understanding of their customs. One incident in a new Jewish village in Galilee was caused by a local sheikh inadvertently trampling on a Jewish garden. The resulting argument, which began verbally, ended in the wounding and eventual death of the sheikh and almost caused the massacre of the Jewish villagers in retaliation.

The Ottoman province was hardly a law-abiding environment. Robbers and marauders attacked Jews and Arabs alike, and neighboring villagers often clashed over land demarcation and grazing rights. At the same time, there were many examples of friendship and cooperation between the Jewish newcomers and the Arab villagers.

Shortly after Degania, the first kibbutz, was established in 1910, two of its members were attacked by armed Bedouin, who shot their mule. But in the letter one of them wrote describing the incident, he stated that the kibbutz members enjoyed "friendly relations" with their Arab neighbors. They learned about farming from the local villagers, supplying them with medicines in return. When one of the pioneers, Miriam Baratz, wanted to learn how to milk cows, she went to the local Arab village, where the women taught her so well that she became better at it than her male comrades were.

The Jewish immigration to Palestine came in several waves, and each new group of arrivals had to find their own accommodation with the local Arabs. For example, it took some time until the Jews understood that, according to Arab custom, it was acceptable for cattle, sheep, and goats to graze on their neighbor's land, unless it was cultivated. In addition, the purchase of land by Jews sometimes resulted in violence, because the landowners selling the plots were town dwellers—often living as far away as Beirut or Damascus. The new owners wanted to farm the land themselves, which meant that the Arab farmers had to move out.

The differences in approach in the new Jewish community can be seen by observing a controversy between Yitzhak Epstein and Zeev Smilansky in a journal of the World Zionist Organization in 1907. Epstein, who started as a farm worker in Galilee, later became a teacher and Hebrew scholar. Smilansky was one of the leaders of the new immigrants. Epstein argued that it was not always advisable to buy any land that was offered by the owners at the expense of the peasants who farmed it, writing: "We have to admit that we have thrown people out of their miserable lodgings and taken away their sustenance." Smilansky responded: "When nations come to settle in a new land, they set about it with swords . . . do we have nothing to worry about except the fate of the Palestinian Arabs?"

"Our purpose is not to Judaize the Arabs," declared Epstein, "but to prepare them for a fuller life so that in the course of time they can become faithful allies of ours, true friends and brothers." To which Smilansky replied: "Everyone will think us mad if we take on ourselves the task of handing out money in order to foster a rival, who will lose no time in putting us out of business."

Significantly, the Arabic-speaking Sephardi Jews were often vociferous in their criticism of their Ashkenazi brethren. Yosef Eliyahu Chelouche was born in Jaffa in 1870 to parents who had come from Algeria. In his memoir *Reminiscences of My Life*, published in 1931, he recalls that when the Jews of Jaffa and Tel Aviv were expelled by the Turkish governor during World War I, over a hundred of them, including his family, found refuge in the Arab town of Kalkiliya. Arab friends helped him find rooms for all of them in a matter of hours. The villagers not only permitted them to bring in Torah scrolls and set up an improvised synagogue, but also facilitated kosher slaughtering. The local Arab commander initially resisted orders from the Turkish authorities to expel the Jews from Kalkiliya, but eventually the pressure was too strong. Nevertheless, he arranged for many of them to be offered hospitality in the nearby village of Kafr Jamal. This, states the memoir, was typical of the relations between Jews and Arabs in Palestine.

Chelouche is scathing about the failure of the Zionist leadership to foster neighborly relations with the local Arabs: "The bitter truth must be told: many of those who came from abroad to build our enterprise did not understand the vital importance of good neighborly relations. Since Herzl proclaimed the Zionist political program, this land was depicted as a desert without inhabitants, and our leaders have acted accordingly."

Chelouche goes on to point out that very few of the newcomers bothered to learn Arabic or to study local culture and customs. He notes that the huge investments in the Zionist enterprise also benefited the local Arab population, but the Arabs did not see this because the immigrants either disregarded them or behaved in an arrogant superior manner toward them. He deplores the indifferent and ignorant attitude of the Zionist press toward the locals. He states that many enlightened Muslims did in fact make efforts to build bridges to the Jewish community, and these could have been fostered with a little tact and sensitivity. He deplores the fact that the Zionist leaders in Berlin and London never listened to Jews like himself, who were part of the local community in Palestine.

His words and sentiments are echoed in *Living with Jews*, a memoir by Elie Eliachar, another Sephardi Jew, whose family lived in Jerusalem for generations. While conceding that Chaim Weizmann, the Zionist leader, did initially take advice from certain Sephardi leaders, he records that "after a short while it became apparent that their services were no longer needed." Although Weizmann was open to the idea of making contacts with the Arabs, he notes, "The sad fact is that the Zionist Executive as a whole was not. Suggestions put forward by Sephardi leaders for improving relations between the two peoples were consistently rejected."

Eliachar, who served in the administration of the British Mandatory government, recalls the words of a Druze colleague, "an erudite writer and extreme nationalist," who confided that "he feared a bloody struggle was liable to develop between Jews and Arabs, which in his opinion would be due to the attitude of Zionists from Europe."

Eliachar recounts numerous examples of unintentionally insulting behavior toward Arab notables by European Zionist leaders, "who did not understand the mentality, customs and manners of the Arabs." The reader might think these incidents trivial, allows the author, "but such niceties create the atmosphere of rapprochement." The Zionist movement, he maintains, "moved toward the idea that our existence in the land of Israel and in the region would depend on our might alone rather than on our relationship with our Arab neighbors."

In his book, which was published in 1980, Eliachar firmly rejects this thesis: "I have never believed that we can live by the sword alone . . . the time has come to think of a policy other than that of reliance on our military prowess for our future survival." Neither Eliachar nor Chelouche ignores the violent anti-Jewish outbursts throughout the period of the British Mandate, in which many Jews lost their lives, but both men maintain that a more sensitive approach by the Zionist newcomers could have prevented or at least minimized the confrontation.

In this context, it should be noted that the bad news syndrome always prevails. An outstanding example is the Hebron massacre of 1929. On the negative side is the fact that the sixty-seven victims were non-Zionist religious Jews who had lived in peace with their Arab neighbors for centuries. Moreover, the slaughter was particularly savage, including beheadings, the murder of women and children, and some grotesque cases of torture. Despite the justified revulsion against this barbarity, however, it should be noted that twenty-eight Arab families risked their own lives to protect the 435 Jews who survived, literally placing their own bodies between their Jewish neighbors and the mob. This fact is almost never mentioned when the 1929 events are recalled.

It is a sad fact that, although it led to an improvement in the administration of Palestine, the British conquest of the country in World War I only served to escalate the confrontation between Jews and Arabs. Early in that war, the British High Commissioner for Egypt promised the Arabs independence, but toward the end of the conflict, Britain's Foreign Secretary issued the Balfour Declaration, which favored creating a "National Home" in Palestine for the Jewish people.

After the League of Nations awarded Britain the mandate to rule Palestine, the struggle between Jews and Arabs became more politicized as the Arabs demanded their promised independent state and the Jews strove to create their promised national home. Both sides endeavored in different ways to exert pressure on their British rulers, which meant that direct contact between the sides was reduced. Despite this, the two most important Zionist leaders, Chaim Weizmann and David Ben-Gurion, made approaches toward the Arab side.

In 1918, Weizmann met with Faisal, who would later become King of Iraq, and reported to his colleagues: "I have seen Emir Faisal, the chief Arab military commander, and I am authorized to say that a *modus vivendi* can be found for the solution of the extremely complex Arab political problem, because we want to live on the very best terms with the Arabs."

For his part, Faisal wrote to American Zionist leader Felix Frankfurter: "We Arabs look with the deepest sympathy on the Zionist movement . . . with the chiefs of your movement, especially with Dr. Weizmann, we have had and continue to have the closest relations. We are working together for a reformed and revived Near East, and our two movements complement one another."

Weizmann envisaged the creation of a large single Arab state after the war, which would enable the Jews to establish their national home in Palestine, but the British and French divided up the Middle East, with France effectively ruling Syria and Lebanon and the British in control of Iraq, Transjordan, Egypt, and Palestine. Faisal had hoped to become King of Syria, historically a Muslim and Arab center. In the event, he had to be content with the kingdom of Iraq, an artificial entity cobbled together by Britain. After assuming that position, he had no further contacts with Weizmann or any other Zionist leader.

Ben-Gurion's overtures took place much later, in the shadow of the rise of Nazism in Germany, which had resulted in accelerated Jewish immigration to Palestine. This influx was one of the factors that caused a full-scale rebellion by the Palestinian Arabs against British rule in 1936. By then the Labor movement had become dominant among the Jews in Palestine and Ben-Gurion was its leader. He wanted to meet with the Mufti of Jerusalem, Haj Amin Husseini, the most important—and most extremist—Palestinian Arab leader, but the latter asked Mussa Alami, a much-respected Arab Mandate official, to represent him.

Ben-Gurion later recorded his impressions of his meetings with Alami and with George Antonius, the Arab historian. Assuring Alami that the Jews did not need more farming land, the labor leader also promised technical assistance and financial aid to improve Arab education and agriculture. Alami agreed that there was room for discussion. With amazing prescience, Antonius predicted "a land of Israel with a Jewish majority and Palestine with an Arab majority." Sadly, these contacts were also broken off.

Apart from Weizmann and Ben-Gurion, several other personalities endeavored to find ways of reaching an accommodation between Jews and Arabs in Palestine. Not only intellectuals, such as Hebrew University President Judah Magnes and philosopher Martin Buber, but Dr. Arthur Ruppin, the head of the Zionist settlement department; Pinhas Ruttenberg, director of the Palestine Electric Corporation; Moshe Novomeyski, manager of the Dead Sea Potash Company; and Henrietta Szold of Hadassah were involved in creating plans based on equality and joint rule of Palestine by Jews and Arabs. Unfortunately, a majority on both sides disagreed with the concept of binationalism. The important Arab leaders rejected partnership with the Jews. The official Zionist movement continued to demand increased Jewish immigration and more land purchases.

In 1937, an official British Commission of Inquiry proposed the partition of Palestine between the Jews and the Arabs. Although the area designated for the Jewish entity was relatively small, the proposal was accepted by the Zionists. The Arab side, correctly seeing this Jewish move as tactical, opposed the partition plan. In a sense, the very idea of partition was a statement against understanding and compromise. The British were saying, in effect: agreement between the two peoples is impossible; at least let us try to keep them apart.

Palestine was comparatively quiet during World War II. Naturally, the Jews wholeheartedly supported the Allied cause against Hitler, their archenemy, and volunteered for service in the British army. The Arabs adopted a more neutral stance, but covertly sympathized with the German side. Indeed Haj Amin Husseini, the mufti of Jerusalem, spent much of the war in Berlin supporting Hitler. Nevertheless, Jews and Arabs lived peacefully side by side in Palestine throughout the period of the war.

The Nazi Holocaust was the final catalyst for the creation of a Jewish state. When the scale of the slaughter became generally known, the Jewish demand for increased immigration became virtually an ultimatum. There were still some contacts between Jews and Arabs of good will, but the movement toward confrontation was unstoppable. The Zionists were absolutely determined to establish their national home to provide a haven for the European survivors; the Arabs did not see why they should pay the price for European crimes.

The victory of the Labour Party in Britain in 1945 generated great optimism on the part of the Zionists, because that party had a long record of supporting Jewish immigration to Palestine. The new government, however, continued the previous British policy of trying to balance the claims of the two sides. As the violence in Palestine escalated, the British government resolved to hand back its mandate to the newly constituted United Nations. The UN came up with a partition plan of its own, this time dividing Palestine more or less equally between the parties. Once again, the Jews accepted the proposal and the Arabs rejected it.

The intermittent fighting, which continued as the British prepared to quit Palestine, broke out into open war when they left, and the Jews declared the establishment of the State of Israel in the territory allotted them by the UN. The local Palestinian Arabs were joined by armies from Egypt, Transjordan, Syria, Iraq, and Lebanon, but, in the subsequent fighting, the new State of Israel managed to hold most of its allotted territory and to gain quite a bit more. In 1949, Israel and the Arab states signed armistice agreements that left the Jews with 78 percent of the territory of what had been Mandatory Palestine.

Most of the Palestinian Arabs fled (or were expelled from) what became the State of Israel, which was left with an Arab population of around a hundred and fifty thousand. Some seven hundred thousand other Palestinians became refugees. The savage all-out war in 1948 thrust the idea of Jewish-Arab friendship into a deep freeze, although even at this time there were instances where Jews persuaded their Arab neighbors to remain, and some Arab communities, notably the Druze and several Bedouin tribes, fought alongside the Jews.

The atmosphere following the war and the establishment of Israel was not conducive to conciliation. The Jews, the "victors," had paid dearly for their success, with some six thousand dead, about 1 percent of their population. Furthermore, this life and death struggle had taken place in the shadow of the Holocaust. There was a huge sense of relief—even of exhilaration—but also a mood of mourning and an awareness of continuing danger. They were in no mood to appreciate the Palestinian tragedy, particularly as the Palestinians and the surrounding Arab states maintained a uniform hostility to the Jewish state. In addition to this, the Jews were focused on bringing in the Holocaust survivors from Europe and an additional wave of immigration from the Arab and Muslim countries of the Middle East.

Infiltration across the borders was frequent. Sometimes Palestinians would come to visit their former homes, to try to harvest their crops, or to steal farming equipment or livestock. In the early 1950s, the Egyptian and Syrian regimes sponsored these incursions, arming the infiltrators and encouraging them to carry out murderous attacks, which cost scores of Jewish lives.

Traumatized and humiliated by their defeat, the Arabs were even less inclined than the Jews were to compromise. Hundreds of thousands of Palestinians had lost their homes and become refugees. The Palestinian state was stillborn: the West Bank was incorporated into the Kingdom of Transjordan, which changed its name to Jordan; Gaza remained under Egyptian military rule. The refugees were housed in camps, mainly in these two areas, but also in Syria and Lebanon. Various military forces were formed under Egyptian patronage, the most important of which was the Palestine Liberation Organization (PLO).

The refugee issue has become one of the main bones of contention between Israel and the Palestinians. Initially, the Arab states demanded that Israel take back all the refugees, while at the same time refusing to replace the temporary armistice agreements with permanent peace accords. Israel, for its part, made a formal proposal to take back one hundred thousand refugees, but the offer was rejected by the Arabs, who organized a comprehensive economic boycott of Israel, forcing the new country to import oil and other vital supplies from far away. A secondary boycott affected countries that were trading with Israel. Many nations were forced to make the choice between economic and commercial relations with the Jewish state or the Arab nations.

Struggling to absorb hundreds of thousands of new immigrants and handicapped by the Arab boycott, the new state was nevertheless compelled to invest much of its resources in security, maintaining a regular army and creating a unique system of calling up reservists, who served at least one month every year. The Palestinian Arabs who remained became Israeli citizens, but, for the most part, did not serve in the army. The majority lived under a military administration based on an emergency regulation of the Mandate regime, which limited their freedom of movement. In these conditions, it was to be expected that they concentrated on their day-to-day existence and refrained from political initiatives.

As for the Jews, in the state of war prevailing after 1948, they treated their Arab citizens with suspicion and reserve. This was true of the government and the population at large. Bearing in mind that the Arab states refused to recognize Israel and would have nothing to do with the Jewish state, there was almost no political engagement between the two sides. The Six Day War of 1967 caused a radical shake-up of the situation. On the seventh day after the outbreak of hostilities, Israel found itself ruling over a majority of the Palestinian people, many of them refugees, in the West Bank and Gaza.

The aftermath of the Six Day War was a disappointment for Israelis, the overwhelming majority of whom were convinced that they would negotiate peace in return for returning the newly conquered territories. The Arabs, however, were in no mood for concessions. In September 1967, at a summit meeting in Khartoum, the Arab heads of state resolved: no negotiations, no peace, and no recognition of Israel.

The PLO, which had been taken over by the Fatah, a military group formed in Kuwait by Yasser Arafat, launched some fifty attacks against Israeli targets, but their networks were quickly defeated by the IDF and their members retreated over the river Jordan. Surprised by the lack of an Arab initiative for negotiations, the Israeli government, which had annexed East Jerusalem soon after the war, seemed uncertain what to do with the newly won territories.

Into this vacuum came two new political movements. On the right, a group of former generals, writers, academics, and some kibbutz members formed the Land of Israel Movement, declaring that Israel should stay put in the territories. On the other side of the political spectrum, left-wing politicians and a different group of academics established the Movement for Peace and Security, calling on the government to declare that it would *not* annex the territories.

Lacking a clear policy, the government failed to prevent the reestablishment of Kfar Etzion, a kibbutz overrun by Jordan's Arab Legion in 1948. Subsequently it launched its own settlement drive. The main thrust of the official settlement policy was in the Egyptian and Syrian areas of Sinai and the Golan Heights, but two Palestinian areas were also included: the Etzion Bloc, south of Jerusalem, where other villages were added near to Kfar Etzion, and the Jordan Rift, considered strategically important by military experts.

A partisan settlement enterprise in the Palestinian town of Hebron was also ratified *post factum*, although it was transferred to the city's outskirts. In addition to this, settlement proceeded apace in the annexed areas of Jerusalem. An artillery war with Egypt broke out along the Suez Canal, and this, together with PLO firing across the Jordan, encouraged a hawkish Israeli policy.

Despite this unpromising atmosphere, a number of Israelis who had advocated dovish policies throughout the 1950s, such as journal editors Uri Avneri and Simcha Flapan, met with individual Palestinians. Later they were joined by Lova Eliav, general secretary of the ruling Labor party, and Gadi Yatziv, a sociologist at the Hebrew University. Levi Eshkol, the relatively moderate prime minister, who had striven unsuccessfully to prevent the 1967 war, died and was succeeded by the far more belligerent Golda

Meir. The new prime minister forced a showdown with Eliav over his espousal of a Palestinian state. Although many in the party agreed with Eliav, none of them dared stand up against Meir and Defense Minister Moshe Dayan, who had become a sort of "Governor of the Territories." Eliav was forced to quit his party position and wrote a book advocating the establishment of a Palestinian state. Few Israelis accepted his arguments, although paradoxically Dayan, who fiercely opposed any political initiative, insisted that Israelis should "listen to the Palestinians," and invited poet Fadwa Toukan to his home for discussions.

Although Palestinian responses to these overtures were cautious, things were moving in the Israeli Arab community. In the early years of the state, the Labor party had endeavored to control the Arab population through supporting local "notables," who had their own faction in the party, but this system of patronage was becoming less effective. Renewed contact with the Palestinians of the territories accelerated the political development of the Israeli Arab community, and in the 1973 elections, the Rakah party won half the Arab vote, putting four members into the Israeli parliament, the Knesset. Rakah, a joint Arab-Jewish party and a successor to the Israeli Communist Party, favored the policy of "two states for two peoples"; in other words, the establishment of a Palestinian state alongside Israel.

In 1970, Nahum Goldmann, an American Zionist leader, proposed to visit Cairo to talk peace to President Nasser, but when Prime Minister Golda Meir made it clear that she opposed the visit, he backed off. One result of the Goldmann affair caused an uproar in Israel. A group of high school students who were about to enter the army published an open letter to Meir asking: "Why should we fight in a purposeless war, while our government's policy is to ignore any chance for peace?" In 1970 Israel, such dissent was unprecedented.

Although the PLO continued to lay claim to all of Palestine, Yasser Arafat allowed his representative in London to write to the *Times* proposing a Palestinian state in the West Bank and Gaza. This prompted a group of Israeli politicians, some of them from the Labor party, to establish the Israeli Council for an Israel-Palestine Peace, which called for the establishment of a Palestinian state next to Israel. The council's members, including Lova Eliav, Uri Avneri, and Matti Peled, a general in the IDF reserve, held a series of secret meetings with PLO representatives in Europe. When the news of the meetings leaked out, both Israel and the PLO rushed to disavow them, but they had taken place with the agreement, if not the approval, of both sides. Moreover, whereas previously only non-Zionist groups had fostered such contacts, this time the Israeli participants included personalities from the country's mainstream.

The Yom Kippur War of 1973, when Israel managed to defeat Egypt and Syria after their initially successful attacks, only served to reinforce the two camps that had emerged in Israel. The left argued that Israel's settlement policy and refusal to initiate any peace proposals had caused the war. The right responded that if the IDF had been stationed on the pre-1967 borders, Israel would have been destroyed. The traditionally dovish National Religious Party had been transformed by the 1967 victory, which it perceived in messianic terms. Its younger members now formed Gush Emunim [Movement of Believers], which fostered settlement all over the territories. When the right-wing Likud, led by Menachem Begin, swept to power in the 1977 elections, settlements were extended into the heart of the Palestinian populated areas of the West Bank and Gaza.

Despite this settlement drive, Begin was swiftly forced to deal with a remarkable peace initiative by Egypt's President Anwar Sadat, who flew to Jerusalem and addressed the Knesset. It was the resulting peace process that gave birth to Peace Now, Israel's largest-ever peace organization. Founded by a group of combat officers in the IDF reserves, the new movement launched an unprecedented series of demonstrations, protests, vigils, lobbying, and media advertisements. Although Peace Now was formed to push Begin to make concessions in the negotiations with Egypt, the movement also resolved that "peace is more important than territory" and opposed "settlement in the territories and domination of another nation." Initially, though, Peace Now, which sought to position itself at the center of Israel's political map, opposed any contact with representatives of the PLO.

After the Israeli-Egyptian peace treaty was signed in 1979, the Likud government stepped up settlement activity still more, causing Peace Now to switch its emphasis to opposing Jewish settlement in the West Bank. In demonstrating against new settlements, the members of Peace Now found themselves in the vicinity of Palestinian towns and villages, which brought them into direct contact with Palestinians for the first time.

A series of meetings led to a public dialogue between Peace Now and a number of West Bank mayors and intellectuals. The two groups found themselves at odds over the official proposal of the Begin government for granting "autonomy" to the West Bank and Gaza. The Palestinians rejected outright the concept of limited self-rule; the Peace Now representatives felt it was a reasonable first step. The Israeli movement also opposed military action, which the PLO maintained were "acts of resistance," but which Peace Now labeled "terrorism." Despite this, two of their leaders held meetings with PLO people in Europe, causing fierce disputes within the movement.

Peace Now also found itself in a dilemma when the Begin government launched a drive against PLO bases in Lebanon in 1982, which quickly escalated into an all-out war and a siege of Beirut, the Lebanese capital. Reluctant to oppose the government while the guns were firing—indeed, as combat soldiers, Peace Now leaders were doing much of the firing—the movement was criticized for its early acquiescence in the campaign. As the war continued, however, the movement returned to leadership of the Israeli peace camp with a large protest demonstration in Tel Aviv.

The movement did not support a new protest group, Yesh Gvul, whose members refused to serve in the IDF in Lebanon, preferring to go to jail. As the war progressed, a number of other protest movements were founded, and after the massacre of Palestinians by Israel's Christian allies in two Lebanese refugee camps, Peace Now organized the largest demonstration in Israel's history. Whether there were really four hundred thousand protesters in Tel Aviv that night is still a matter of dispute. What is beyond controversy is that there has never been a larger demonstration in Israel before or since. It led to the establishment of a State Commission of Inquiry, to the dismissal of Defense Minister Ariel Sharon, and ultimately to the resignation of Prime Minister Begin.

In the wake of the Lebanon war, more peace groups were established, among them East for Peace, a movement of Sephardi Jews, and Paths to Peace, a religious movement. Peace Now and the other movements tried to influence the elections that followed Begin's departure, focusing on the occupation of the Palestinian territories. As a result, some twenty Knesset members in four parties supported a policy of withdrawing from the territories, although there were differing opinions about the extent of the pullback envisaged.

Several movements were now fostering contacts between Israelis and Palestinians and between Jews and Arabs in Israel. The Jewish-Arab village of Neve Shalom, founded in the early 1970s, established its School for Peace, and Givat Haviva, the educational center of the Kibbutz Artzi movement, started a special program for Arab and Jewish high school students. A joint youth movement called Re'ut ran community projects, hikes, and camps for Jewish and Arab children. Beit Hagefen, Haifa's Arab-Jewish Friendship Center in Haifa, stepped up its activities and the intercommunal Olive Tree Festival became an annual event in Galilee. Gesher [Bridge] was one of several Israeli-Palestinian encounter groups established in the mid 1980s.

There were so many meetings between Israelis and Palestinians at this time that the National Unity Government of Likud and Labor enacted legislation that made it illegal for Israelis to hold meetings with members of the PLO. Although it officially opposed contacts with the PLO, Peace Now continued holding regular meetings with the younger generation of leaders in the territories, all of whom were fervent supporters of that organization.

Despite all this activity, it was clear by the mid 1980s that the Israeli peace movement had lost out. The agreement with Egypt had turned out to be a "cold" peace and there were no new official peace initiatives. Moreover, there was no sign of withdrawal from the territories—quite the opposite: Israel was digging in and the settlement enterprise was flourishing.

In December 1987, the first Palestinian *Intifada* erupted. The word Intifada means "shaking off" in Arabic, and the young Palestinians aspired to shake off the Israeli occupation of their territories. A spontaneous uprising aimed at asserting their independence, the Intifada took both the Israeli and the Palestinian leaderships by surprise. Israel took it so casually at first that Defense Minister Yitzhak Rabin did not even return from a trip abroad to deal with it. For its part, the PLO took several months to realize its importance and assume the leadership.

Although it was the clashes between stone-throwing Palestinian youngsters and Israeli troops that made the headlines, an economic boycott was in some ways more significant. The Palestinians served notice that they could manage without Israel and endeavored to become self-sufficient in at least some products. It was a sort of declaration of independence from Israeli rule.

Responding to the new situation, some of the marginal Israeli groups organized visits to the occupied territories and joint protest demonstrations with the Palestinians. The Moked for the Defense of Victims of Violence, which assisted Palestinian victims on an individual basis, and Betzelem, which monitored human rights violations in the territories, were established shortly after the outbreak of the Intifada. Yesh Gvul, the IDF reservists protest group, gained a new lease on life. Only 150 soldiers were imprisoned for refusing military service during the Intifada, but it became clear that several thousand more found ways of evading call-up.

While Peace Now, the largest group, opposed the refusal to serve, it did call a meeting to advocate disobeying illegal orders in combating the Intifada. At the same meeting, Palestinian editor Hana Seniora told the Israeli protesters that the Intifada was directed against the occupation—not against Israel.

Even as the Intifada raged, meetings between Israelis and Palestinians continued. In an unprecedented development, Moshe Amirav, a member of the Likud Central Committee, met with Palestinian leader Faisal Husseini and some colleagues and proposed an Israeli-Palestinian confederation that would avoid repartitioning the Land of Israel. Amirav was later forced out of his party for such "daring" actions.

The uprising also resulted in a radical political development as King Hussein of Jordan formally relinquished responsibility for the West Bank. The PLO responded with a declaration founding a Palestinian state, mentioning the UN Partition resolution of 1947, previously rejected by the Palestinians. At the end of 1988, Arafat announced that the PLO "rejected terror" and accepted the right of Israel to live "in peace and security." Peace Now called for immediate negotiations with the PLO.

Around this time the Israel-Palestine Center for Research and Information (IPCRI), a new think tank with equal numbers of Israelis and Palestinians on its board, launched a series of meetings between Israelis and

Palestinians and established committees to discuss Jerusalem, borders, security, trade, refugees, and the environment. At the end of 1989, Israelis and Palestinians linked hands in a joint demonstration around the walls of the Old City of Jerusalem.

The momentum for peace and dialogue was interrupted by Iraq's invasion of Kuwait in 1991 and the subsequent American-led counterattack. During the conflict that would come to be known as the first Gulf War, dozens of Iraqi missiles were fired at Israel. Although the damage was minimal, some Israeli media experts warned that the rockets might be tipped with chemical or biological warheads.

Israeli citizens, who were instructed by their government to shut themselves in sealed rooms in case of unconventional attacks, suffered severe psychological shock. Their trauma was made even worse by Yasser Arafat's openly voiced support of Iraqi leader Saddam Hussein. Many Israeli Jews believed reports that Palestinians "danced on the roofs" as the rockets sailed over their heads toward Tel Aviv. Hostile feelings on both sides followed a renewed series of violent Palestinian attacks, and the territories were sealed off from Israel.

Throughout the Intifada, Palestinians had continued passing freely into Israeli territory, but now, for the first time, over one hundred thousand Palestinian workers could not reach their jobs in Tel Aviv and other Israeli towns. Furthermore, Arafat's ill-judged support for Saddam Hussein also led to the expulsion of some four hundred thousand Palestinians from Kuwait. As the breadwinners in Kuwait had been mailing money back home, the economic situation in the territories deteriorated even further. It has been estimated that the wages earned in Israel and Kuwait at that time amounted to half the Palestinian GDP. This income was now lost to the Palestinian economy.

In the face of these negative developments, following the first Gulf War the United States convened a peace conference in Madrid, in which Israelis faced a joint Jordanian-Palestinian delegation in addition to other Arab representatives. The Palestinian delegates from the West Bank and Gaza, who had been approved by the PLO in Tunis, coordinated their moves with Arafat throughout the talks. Coincidentally with the Madrid talks, some West Bank Palestinians launched a local "peace initiative," handing out olive branches, flowers, and balloons to IDF soldiers and even to Jewish settlers. Unfortunately, other Palestinians subsequently launched a further wave of terror attacks.

Then, in 1992, the Labor party, led by Yitzhak Rabin, won the Israeli elections, forming a government pledged to bring peace. Starting with secret talks in Oslo, Norway that became more official as they went along, Israel and the PLO negotiated a declaration of principles (DOP), which was signed on the White House lawn. In the DOP, Israelis and Palestinians for the first time recognized each other's national rights. Yitzhak Rabin and Yasser Arafat shook hands on the deal and, for a time, an entirely new atmosphere prevailed. Israel withdrew from Gaza and the Jericho area of the West Bank to be replaced by the PLO-led Palestinian Authority (PA). In subsequent months, Israel withdrew its forces from the main Palestinian towns, enabling the PA to extend its rule over most of the Palestinian population.

The Oslo years, 1993 to 2000, saw an unprecedented increase in Israeli-Palestinian dialogue and cooperation at all levels. Today, despite all that has happened since, there are more than a hundred NGOs and grassroots organizations fostering Israeli-Palestinian and Jewish-Arab coexistence and dialogue in the fields of information, environment, media, education, culture, music, sports, and even religion. It should be pointed out that (with the notable exception of the groups described in this book) most of them have been short-lived, and many of them involved relatively small numbers of people. Nevertheless, although the vast majority of people on both sides remained unaffected by their activities, they demonstrated the enormous potential for coexistence and cooperation between the two sides.

One of the most intriguing developments of the Oslo years was "Operation Charlie," a series of secret meetings between leaders of the Jewish settlers and Palestinians who were quite senior in the PLO hierarchy. Organized by Yossi Alpher, at that time the representative in Jerusalem of the American Jewish Committee, the meetings mostly took place in Jerusalem, but one important get-together was in an English manor house near Oxford.

Although both sides insisted on secrecy, partly for fear of the reactions their friends and associates, the talks were remarkably frank and probing. The Palestinians were exposed to the attitude of the settlers, who made it clear that their attachment to all parts of the Land of Israel was non-negotiable.

"If we lose Shilo and Ofra," said a settler, referring to two settlements in the heart of Palestinian population concentrations, "we are giving up on the whole Zionist enterprise. Zionism is a return to our roots, and our roots are there."

Another settler leader said that he much preferred talking to the Palestinians than to the "Israeli left." The Palestinians, he asserted, had the same attitude of devotion to their land. On one occasion, there was even a lighthearted discussion between a settler and a Palestinian official about a proposal that Israel should be established in the hills of Judea and Samaria and Palestine should be in the coastal plain, where Tel Aviv and Haifa are situated. This, they noted, would be more in line with historical precedent.

There was considerable discussion about whether Jewish settlements could remain under Palestinian rule, with some settler representatives looking on this as a possibility. A Palestinian representative asked why such settlements should be exclusively Jewish. He felt that Palestinians Arabs should be entitled to live there alongside Jews. He also made the point that, although he was against the existence of Jewish settlements, he did not oppose the right of individual Jews to live in Palestine.

The discussions did not bring the sides close on any issue, but they did add to understanding and were important in countering the Israeli picture of the PLO men as "terrorists," and the Palestinian picture of the settlers as "colonialist land grabbers."

Sadly, the conciliation process of the 1990s has been set back by recent events on the ground. The outbreak of Palestinian violence in September 2000, the harsh Israeli response, the escalation of the violence, the IDF reoccupation of most of the PA-administered territories, the consolidation of the closure, and the construction of the separation fence have made it far more difficult to maintain ties between Israelis and Palestinians.

The unilateral Israeli disengagement from Gaza did not improve the situation. Indeed, it may have made it worse. The withdrawal of Israeli settlement and the IDF from Gaza was carried out unilaterally, No attempt was made to reach agreement with the Palestinian side. Furthermore, Gaza was cut off on all sides with the result that its economic situation, always bad, became even worse. Extremist groups in Gaza daily fired primitive rockets into the adjacent area of Israel, the town of Sderot and several kibbutzim. In response, Israel launched a series of air strikes and land attacks, but had very little success in stopping the rockets.

Prime Minister Ariel Sharon, the architect of disengagement, suffered a massive stroke. Following his departure from public life, there were elections and a government espousing "unilateralism," the separation of Israelis and Palestinians, took office in Israel.

The new government became embroiled in an armed conflict with Hezbollah, a fundamentalist Shiite Muslim militia stationed on the border with Lebanon. The monthlong conflict, causing death and destruction on both sides of the border, only added to the atmosphere of hopelessness and depression in Israel and the Palestinian territories. It has become almost impossible for Israelis and Palestinians to get together, increasingly separated as they are by physical, legal, and psychological barriers.

Despite these negative developments, some see the disengagement from the Palestinians of the West Bank and Gaza as an opportunity for reengaging with the Palestinians who are citizens of Israel, the Israeli Arabs. At a conference in the Israeli Bedouin town of Rahat, Safa Abu-Rabiya made the following points:

> In disengaging from Gaza, we at last see a return to sanity by the State of Israel and its citizens. The restoration of territories to their natural owners has

implications for stabilizing our relations with our Jewish fellow citizens. We Palestinians who are citizens of Israel now have a new opportunity to establish our own identity. Relinquishing the dream of Greater Israel is a move toward healing the bleeding wounds in relations between Israelis and Palestinians, wounds that also affect Jewish and Palestinian citizens of Israel.

This disengagement is not from us Palestinian Israelis, and has not made us disappear. On the contrary, leaving Gaza has placed us more firmly on the map of Israel. We are here and we are demanding that our situation be addressed. We have disappeared in the past, but we are not going to disappear again.

We Palestinian Israelis do not want to be regarded as a security danger. Nor do we, Palestinian Bedouin women, want to be defined as wombs that threaten the demographic balance in Israel. We demand to be recognized as individuals. We hope that part of this process of returning to sanity will lead to our acceptance as equal citizens and as human beings worthy of full rights.

The meeting addressed by Safa was organized by Sikkuy [opportunity], an Israeli association dedicated to closing the economic, social, and political gaps between Jews and Arabs inside Israel. In the next chapter, we will visit this NGO and examine its drive for full social, economic, and political equality among the different communities in Israel.

9

Building Blocks of Equality

> I am not Sisyphus, who rolled a stone up a hill, knowing that it would roll down again. Every stone that I roll up the hill remains there. The stones are the building blocks of the structure that we are trying to create: a state in which every citizen is equal. It doesn't matter what solution there is to the Israeli-Palestinian problem. There can be two states, a Jewish democratic state, a binational state, even a traditionally religious state. The point is that in Israel there must be absolute equality.

Shalom "Shuli" Dichter's emphatic statement comes at the end of a long conversation, when he is asked whether he ever becomes discouraged. Dichter, the Jewish codirector of Sikkuy, has been involved in Jewish-Arab relations all his life. In the yard of the nursery school at the kibbutz where he was born, he and a friend were banging on the ground with hammers. When the teacher asked them what they were doing, the young Shuli replied that they were "building a house for the Arabs because they don't have anywhere to live because they were expelled." He had heard about the Arab refugees of the 1948 War of Independence and decided to do something about it. The nursery school "foundations" were soon abandoned by the children, but a sense of personal involvement has remained with him ever since.

Before he came to Sikkuy, Dichter taught Arabic in kibbutz schools, served as secretary of his kibbutz, and founded Children Teaching Children, a program where Jewish and Arab children in Israel taught each other Hebrew and Arabic. This swiftly expanded into a project dealing with all aspects of coexistence between the two communities and bringing in teachers as well as students. The program now deals with "the pluralistic, multicultural nature of the state and the complex vision of living in the reality of the Arab-Israeli conflict."

In 1998, Dichter was invited to become codirector of Sikkuy, a Jewish-Arab advocacy group founded in 1991 to work for complete equality between Jews and Arabs in Israel. He has served with two Arab co-directors, first Asad Ghanem and today Ali Haider, an attorney from Ibillin, an Arab community near Haifa. "It is a Zionist mission," stresses Dichter, a stocky, sunburned man with thick wiry gray hair. "We Jews will benefit from equality for the Arabs just as much as the Arabs themselves."

This became even clearer to Dichter when he attended the Durban Conference, the UN forum of NGOs held in South Africa in the fall of 2001. His friends warned him that he would be disillusioned by the behavior of the Israeli Arabs at the conference. The Arab delegates often behaved as separate representatives with a strong tendency toward regime change, in effect delegitimizing the State of Israel.

After a lifelong commitment to Jewish-Arab equality, Dichter is resilient enough to confront such a situation realistically. He acknowledges that efforts at so-called coexistence in Israel's first years after 1948 were directed toward persuading Israel's Arab citizens to accept the status quo, a coexistence of rider (Jews) and horse (Arabs). He understands that this situation has become unacceptable to Israel's Arab citizens, who today demand genuine equality. He defines the current situation as an ongoing conflict—not coexistence—but he urges the Israeli Arabs not to sever their links to their Jewish fellow citizens. Jews and Arabs must, in his view, engage in continuous dialogue.

In October 2000, together with the eruption of the second Intifada in the Palestinian territories, there were also violent demonstrations in several Arab communities inside Israel, to which the police responded with considerable force. After thirteen Arabs, all but one of them Israeli citizens, were shot to death by the police and a Jewish citizen was killed by a rock dropped on his car, the government was forced to establish an official inquiry commission, headed by Supreme Court Justice Theodor Or. The codirectors of Sikkuy were among those giving expert evidence.

After three years, the Or Commission published its report, which reviewed the violent confrontation in detail and blamed the government of Israel, the police, and some of the leaders of the Arab community for allowing the situation to get out of control. However, the report also surveyed the background to the events, determining that Israel's Arab citizens "live in a reality in which they are discriminated against as Arabs." This discrimination, it was emphasized, related both to status and to the allocation of national resources. In fact, the Or Commission restated what Sikkuy had been saying for more than a decade: the Arab citizens of Israel are not receiving their fair share of the national cake.

The commission stated that "the attainment of complete equality for Israel's Arab citizens must be a central aim of the state" and recommended that the government "initiate, develop and implement programs to eliminate existing disparities."

Sikkuy immediately established the Or Commission Watch, a team of Jewish and Arab volunteers to monitor the implementation—or as it turned out mostly the nonimplementation—of the commission's recommendations. The Sikkuy leadership is convinced that the Or Commission report is a potential turning point in the situation of Israel's Arab citizens, and the organization is focusing its efforts on advocating that the recommendations be carried out.

Following official approval of the report, the government appointed a committee headed by Yosef Lapid, who was serving as Justice Minister at that time, instructing it to come up with a concrete plan for implementing the recommendations. Lapid subsequently addressed a Sikkuy conference, where he promised that the Or Commission proposals would be carried out, but he also stated that equality demanded "obligations," a thinly veiled reference to the fact that the majority of Arab citizens of Israel do not perform military service.

Sikkuy leaders hit back at the minister, saying that equality could not be conditional and also charging that the government committee headed by him had not come up with a realistic program for implementation. Dichter announced that Sikkuy would monitor the Or Commission proposals—not those of the Lapid Committee. Sikkuy would further work to mobilize public support for the proposals, as this was clearly lacking.

Historian Shimon Shamir, a member of the Or Commission, also addressed the Sikkuy Conference, noting that it was clear what had to be done and reiterating that the key was implementation. This is consistent with Sikkuy's activities since its inception. The organization's latest annual report contains a wealth of information about discrimination and inequality, but the report goes on to state, "the acquisition of this information is not the objective, changing the situation is the goal."

Among other things, the report refers to the 2005 evacuation of the Jewish settlements and the IDF from Gaza, calling it an "instructive lesson in the power of the Prime Minister." Without going into the pros and cons of the so-called disengagement, the report noted: "The Prime Minister proved that when he wants it he can do it. It would be desirable if the same approach were applied to instituting equality between Jews and Arabs in Israel."

In his remarks, Professor Shamir concluded: "There is a very positive breath of fresh air regarding recognition of the lack of equality and in regard to the desire to solve this inequality. I mention this because it is important to remember that this spirit is blowing among a minority in Israeli society. Unfortunately the wind that is blowing among the majority of the Israeli population is very negative and it categorically rejects the positive things that can be found in the Or Commission and the Lapid Committee."

This is precisely the reason for the establishment of Sikkuy's Civic Action Committees, which seek to persuade the Jews that equality is in their interest also. This cannot be taken for granted. "The Arabs know very well that they are not equal," explains Dichter, "but this is not always so clear to the Jews."

The national director of the Civic Action Groups, Hassia Porat, lives in western Galilee in a Jewish village surrounded by Arab towns and villages. She relates with relative equanimity the violence in the fall of 2000. "We knew that an explosion was coming," she declares. "When it happened, it was frightening and shocking. Many Jews were deeply offended, but those of us who knew the depth of frustration in the Arab community were surprised it wasn't much worse. You have to understand that the real violence only happened after the police opened fire."

Porat and her husband sought to change their lifestyle when they moved to Yaad with their two sons in 1991. They were looking for a less materialistic environment and one where they could make their influence felt. Porat was a publisher's assistant who was able to continue working from home on her computer. Her husband, Tzur, moved his architect's office to his new home in Galilee.

Their light, airy, spacious house, decorated with modern art and sculpture and surrounded by trees and lawns, was enlarged by Tzur from a standard village unit. Hassia, a sturdy, middle-aged woman, serves coffee and biscuits and sits across the table from me, gesturing vigorously as she talks. The first Saturday after their arrival in their new home, she relates, Tzur went to the nearby Arab town of Sakhnin, ordered a coffee, and announced to all and sundry that he wanted "to meet people." Over the years, the Porats have made numerous Arab friends, so it was natural that, after the 2000 riots, they were among the activists who set up a special peace tent. Many Jews and Arabs visited the tent, including the head of the local regional council, the Misgav Council. He asked Hassia to establish a forum of representatives from the Jewish and Arab communities. When she tried to do this, she found that the Jews turned up, but the Arabs, still smarting from what they felt was overreaction by the police to the recent demonstrations, refused to attend. "At this point I realized that if I waited for Arab partners I would wait for a long time," recalls Hassia, "so I accepted a proposal from Sikkuy to establish a purely Jewish Civic Action Group. We acted as Jews toward the Jewish establishment."

A number of local Arabs soon perceived that the Hassia's group was successfully targeting both local officials and the local media, and this showed them that there were some Jews who really believed in equality. They soon established contacts with Hassia and her committee, and today Arab officials from Sakhnin and the other towns and villages in western Galilee are eager to cooperate with her group. "Although the idea of the group is to get Jews to take action, our contact with the local Arabs makes sure that we get it right," explains Hassia. "After all, they know better than we do what is really needed."

Most Jews don't know about the extent of the inequality between Jews and Arabs in Israeli society, she asserts. They also think that because they don't serve in the army, the Arabs don't deserve civil rights, so there is a lot of work to be done among Israeli Jews. On the other hand, she finds that those who do understand the problem are tired of hearing the statistics and want to do something concrete about it. The all-volunteer Sikkuy group has a core of twenty-five members, all volunteers working in their free time. They meet every few months and in between keep contact via e-mails. Since the formation of the first Civic Action Group in Misgav, several other groups have been formed all over Israel.

"We are constantly fighting the authorities," relates Hassia. "I'll give you an example: the Jews who live in Carmiel and the others who live in the Misgav region receive the various services given to citizens by the Interior Ministry in their town. On the other hand, the Misgav Arabs, mostly Bedouin, have to go to Acre or Nazareth to receive those same services. Do you know why? It dates back to the time of the British Mandate—or even to Ottoman times!"

Hassia has a long list of cases of discrimination. The chairman of the Misgav Regional Council takes pride in the fact that he has helped the Misgav Bedouin. Hassia agrees that this is true. He raised money to build a fine community center in one of the local villages, but because there was no master plan for the village, complications arose about its location. He proposed to go ahead with the building anyway and promised to transfer the ownership of the land to the village subsequently.

When the local villagers showed that they were suspicious and wanted some sort of guarantee from him, he was hugely insulted, but Hassia says she understands why the Bedouin have learned to distrust the authorities. The Misgav chairman has done some good things, she concedes, but he has a lot to learn about his Bedouin constituents. She contends that he has been working *for* the Bedouin, but he must learn to work *with* them.

Then there is the matter of the Kariv Foundation, which funds a school enrichment program that pays for extra classes in English and math as well as art, music, and theater groups. The foundation pays part of the expenses, the local community puts up matching funds, and the parents make a modest contribution. The Jewish schools in Western Galilee have been benefiting from this project for fifteen years; the Bedouin schools have not been receiving this assistance. There is a problem about the matching funds, concedes Hassia, but no real attempt has been made to solve the problem.

Officials of the National Insurance Institute promised to open a branch in Sakhnin, an Arab town of twenty-five thousand residents, but then they changed their minds. They now propose to build it in the Misgav Industrial Park. This means that the Arabs will have to trek into a Jewish area to receive the services. A proposal to build a hospital in Sakhnin was turned down on the grounds that the town was not large enough to merit a hospital. Instead, there are plans for a hospital in Kiryat Ata, a Jewish satellite town of Haifa.

"Has there been any consultation with the Arabs themselves?" demands Hassia. "I asked that question, even though I knew the answer. Of course there had not been any consultation. The prejudice and discrimination are so deeply ingrained that they are almost unconscious. The hospital plan is particularly shameful, because it is predicated on the assumption that Jews won't go to Sakhnin for hospitalization because it is an Arab town. In fact hospitals are one of the few bright spots in this country. They are the best examples of cooperation and integration between Jews and Arabs that we have."

Hassia and her colleagues on the Civic Action Groups are dealing with day-to-day matters on a local basis, but Sikkuy is also dealing with the overall situation in the country as a whole. During the monthlong war between Israel and the Shiite Hezbollah in Lebanon in the summer of 2006, the world media focused on the casualties and destruction in Lebanon. Certainly, the Lebanese suffered more damage than the Israelis, but in northern Israel Jewish and Arab communities were indiscriminately shelled by Hezbollah forces. The damage was wide-scale and, as a consequence, the government came up with a rehabilitation plan for the region, budgeting large sums for development.

In fact, plans for developing Galilee were in the pipeline before war broke out. The new government, headed by Ehud Olmert, was committed to this. In the 2006 elections, the new Kadima Party, founded by Ariel Sharon but subsequently led by Olmert, promised to withdraw from large areas of the West Bank. The party platform stated that investment would be redirected from the West Bank to Galilee in the north and the Negev in the south.

As both regions, which are heavily populated by Arabs as well as by Jews, have seriously lagged behind the rest of the country, this was good news indeed. The bad news, as Sikkuy swiftly demonstrated in a special report, was that the plans were almost exclusively directed at Jewish towns and villages. Sikkuy pointed out that even equality of investment was insufficient: a policy of affirmative action was required to bring the Arab residents up to the level of their Jewish fellow citizens. Equality of opportunity is not enough; the aim must be equality of results.

The report notes Israel's proven ability to get things done. The disengagement from Gaza has already been mentioned, but even more notable is the immigration of almost a million people, mostly from the former Soviet Union, during the 1990s and their integration into Israeli society. National institutions demonstrated an impressive ability to cut red tape and provide housing, employment, health, and education for this relatively large influx. Sikkuy calls for a similar effort to carry out the recommendations of the Or Commission to bring the Israeli Arabs up to the standards of their Jewish fellow citizens.

Housing, employment, and education must be dealt with as a matter of urgency. Laws must be promulgated; money must be invested. Most Arab towns and villages still lack master plans, which would enable them to build housing and infrastructure for their growing populations. Mortgages must be made available for purchasing houses and apartments. Industrial parks, almost nonexistent in the Arab sector, must be planned and constructed. Arab entrepreneurs have to receive the same incentives given to Jews. The proportion of Arabs employed by government ministries, local authorities, and national institutions must be increased exponentially. Most importantly, all this must be carried out in consultation with the Arabs themselves, with their mayors, local councils, and NGOs.

Special committees must be established, similar to those set up in the 1990s to deal with the immigrants, which will be able to circumvent decision-making barriers and sometimes even overrule the planners. Those special committees approved zoning and planning for the immigrants. Now the same can be done for the Arabs. Moreover, these committees must include Arab members. The Sikkuy report suggests the establishment of a special authority or directorate to speed up the planning in Arab communities. The system of national priority zones, which is currently biased in the direction of the Jewish population, must be restructured to favor the development of the Arab towns and villages.

Several new schools must be built in Arab communities, including two regional high schools, and existing schools must have classrooms added. In addition, the Sikkuy report proposes the establishment of technological colleges in Nazareth and Western Galilee.

The development plans for Galilee and the Negev, concludes the report, offer a unique opportunity to change the priorities of Israeli society. The physical planning of Arab communities is a bottleneck, says the report, but not the barrier. The barrier is the attitude of the Israeli state, and this can be changed. The development tracks for Jews and Arabs must be fused into a single impartial development track that will lead to equality.

Hassia has pinpointed some of the problems in Galilee. The Negev is less in focus, as it was unaffected by the recent war, but its problems are no less acute. In some ways, they are more serious. In the previous chapter, we met Safa Abu-Rabiya delivering an impassioned speech at a Sikkuy conference in the Arab town of Rahat in the Negev. Her presentation was delivered in impeccable Hebrew with the body language, confidence, and accent of an Israeli-born Jewish citizen of Israel. In her presence and personality, Safa, a doctoral student and lecturer in anthropology at Ben Gurion University, demonstrates how an Israeli Arab woman from the country's least developed community can become an integral part of Israeli society and advance to the center of academic life in this country.

Formidable on the platform, Safa is less intimidating but just as impressive close up when we meet on the campus of the Ben-Gurion University of the Negev in Bersheba. A slim, almost frail figure in slacks and a short-sleeved top, she makes her points quietly but emphatically. She has slightly modified the opinions she stated so emphatically at the Rahat conference.

"I said then that we have to start worrying about ourselves after lobbying for the Palestinians and neglecting our own problems inside Israel," she explains. "That is correct, but we cannot entirely separate the two issues. Today I see that they are closely entwined. We all have family ties with our fellow Palestinians. Still, we should leave the Palestinian problem to the residents of the West Bank and Gaza. We should continue to show solidarity with them. There should be a Palestinian state, but that won't solve our problems as Palestinian citizens of Israel. Our real problem is right here at home."

Safa is the second daughter of Yunis Abu-Rabiya, the first Israeli Bedouin to become a physician. A longtime campaigner for Bedouin rights, he currently heads the medical center in Rahat. Safa's elder sister earned her PhD in the sociology of education for her research on Israel's Bedouin schools. Her younger sister has a law degree and plans to work in the office of the state prosecutor, her youngest sister is a nursery teacher, and her brother is about to enter medical school.

This remarkable record is the result of the family tradition: Yunis, her father, was sent by his parents to study in Nazareth as at that time the standard of Bedouin education was low. He in his turn always emphasized the importance of education to his children. Safa herself studied to fifth grade in the Bedouin school at Tel Sheva and continued at Jewish schools in Beersheba. She learned Hebrew from sixth grade and later went on to Ben-Gurion University, where her first degree was in Middle East studies, her second was in anthropology, and her doctorate is in the framework of Middle East studies, but using anthropological tools. Her MA thesis was on the identity of the Bedouin of the Negev. "As I had been to a Jewish school, I lacked knowledge of my own history and culture," she states. "My research was also a search for my own identity."

Although her doctorate will deal with the Bedouin feminine society, her MA, which researched the Bedouin attachment to land, was focused on the men of the older generation. A single young woman could not hope to interview elderly male Bedouin, so her father accompanied her everywhere. "I asked the questions," she recalls, "but they always replied to my father. They looked at him—not at me. I was not in the least offended. I knew that they behaved in this way out of respect for me."

Much of the research into Bedouin life has concentrated on the folkloristic aspects, but Safa was determined to look into the social and political issues. There is a general perception that because of their nomadic tradition, the Bedouin are not attached to the land, she notes, but this is an oversimplification. She surveyed the generation of 1948, seen by Arabs as the Nakba, the disaster, when the Jews won the war and established the State of Israel. Traditionally the Bedouin did move from place to place, but their wanderings were within a certain territory and they felt a strong attachment to that location.

Her own tribe, the Abu-Rabiya, remained on its land after the 1948 war, but many other Negev Bedouin were relocated. Today they visit their former lands with their children and have rituals connected with them, proving that their past is part of their present. She estimates that this population has grown to 175,000 individuals, half of them living in unrecognized villages. They have no roads, water, electricity, schools, or municipal services, she notes, but even the official Bedouin communities, such as Rahat and Tel Sheva, where these things are available, are failures. They have no industrial zones and they have the highest rates of poverty and unemployment in Israel. She emphasizes that the problems of the Bedouin are already beginning to have an impact on Jewish society as crime increases because of the bad conditions.

It can all be worked out, suggests Safa. All that is needed is goodwill. There has to be a compromise. Clearly, not all of them can go back to their lands, but some of them can. A number of the unrecognized villages should receive official recognition so that roads, electricity, water, and phone lines can be installed and schools built. Many Bedouin who are prepared to move into modern towns and villages would still like to maintain symbolic links to farming and raising livestock by pitching a guest tent in the yard and keeping a few animals. This would be taken into consideration in the design and layout of Bedouin communities if they themselves were partners in the development.

Although she grew up in a Jewish society and many of her Jewish friends did not even know she was an Arab, Safa emphasizes that she never felt the temptation to become part of that society. Her mother, until recently a supervisor of nursery schools for the Ministry of Education, was born in Nazareth, but her family was from a village by Lake Kinneret and she always felt attached to it. Both her parents were proud of their identities, and she always felt Bedouin, Arab, and Palestinian.

Like her father, Safa has worked for coexistence, fostering contacts between her own Bedouin community and the Jews, but today she feels the priority should be to develop Bedouin society so that coexistence will be between equals. She has worked among Bedouin women, teaching them about empowerment and making them aware of their rights.

Switching to English, Safa talks about the Bedouin women sitting near us in the university cafeteria, all of whom wear *jilbab* dresses and *hijab* head scarves. Their dress does not necessarily mean that they are devout Muslims, she explains. They wear traditional clothes as part of the agreement with their families, who permit them to study on condition that they don't abandon their way of life. There are about one hundred Bedouin women studying at Ben-Gurion University, many of them supported by the campus Bedouin center, which is financed by an American Jewish donor.

Safa is not optimistic. She is not sure that even her eight-month-old daughter will live in a time of peace. In her own short lifetime, she has seen too many moments of hope collapse. The second Intifada, the violent confrontation between Israelis and Palestinians that started in 2000, has set back coexistence by many years, she asserts. Her generation is very aware of reality of life in Israel today.

"We are not intimidated," she declares. "We are much more confident than our parents were. We are prepared to shout for our rights, but there can only be progress if the situation in Gaza and the West Bank calms down. My first priority is my own people, the Bedouin of the Negev, but that doesn't mean that I am not aware of the wider picture."

The latest Sikkuy annual report for monitoring civic equality has four headlines on its cover: "Government Development Plans for Arab Citizens"; "Inequality in Social Welfare Funding"; "Fair Representation of Arab Citizens in the Civil Service"; "Two Years to the Or Commission Recommendations." It was the last report to be edited by Shuli Dichter. In a personal note handing over the editorship to his codirector Ali Haider, Dichter noted that the first report in 1999 received no coverage in the Israeli media. Since then the situation has improved in that today there is an awareness of the discrimination against Arabs in Israel. Now the emphasis must be on changing the situation.

Sitting in the Sikkuy office in the northern Israeli town of Haifa, Ali Haider, codirector of Sikkuy and the new editor of its annual report, notes that when he took up his present position, there was no permanent Sikkuy office in the north, where most of Israel's Arabs live. A relaxed, self-confident man of thirty-four, Haider offers me something to drink despite the fact that he is fasting for Ramadan. I decline, but he presses me, insisting that "there is no problem." I again refuse his offer and we proceed to the interview.

Haider was born in the Galilee village of Ibillin, where he now lives again after spending several years away with his wife and two children. Educated in village schools, he began studying political science and education at Haifa University before switching to law, which he learned at Bar Ilan, a religious university near Tel Aviv. "Socially I was an outsider at Bar Ilan," he recalls, "but I was well taught and I hope I became a good lawyer."

He was employed for a time at the State Prosecutor's Office in Tel Aviv before going to Jerusalem to work in several NGOs connected with human rights. He worked for the Moked for the Defense of the Individual and then spent three years in Sikkuy directing a special project for affirmative action and fair representation. He then left to establish a private law firm in Haifa, which is now run by his brother.

Returning to Sikkuy as codirector in 2003, he now doubles as editor of the annual report. The next report will feature a special "equality index," he tells me. Four prominent university lecturers, two Jews and two Arabs, are assessing the fields of education, employment, poverty, and welfare to come up with the index. The equality index will be a permanent feature of Sikkuy's annual report.

There are two classes of citizen in Israel, suggests Haider, Jewish citizens, who have full rights, and Arab citizens, who have diminished and conditional rights. This has to be remedied for the good of society as a whole. When a minority is deprived, there is an explosion, and this is what happened in October 2000. The second Lebanon war of July 2006 drove a further wedge between Israeli Jews and Arabs, with many of the Jews accusing their Arab fellow citizens of supporting their Hezbollah enemies. Haider maintains that this is a complete misunderstanding.

"Most of us opposed the war from day one," he states. "We thought it was hasty, unconsidered, and unnecessary. Later on, many Jews came to the same conclusion, but at the outset there was almost universal Jewish support for the war, led by a 'mobilized' media. This led to the canard that we support Hezbollah. It is simply untrue."

Haider rejects the demand, which is voiced by many Jews, that the Arabs in Israel do national service. He points out that there are many Jews, such as the ultra-Orthodox, who don't undertake military service, and they have full rights. Conversely, Arabs who do serve in the IDF, such as Druze and some Bedouin, do not have equality with the Jews. Equality cannot be conditional, he insists. The Arabs of Israel do not have to earn it: it is their right. The basic problem is one of mistrust, he avers. There is suspicion and a complete lack of confidence. If the Arabs became full partners in Israeli society, the situation would be transformed.

"I would not be sitting here in this office unless I was basically optimistic," he declares. "But I must be realistic. I recognize the barriers that still exist between Jews and Arabs and I'm seeking ways to break them down. I am part of a new generation. We are Palestinians, Arabs, and also Israelis. We know Israeli society and we relate to it as equals. We expect and demand equality."

After this chapter had been completed, a prestigious group of forty Israeli Arabs, including Ali Haider and his predecessor Asad Ghanem, published "Future Vision of the Palestinian Arabs in Israel," which many Jews who regard themselves as sympathetic to the Israeli Arab community find profoundly disturbing. The demand for equality was acceptable to them, but many saw the document as a refusal to accept the Jewish connection to the land of Israel and saw an exclusive concentration on the Arab version of Israel's establishment.

Dichter was not really surprised by the document, nor does he find it threatening. He is, however, highly critical of the way it was presented. He feels that his Arab friends—most of the framers of the document are personal friends and colleagues—should have brought it before a Jewish forum for discussion. He stresses that this is not for censorship, but to discuss how it should be presented to the Jewish community of Israel. In presenting it directly to the media, they were harming themselves and all those working for equality and coexistence.

That being said, he is also critical of some of the content. In describing the Zionist enterprise as "colonialist," he thinks that the Palestinian Israelis are "making things easy for themselves." The solution to colonialism is simple, he notes. The colonists return to their countries of origin. This does not apply to the Israeli situation.

"The Jews are always asking us to state clearly what we really want," observes Ali Haider. "This is the first time that we Israeli Palestinians, intellectuals, activists, others involved in the Arab community, have come out with an initiative—not a reaction, but an initiative. This is significant." What should be appreciated, continues Haider, is that this is a consensus document. There were some who would have formulated it in even more radical terms, and others who are more pragmatic. The document represents an internal discussion within the Israeli Palestinian community. Any document put out by a minority that slaughters sacred cows will attract anger, he says. "In fact the Vision Document doesn't really say anything that hasn't been said before," suggests Haider. "The problem is there, right in the midst of Israeli civil society. That is the reason for the establishment of Sikkuy."

One of the fields where some points of light exist is that of culture in its widest sense. Israeli Jews, Arabs, and sometimes Palestinians from Gaza and the West Bank, cooperate in sporting endeavors, in music, and in theater. The Israeli soccer team of Bnei Sakhnin is an Arab team, but it has a Jewish coach and some Jewish players.

The Arab players often suffer racial slurs and insults from opposing fans when playing Jewish sides, but the team's success has done wonders for the morale of the citizens of Sakhnin. Bnei Sakhnin's captain, Abbas Suan, plays for the Israeli national team, and his last-minute equalizing goal against Ireland kept Israel in last year's World Cup. In a subsequent interview, Suan declared: "It is time to stop talking about Jews and Arabs; we are all one people; my goal is dedicated to everyone in Israel." In a newspaper article, a Sakhnin resident was quoted as saying that soccer would achieve more for Israel's Arabs than years of political struggle.

Daniel Barenboim, the world-famous pianist and conductor, directs the East-West Diwan Youth Orchestra with Israeli Jewish, Palestinian, Jordanian, and Syrian players. The orchestra has performed in Britain, Spain, Argentina, Brazil, and Germany. Last summer the IDF opened its roadblocks to allow the Israeli musicians to pass through to participate in a concert in the Palestinian city of Ramallah before an audience of more than a thousand. "Beethoven's Fifth isn't interested in what you are, or where you came from," said Barenboim.

The Efroni Choir with members from Jewish villages in the coastal plain north of Tel Aviv sings together with the Sawa Choir from the Arab town of Shefaram further north. Recently they performed together in Barcelona. There have also been contacts with choirs in Bethlehem and Nazareth. At a Christmas concert in the Arab village of Abu Ghosh near Jerusalem, the two choirs together with the Choir of London performed the Middle Eastern premier of *Lament for Jerusalem* by British composer John Tavener with texts from Jewish, Christian, and Muslim sources.

These are three of the best-known projects where representatives of the two peoples perform side by side. In the next chapter, we will discuss lesser-known examples of Jews and Arabs having fun together: White Flag, an Israeli-Palestinian musical group; the Arabic-Hebrew Theater of Jaffa; and the Tennis Coexistence Project. These three enterprises illustrate that Jews and Arabs, Israelis and Palestinians, can compete against each other in friendship, create music together, and act alongside each other.

10

Creativity and Recreation

When the violence broke out between Jews and Arabs in the fall of 2000, the Tennis Coexistence Project was just getting off the ground. The brainchild of retired businessman Freddie Krivine, it was designed to bring tennis to the Arab towns and villages in Israel and to enable Jewish and Arab kids to train together and play against each other.

Because of the mood in the country, Krivine was urged to abandon the program or at least to put it on hold until the situation calmed down. Rejecting the advice outright, he instructed the coaches whom he had recruited to hold themselves ready and visited the Arab communities involved in the project, persuading the officials of the local authorities and sports centers to go ahead. Today more than two thousand Jewish and Arab children play tennis against each other, train together, and forge firm friendships in a dozen Arab and Jewish localities all over northern Israel. Sadly, Krivine died four years later, but the project he initiated carries on with growing success.

Born in Harrogate in northern England, Freddie Krivine was the quintessential English gentleman, but there were several extra layers beneath the outer image. When he was in his teens, Krivine's parents took him out of his local school and sent him to agricultural college in Palestine, then under the administration of the British Mandate. It was a life-altering experience: he learned Hebrew, made friends with men who would become Israeli cabinet ministers and senior government officials, and formed a lasting attachment to the land and the Zionist enterprise.

Returning to England on the outbreak of World War II, Krivine enlisted in the Royal Horse Guards, a prestigious British regiment. After the war, he went into business in London, succeeding first in manufacturing and later in real estate. In the early postwar years, he found himself living next to a young Pakistani diplomat and his family. In the Britain of the 1950s, a man with a dark skin—even a diplomat—was not an appreciated neighbor. Krivine was one of the few who offered friendship, and the two families became close. Over the following years, Krivine and his wife Sheelagh visited their Pakistani friends at their new postings in several Arab countries, where at that time Jews were officially barred from entry. When he wound up his business and came to live in Israel, his ties of friendship with the Muslim diplomat remained strong.

Prior to his retirement, Krivine, a keen amateur tennis player, had collaborated with a group of American and South African philanthropists to establish a network of tennis centers in Israel, bringing the game to numerous deprived neighborhoods. Coming to live permanently in the country in 1984, he resolved to focus his attention on improving women's tennis and became the non-playing captain of the Federation Cup team. In 1992, he was elected president of the Israel Tennis Association and a few years later he attended Israel's National Junior championship at the Ramat Hasharon center. He was enormously gratified by the fact that there were some six hundred competitors, showing how popular the game had become in Israel, but it seemed to him that all the players were Jewish. He asked how many Arab children were competing and was informed that "just two" had registered.

Within months, Krivine established an Arab-Jewish committee that evolved into the Tennis Coexistence Project. Demonstrating formidable energy for a man of his age, he raised the funds to finance the program, which included the building of a tennis center in the Arab village of Jisr al-Zarka, south of Haifa. Visiting the project in its earliest days, I have a vivid memory of Krivine, dressed in blazer, cravat, and Panama straw hat, talking with narghile-smoking Arab elders at the Jisr al-Zarka coffee house in his British-accented Hebrew, gently persuading them that tennis would give the local children something constructive to do and keep them off the streets. At his funeral some years later, an Arab villager movingly eulogized Krivine, referring to him as "our father."

Today the Freddie Krivine Foundation is run by his daughter, Jane, who proudly takes me around several of the centers to show me the children of both communities—and both sexes—thumping the yellow balls across the net with a skill and power that I can only envy. Starting at the place where the coexistence project was launched, Jisr al-Zarka, we stand in the hot sun as Radwan, the patient coach, himself a local villager, encourages the kids, some of whom seem smaller than their rackets. So far, the center has only one court, which is host to four hundred youngsters in the morning program of general physical fitness and ninety older kids playing tennis in the afternoon. Jane hopes to build a second court, which will enable them to expand the scope of the program. "Jisr is a traditional village," she points out. "We don't know how many of the girls will be able to continue playing as they get older. At Fureidis down the road, several of the teenage girls are already competing in national tournaments."

In Pardess Hanna, local Jewish kids play with children from Baka al-Gharbiya and the Caesarea youngsters play with the Fureidis children. The sweat-suited children play with enormous zest and manifest enjoyment. It really is impossible to tell them apart.

"My generation never had a chance to have this sort of fun," exclaims Nadia, a petite Arab lady from Fureidis, "but I love watching my kids play."

"I have no words to describe what Freddy did for our children," chimes in Na'im, her husband. "What a wonderful man. He is with us even today. Playing tennis is absolutely marvelous for Ibrahim and Matar. I am so proud of them."

Na'im, a welder and building worker, has just returned to work after a long lay off because of an operation. In his opinion, tennis does not have to harm the traditional Arab way of life. The kids can play tennis and be good Muslims. Tennis is a positive factor in the life of the village children, he stresses.

"We always try to have two coaches, one Arab and one Jewish," Jane explains. "We don't want to have Jews telling the Arabs what to do; everything is on the basis of equality. Also it is important for the Arab youngsters to have role models from their own community."

In Binyamina, the children sit in a circle on the court and receive prizes from the coaches for a recent tournament. The local kids are joined by Arab children from Kafr Kara. So far, there are only two tennis centers operating in Arab villages, but the Nazareth courts are being refurbished, and others are in the planning stage. Meanwhile the very fact that the project brings Arab children to play in the Jewish villages near to them is important. "Many of the Arab kids had never met Jewish kids and vice versa," notes Jane. "It's surprising, but if not for the tennis, they would never get together."

Some of the statistics are impressive: this year the combined Caesarea-Jisr al-Zarka club fielded two teams, beating the team from Zichron Yaakov, a nearby Jewish town, in the final of the national youth tournament; four teenagers from Jisr and Fureidis earned assistant coaching certificates and three others attended an international tennis camp in Slovenia. A further eight hundred Arab children are set to play in joint programs with Jewish children in Galilee, Haifa, and Jerusalem.

Danny Meder was working as a senior coach at the Israel Tennis Center when he was recruited by Krivine in 1999 to launch the new project. A resident of Kerem Maharal, a Jewish village not far from Jisr, he was familiar with Arabs and knew some Arabic. Meder has had to give up private coaching. He is simply too busy. He now divides his time between coaching at Haifa University and the Freddie Krivine Foundation.

"Freddie's project is more than just tennis," he declares. "It is bringing pleasure to hundreds of children who were not fully part of our society. Several kids from Jisr and Fureidis went to Tel Aviv this year to participate in the tennis coaching program. It was the first time they had traveled by train. When we started with them, they were only eight years old. Today some of them are coaches. You should see them: they are enthusiastic, they communicate well, and they work hard. It's a real pleasure to be with them."

Meder says that whereas the Caesarea program is of a high level and has produced some excellent players, the standard is lower in Jisr al-Zarka, but at least the children are hitting tennis balls on court and not throwing stones in the streets. He believes that he can improve the quality of the tennis there in time.

He is excited about the foundation's new program in the Druze-Christian village of Maghar, where the foundation has converted a basketball pitch into a tennis court. Coexistence, he explains is not just about Jews and Arabs. In Maghar, there is a dispute between the Druze villagers and the Christian neighbors. There are already thirty Druze kids playing regularly and he hopes to have a similar number of Christians playing with them in the coming year. "The children will teach their parents how to be friends," he suggests. "So far the program is going really well."

Other Druze children from Ussafiya travel to the prestigious Reali High School in Haifa to play tennis with the Jewish kids. "It's not just a question of playing tennis," Meder points out. "Ussafiya and Haifa are neighbors, who never mixed. Now their children are getting to know each other."

He cautions against being too ambitious. There is one superb Arab youngster, Nadine Fahoum, who is one of the best young players in the country, but she is from a modern family in Haifa. Her mother is an attorney who plays the game herself, and she realizes that her daughter must train five hours a day if she is to continue playing competitive tennis. "As a child I dreamed about playing tennis," recalls Wafa Fahoum, Nadine's mother. "We lived near a court and I admired the players so much. I fantasized about playing, but we were ten brothers and sisters, and my parents insisted on studies and more studies. I only started playing when my own children started."

Nadine, her daughter, has been playing since she was nine years old. Her whole life is school and tennis, starting with practice in the early morning and further play or practice after school. She finds it difficult, but she has always enjoyed it. She has good grades at school and hopes to complete her matriculation before embarking on a full-time professional career. Later, after her tennis career, she plans to return to studies, probably law like her mother or business administration. "Freddy believed in me," she recalls. "He wanted me to succeed and gave me the motivation. There is plenty of talent in our community, as in all communities. I am proud to be an Arab representing Israel."

Her next event is the Orange Bowl Championship in Florida for girls under eighteen. She hopes to reach the later rounds, "at least the quarterfinals." Nadine, just seventeen, is currently number two in her age group in Israel; Fahoum, her fifteen-year-old brother, is also a promising player.

Their mother Wafa acknowledges that tennis is a "problematic" career choice. It is no good being mediocre, or even quite good, she notes. The players have to be excellent and they have to work really hard, but she is prepared to give both her children the chance. "It's now or never," she stresses, going over to English for emphasis. "They can study later on, but they can only play at top level when they are young."

She is full of praise for Haifa's Reali School, where Nadine is studying for her matriculation. The principal is on the board of the Freddie Krivine Foundation and recognizes the importance of sport. Reali is a good school, not just a factory for good grades, she notes, although in fact Nadine's grades are excellent.

Wafa is the attorney of the Freddie Krivine Foundation, a job she carries out pro bono. Her husband is a successful businessman. They are part of Haifa's modern Arab community. Wafa has also devoted considerable time to fundraising for the foundation in Israel and abroad. The tennis coexistence project transcends sports, she emphasizes. More and more Arab children are playing, and Nadine and Fahoum are role models for a new generation. Hundreds of Arab children who would not have encountered Jews until work or university are meeting, playing, and making friends on a regular basis.

"These village kids are getting all sorts of new ideas," points out Wafa. "Many of them are exposed to concepts such as careers in sport, or even higher education. The fact that they mix with Jewish kids broadens their horizons. Of course it will take time. We have to be patient and show, for example, that sport is not anti-Muslim."

Most of the Arab kids won't reach the standard of Nadine Fahoum and her brother, notes coach Danny Meder, but they can still play the game and enjoy it. It has to be admitted that the traditional nature of Arab and Druze society is a real problem. Two promising girls from Jisr have been removed from the program by their father on reaching the age of twelve, he says sadly. Now that they have started to grow up their family cannot accept them continuing to play tennis with boys. The Druze are also keen to preserve their traditional ways, he notes, and he doesn't know how that is going to work out as the children grow up.

Traveling southeast from Caesarea brings one to Kfar Yona. Founded as a moshav cooperative farming village in the 1930s, it has become urbanized and has grown considerably but still retains a rural ambience. In a shady corner of the village, Mark Smulian lives in a modest house on a plot of land that that he bought thirty years ago. His friend Shadi Alhaj, from the Gaza Strip town of Khan Yunis, lived there illegally for almost a year, trapped in Israel by the outbreak of the second Intifada in October 2000.

Shadi, Mark, and their friends are the founders of White Flag, an Israeli-Palestinian musical group, playing what they call "Palestinian-Israeli street fusion." They were performing at a music festival at Megiddo in the Jezreel valley in the fall of 2000, the day after Ariel Sharon sparked the outbreak of violence with his visit to the Temple Mount in Jerusalem.

"We didn't know whether to go on or not," recalls Shadi. "We had seen the violence on television and we weren't sure if we ought to be playing in front of an Israeli audience. We felt it was the wrong time. The Israeli members of the group said it was up to us Palestinians to decide. In the end we came to the conclusion that playing was a sort of message, and it was a message we wanted to transmit."

"It was one of our best concerts," says Mark. "At first there were only a few people in front of the so-called 'ethnic stage.' By the end of our performance, there were hundreds dancing and clapping and stamping their feet."

After nine months of living illegally in Mark's home, Shadi fled from the Israeli police and crossed over into the territory of the Palestinian Authority only to be arrested by Palestinian security forces in Ramallah. He was harshly interrogated but was released after being told: "Apparently you are not a collaborator with the Israelis—simply an idiot." In due course, Shadi managed to get to Switzerland, where he now lives with the Swiss girl he plans to marry. He and Mark maintain regular phone and e-mail contact and continue to create the music that both of them love.

Mark Smulian was educated in England and Israel and feels he was "lucky to have received a cosmopolitan education." He has been playing music for many years, and at some stage started "hearing" melodies. Since then he has also been a composer. A teenager at the time of the 1973 Yom Kippur War, he was recruited to entertain the troops: "I had a guitar and knew how to perform 'Imagine,' so they put me with some others and we traveled all over."

Subsequently mobilized into the IDF, Mark served in the paratroop brigade before going to the United States to study music at the Mannes College of Music in New York, where he earned a degree in classical music. "I love classical music," he asserts, "but I've never played it professionally. My scene is ethnic jazz and rock."

Mark's wife, Gani, born in the veteran moshav cooperative Nahalal, also studied at Mannes, but they both deliberately avoided meeting "the only other Israeli in the school." They got together some years later at a gig in Israel. Gani, one of White Flag's two vocalists, made her living singing jingles and doing voice-overs for advertisements for several years. They have two daughters, Talia, twelve, who is learning piano, and Micah, nine, who studies the guitar. Mark himself plays electric guitar, bass guitar, and double bass.

For many years, he had a small band that performed in schools around the country, and he also taught music at schools and community centers. In 1998, he received a phone call from Ruti Atzmon asking him to help organize a jam session with a bunch of young Palestinians to raise money for Windows (the project described in chapter two of this book).

"I was a keen member of Windows," states Shadi Alhaj, "and for two years I was co-editor of the magazine." Shadi was born and raised in Khan Yunis, the Gaza Strip's second-largest town. Both his parents were teachers, with his father becoming a headmaster. After matriculation, he studied pharmacy at Gaza University but did not complete the course. He started making music on a synthesizer at home. After a few years, he joined the local Palestinian folklore and dance troupe. As a member of Windows, he willingly responded to the proposal for a jam session and a dozen Israelis and Palestinians assembled at the Tel Aviv cultural center of Beit Lessin. "We spent a couple of hours together before the performance, working out what to do," recalls Shadi. "Then we just played and it worked out pretty well."

"It was a wonderful evening," enthuses Mark. "It was very spontaneous. People came up on stage and joined in and then returned to the audience. I think there were about twenty-five people from Gaza. Afterwards we had coffee together and someone said that we should do it again."

After the second concert, they decided to establish something more permanent, but they were not sure how to do it. Some of the participants were reluctant to continue without a financial guarantee, but eventually a core group of three Israelis and three Palestinians resolved that they would go ahead and form a band no matter what. Zaher Abdel-Jawad from Dir al-Ballah, who plays the oud, a traditional Arab string instrument, suggested the name White Flag to symbolize peace and the fact that they were supranational.

White Flag didn't manage to perform in Palestinian locations, but during the next two years it played some twenty concerts all over Israel in towns, villages, and kibbutzim. The earnings were very sparse, but the members felt they were on to something promising. "I've been in successful bands," declares Mark, "and this was it: we were on a roll. At some point we just clicked. We became friends and the joy of the music came out. We just played what we wanted, a mixture of oriental and western music. Gani and Yassin sang in Hebrew, Arabic, and English. The fact that we were Palestinians and Israelis playing together created an atmosphere of euphoria at our concerts. The people in the audience were up and dancing."

"Although it started as a project of Windows," explains Shadi, "I felt at some point that Windows and White Flag were on separate tracks. I don't want to say anything against Windows. It is a great project, but to be honest it is an Israeli program. We Palestinians joined in, but the initiative came from the other side. At White Flag we were just a bunch of friends playing together without it mattering who we were or where we came from."

"One problem was organization," admits Mark. "I refused to be the director. We didn't want a director, but somehow it all worked."

The Meggido concert proved to be White Flag's last hurrah. The border between Israel and the Palestinian territories closed down and the members of the band were simply unable to get together. While Shadi lived with Mark and Gani, they continued creating music.

"We both took risks," observes Mark. "He is a Palestinian from the Gaza strip and I'm a former IDF paratrooper, but our friendship is basic. We had nine months to discuss it all. Our conclusion: nobody is right and nobody is wrong. You cannot blow yourself up in a supermarket and you can't just send in planes to bomb. Fuck the violent people on both sides. I am against barbarism."

"I must be honest: I'm not a 'nice Palestinian,'" confesses Shadi. "I am an extremist and I hate Israel for what it is doing to us Palestinians, but I don't hate Israelis. In the band we make music together and I love all of them. I don't say that White Flag is an Israeli-Palestinian coexistence project. It is a beautiful coincidence. We have no nationality. We are a group of friends. It is a very personal thing."

After Shadi moved to Switzerland, Mark visited him several times and they conceived the idea of a reunion. The core group was expanded to a band of nine: five Israelis and four Palestinians. They spent three months in Switzerland, making a television program and giving several concerts. The municipality of Lucerne financed the project and the group performed in the city's splendid concert hall.

Watching a DVD of the concert, one cannot fail to be amazed at the enthusiasm of the stolid Swiss at the sight of Israelis and Palestinians playing together. They clap, cheer, and stamp their feet with huge enthusiasm. The Israelis might be a majority by five to four, but the Palestinian-Israeli street fusion, while a mixture of styles, is definitely dominated by oriental sounds. Introducing the band, Mark tells the audience, "Please leave your nationalities at the door!" Yassin and Gani sing in Arabic, Hebrew, and English. The others play a variety of instruments. Talia and Micah, Mark and Gani's daughters, come on stage to sing a number.

"Thanks, Yassin, for singing on the same stage as me," proclaims Gani.

"I'm not your friend," declares Yassin, shaking his head emphatically—dramatic pause, during which he puts his arm around her shoulders—"I'm your brother!"

So far, the band has had only limited professional and financial success, but Mark is optimistic about a recording contract. He is in touch with a number of German companies.

"White Flag is going to continue," sums up Mark. "The show must go on. You can't separate people artificially. It's bullshit. The wall must be pulled down!"

"When I look at the situation from Basel, it seems terrible," states Shadi. "Six years ago I felt there could be peace, but today it looks unfixable. How can there be peace after all that has happened? And yet I want to come back to live in Palestine. I don't feel at home in Switzerland. I hope I can persuade my wife to come with me. Maybe, somehow, the situation will improve."

Under the stone arches of the cavernous five-hundred-year-old building in Jaffa, which used to be the residence of the governor in Ottoman times, we sit on swivel chairs watching the performances all around us. The actors "attack" us from all directions. We face first this way, then that, trying to pay attention, to look, to listen, to understand, and to absorb the differing and diffuse messages. The effect is confusing and at the same time stunning and powerful, a deliberate assault on our sensibilities.

The experimental play *Longing* was written by the six actors themselves: three of them Jews, three Arabs. They seek to narrate their own stories. The Arabs tell of dispossession from their lands, describing their frustrations and their longings. The Jews look back to their countries of origin, conveying their mixed feelings, their hopes and dreams. Only after each of them wrote about his or her own experiences did they come together to synthesize their presentation. The result is a kaleidoscope or a collage: a complex, contradictory depiction of the variegated, multicultural reality that is Israel.

The fun starts while the audience is still in the lobby. Christian Arab actor Norman Issa announces that he will sing in Arabic—"Don't be alarmed, it *is* an official language you know!"—in Russian, and finally in Hebrew ("So that you can feel at home"). The music is very oriental, very loud. It is followed by actress Rauda Suleiman reciting "My Home Is a Suitcase" by the famous Palestinian poet Mahmoud Darwish.

The play is performed mostly in Hebrew, with some Arabic, Russian, and German. An elderly Jewish lady from Cairo greets her sons who are visiting her from the United States and remembers her life in Egypt before she immigrated to Israel: her fine house, her mother's two servants, the theater they used to enjoy, the beautiful clothes they wore. She contrasts this with her first days in Israel in the *ma'abara* [transit camp] in the 1950s.

Magdi, an Arab, is working in the fields of Ein Hod, a Jewish artists' village, which used to be his village of Ein Hud. He is rebuked by his uncle for continuing to cultivate the land that belonged to his family. Norman Issa holds a different dialogue with his uncle, who died before the Jews conquered his northern Galilee village of Biram. The uncle assumes that the

Jews were beaten in 1948 and urges his Arab friends to behave magnanimously toward the surviving Jews. When it is Norman's turn to speak, he is hilarious about the Jewish food that he is offered; he forces himself to eat it out of politeness.

Oleg, his wife, and his son are from Uzbekistan. They recall their difficulties with the Israeli authorities as they try to resume their theatrical careers in their new land. Gaby is an Israeli who has returned to Berlin (of all places), a Jew full of complexes in the former capital of the Nazi Reich. "Telenovella" (Hebrew for television soap opera) is nostalgic for what might be. She is against violence from the biblical age to the present and dreams about a better future.

The bad guys are the state, the authorities, the officials; the good guys are the little people—Jews, Arabs, Russian immigrants—struggling to survive and make sense out of their lives. The stories jump from one to the other with bewildering speed. At the end of the performance, the actors pass around food and wine to the audience.

In the subsequent discussion, director Yigal Ezrati is asked whether this is not, in fact, an anti-Israeli play. No, he explains patiently, they were simply trying to present the reality. The concept of longing—or of "exile at home"—merely explores the nostalgia of different people.

"We have everyone here in our theater: Jews and Arabs, Muslims, Christians, Russians, Germans, Italians, immigrants and natives, gays and straight people. We were afraid that this play would turn into a competition about guilt or suffering, but it didn't: all the narratives, all the nostalgia, can co-exist in this situation, without rancor."

"I live in Jaffa with Jews and Arabs," adds actress Gaby Aldor. "At weekends Jaffa fills up with Israeli Jews who come to buy and eat in the restaurants. I always think how good it would be if we all actually *lived* together on a day-by-day basis! The reality would destroy the demonizing of one another. We have been amazed at the different groups that come here to our theater. There is a Jewish-Arab embroidery circle, a group of Russians learning Arabic—no one ever hears about such phenomena, which completely obliterate all the stereotypes."

They decided to call themselves the Arabic-Hebrew Theater, explains Ezrati, because they did not want to get into the complications of Arab, Jew, Muslim, and Christian identities. In the theater, there is language; Hebrew and Arabic are languages. The theater produces plays in Hebrew, Arabic, and both of them together. Situated in Jaffa, where Jews and Arabs live side by side, and supported by the Tel Aviv Municipality and the Israeli Ministry of Culture, it aims to promote understanding and interaction between Israeli Jews and Arabs.

In the words of Shai Bar-Yacov, a journalist at *Yediot Aharonot*, the mass-circulation Hebrew newspaper, "It presents materials that enable a sensitive response, reflective and non-confrontational. The endearing spirit of innocence is the key to the special charm of the small theater in Jaffa, a place where the cruel reality is moved aside for a moment to make place for a sort of delicate dream of a reconciled and bubbling co-existence."

In fact, "cruel reality" is not moved aside either in the play we have just seen or in *Winter in Kalandia*, another offering of the theater, a hard-hitting depiction of the harsh reality of a military check post on the border between Israel and the Palestinian territories. Nor is it evaded in *Song of Death*, an uncompromising play by Egyptian writer Tewfik al-Hakim about revenge killings. At the same time, the theater differs from the harsh reality of today's Israel in conveying a vision of the sort of country it could be if people learned to live and work together as the actors, directors, producers, and managers of the theater already do.

Yigal Ezrati, the Hebrew artistic director, has been politically aware all his life. His mother's family, helped by an Arab friend, fled from their village of Kfar Uriya during the Arab riots of 1929. "It was an Arab who saved us, defending us from his fellow Arabs," notes Ezrati. "That was the narrative on which I was raised."

During his army service, he became active in Yesh Gvul, a protest movement of soldiers who refused to serve in Lebanon or the occupied territories. Going on to Tel Aviv University, where he studied directing, he felt that theater and politics were inevitably entwined. Later, while teaching at the university, it was natural for him to gravitate toward projects where Arabs and Jews worked together. In 1998, he linked up with Adib Jahshan, a Christian Arab actor, and the result was *Alley of White Chairs*, a theatrical presentation in a Jaffa warehouse, which conveyed a picture of an apartment block with a mixture of inhabitants. The Tel Aviv Municipality allowed them to rent the former governor's residence and also granted them a small budget. The building was terribly run down and they had to work hard rebuilding it, painting it, and cleaning it up to make it usable.

The Hebrew Theater is separate from the Arabic, which means that each outfit has its own director, its own management committee, and its own team of actors. This preempts the problem of one side dominating the other. The Arabic Theater puts on plays in Arabic, the Hebrew Theater presents Hebrew plays, and they collaborate to put on shows in both languages. For example, there is an Arabic version of *Longing* where the Arab actors act in their own language and translate the Hebrew parts for an Arabic-speaking audience. The company has also revived Aramaic, the language spoken in the time of Jesus, for a children's play that has also been presented abroad. *Longing* has been seen in several countries with simultaneous translation.

Adib Jahshan, Ezrati's Arab counterpart, has a long history of acting, directing, and producing. Relaxing over a cup of bittersweet cardamom-flavored coffee in his Jaffa apartment, the Arabic artistic director proclaims: "Even as a kid, I was attracted to the arts: I was the school artist and also the school clown. I always loved performing." He was fascinated by the story of Habima, Israel's national theater, which began as a Hebrew theater in Russia before its members immigrated to Palestine. He became obsessed by the idea that the Jews could put on plays in their national language in Russia, whereas the local Palestinian culture had disappeared. He was determined to revive the Arabic theater that had existed in Jaffa and other places.

Born in Haifa to Greek Orthodox Christian parents, Jahshan fled with his family to Acre during the 1948 war, returning to Haifa after it was over. The youngest of four brothers and six sisters, he wanted to study theater in England after finishing school, but his father, a builder, vetoed the scheme. He got a job at a Jewish-Arab community center in Haifa putting on plays and teaching art, and later managed to gain admittance to the Beit Zvi acting school in Tel Aviv. There were only two Arabs in his year, both of them from Haifa, he recalls, and there was a sense of alienation between them and their Jewish fellow students, which evaporated quickly as they got to know each other and became friends. "That taught me my first valuable lesson," he notes. "I learned that, when the walls come down, friendship ensues."

He spent the next two decades struggling to bring Arabic theater to the Arab towns and villages in Israel. Among the early performances were translations of Eugene O'Neill's *In the Zone* and Samuel Beckett's *Krapp's Last Tape*. He was the first Arab to act in Hebrew on an Israeli stage at the Haifa Theater and also worked with Reuven Morgan, an Israeli of Welsh origin who directed plays in Jerusalem, but he had a sense of mission about reviving Arabic theater.

His Rising Arab Theater company put on performances in Arab villages where there was no electricity using gasoline pressure lamps. Later they managed to obtain a generator, which enabled rudimentary stage lighting. Jahshan also worked with children, establishing an Arab Youth Theater. After studying in London, he continued putting on performances in high schools and clubs in many Arab towns and villages.

It was his love of theater that brought him into contact with children with special needs. He started teaching acting to the children and putting on plays, calling his work "psychodrama." "I was helping these kids by getting them to act out their frustrations long before art and dance therapy became popular in Israel," he says with pride. After he married, Jahshan moved to Jaffa, but still commuted to Sakhnin and other Arab villages in the north to produce plays. At the same time, he began to earn his living by working with handicapped children, something he still does today.

One of his first projects after meeting up with Yigal Ezrati and establishing the Arabic-Hebrew Theater was Beckett's *Waiting for Godot*, which he staged as a sharp political satire about his own Arab community. "What are we waiting for?" he asks in his version of the classic play, "Nasser, Saddam Hussein—or maybe the first Arab prime minister of Israel?"

Ezrati and Jahshan are busy with plans for the future. Next summer they are planning to present *A Thousand and One Nights*, a large-scale pageant in the open air, with funding from the European Community. A joint production with the Israel National Opera is also in the works.

For all their dynamism and manifest optimism, both directors complain about a lack of funds. Ezrati adds: "We still don't reach enough of the Israeli public, the sort of people who watch commercial television—and they are the majority. There are still many Israelis who simply don't want to know about us and the subjects that we deal with."

As the foregoing demonstrates, partnership between Jews and Arabs is wide ranging. In my voyage through the landscape of Jewish-Arab cooperation, I found some unexpected phenomena, but none of them is more surprising than the project depicted in the following chapter.

11

Donkey Garden of Eden

The donkey is the archetypal nudnik. When you approach the compound, a dozen or so donkeys amble over, butting you with their big heads, sticking their noses out to be stroked, shoving you with their shoulders, and—if you let them—treading on your feet with their hooves. "Donkeys are phenomenally sociable," asserts Lucy Fensom, scratching a pair of large ears. "They are naturally playful and much more intelligent than horses."

Domesticated for at least four millennia, the donkey was traditionally preferred as a working animal to the ox, which had to take a rest every now and then to chew the cud. Donkeys have served humankind faithfully and effectively, but not only have we humans been ungrateful, often treating them appallingly, we have added insult to injury by labeling the faithful beasts as stupid, dumb, and obstinate.

The blond, laughing, English-born Fensom is determined to rectify this state of affairs and has mobilized a team of Jews and Arabs to assist her. Safe Haven for Donkeys in the Holy Land (SHADH), located on four acres at the cooperative farming village of Gan Yoshiya near Netanya, has been up and running for five years. An improbable, eccentric dream, a project where Israelis and Palestinians work together with a common purpose, it is run in a purposeful, professional, and eminently practical manner.

Fundamentally, it is a rescue operation, collecting abused and neglected donkeys and bringing them to Gan Yoshiya to enable them to live out their days in dignity and contentment. There are just over a hundred donkeys of various shapes and sizes in the sanctuary, half a dozen mules, and three horses, munching contentedly in the sun, rolling in the red earth, drinking, strolling around, or simply standing, flicking their ears.

SHADH also runs an outreach program, treating sick and injured donkeys, mules, and horses at half a dozen locations in Israel and Palestine. Far removed from the tranquil ranch in Gan Yoshiya, at a garbage dump on the edge of the Palestinian town of Kalkiliya just beyond the separation fence, this operation gets underway. Two pickup trucks, a tall van, one trailer with an electric generator, and another with a water tank have drawn up among the rusting chassis, plastic bags, and other refuse. Donkeys, horses, and mules, some pulling carts, many with visible wounds and sores, stream with their human owners toward the assembled vehicles. Lucy, Adi, Muhammad, Ahmad, Pierre, and Amer, all wearing black T-shirts labeled "staff" in English and Arabic, struggle to contain the mob.

They string up a rope, creating a temporary corral, and open up the tall van, revealing dozens of drawers and shelves bursting with equipment of all types: medicines, sprays, syringes, needles, scalpels, scissors, and harnesses. The van, labeled "Safe Haven for Donkeys in the Holy Land in partnership with Brooke," is a mobile clinic that travels regularly to six locations in Israel and the Palestinian territories.

Adi and Lucy hand out bright red, green, and mauve harnesses, replacing the frayed ropes and wires around the animals' necks and showing the owners how to tie them on. They charge a nominal sum. Muhammad, from the Israeli Arab town of Taiba, fills out file cards for each animal treated. Pierre the vet is in perpetual motion, squirting anti-worm medicine into mouths, examining teeth, dressing wounds. A large horse has a more serious wound and Pierre cuts off pieces of infected flesh before stapling the bleeding gash and injecting antibiotic fluid. He is assisted by Amer, who holds the animal's head firmly while explaining the procedure in Arabic to the horse's owner.

White-haired Ahmad from the village of Bakr al-Gharbiya takes a bunch of leaflets on correct animal care and, sitting on a cart nearby, gives an impromptu lecture to a dozen Kalkiliya teenagers. They pay attention to his words and pocket the literature. Muhammad stops writing his cards and tries to create a semblance of order, haranguing the unruly owners and forcing the horses, donkeys, and mules into a proper queue. "We'll pack up and leave, if you go on pushing and creating chaos," he warns them. "Lucy has come from abroad specially to help you and your animals: is this how you thank her?"

Lucy and Adi distribute hay and fill a couple of troughs from their black plastic water tank. Lucy explains to a young boy that the harness should be looser. Amer interprets for her. She dabs iodine on some of the sores and smears ointment on others.

Pierre tells the owner of the white horse that all his efforts will be in vain if he doesn't let the animal rest. "Tell him that I understand he is a working animal," he says to Amer, "but if he wants to get good work out of him, he has to rest him for at least two weeks." He is called to a donkey with a raw wound on his back, which he covers with large gauze, securing it with wide strips of cellophane tape.

"It was much better last week," remarks Lucy apologetically as we drive back in the pickup. "I don't know why they were so unruly this time."

"That's what misfortune does to you," suggests Pierre. "They are under terrible pressure."

Amer Issa, the interpreter and assistant, an athletic youngster from the Israeli Arab town of Kafr Kassem, is due to go on to his other work as riding instructor in a Jewish village. All his customers are Jewish, he tells me. They come from Tel Aviv and the surrounding towns and villages. He has earned an official certificate as an instructor from the Wingate Sports Center.

Burly, bass-voiced Muhammad Mussawa, a retired teacher from the nearby town of Taiba, has pursued a variety of activities in his town, establishing the first football club, holding road safety classes, and leading the local children in painting pedestrian crossings. Growing up in a farming family, he always loved animals. The family donkey lived under the house, and his father gave him a goat when he was very young. Before he finished school, he had a dozen goats. He currently raises lambs, rabbits, and doves.

"People who like donkeys and other animals, also love human beings," he insists. "It is a matter of education. I totally support what Lucy and Adi are doing." When the local municipality demolished a treatment center they built in Taiba, he rebuilt it on his own land. He gives them water and electricity free. Since then nobody has dared to touch it. Recently he gave an interview to the Taiba paper about the treatment center and more than a hundred local people called to congratulate him.

Muhammad's wife is a probation officer and the couple has a son and five daughters, the eldest of whom has completed a degree at Tel Aviv University. The son is a teacher at the local school. Muhammad himself is due to become a member of the Taiba Town Council in about a month's time under a rotation agreement. "As a councilor, I'll continue pushing the donkey project," he declares. "As long as I live, I will support this project."

Lucy Fensom first came to Israel in 1989 as a kibbutz volunteer. After working on two kibbutzim, she ended up in Jerusalem volunteering for the local Association for the Prevention of Cruelty to Animals. She stayed for five years. "I'm not Jewish," she remarks, "but my mother is more 'Jewish' than most Jews. She is crazy about Israel and it was she who urged me to come here."

While she was working at the animal refuge in Atarot in north Jerusalem, Lucy adopted Donk, a large male donkey left tied up outside by local Bedouin. "I used to sit there reading a book," she recalls, "and Donk would rest his head on my shoulder. I became very attached to him. Of course the Bedouin guy came back to claim him and, as he led him away, Donk kept stopping and looking back at me. It broke my heart."

Lucy enlisted the aid of an Arab wholesale butcher, and they went and bought Donk from his Bedouin owner, bringing him back in a meat van. When Lucy returned to England for her sister's wedding, Donk was fed and watered, but not exercised. When donkeys stand still, their hooves grow and turn up at the ends, virtually crippling the animals. After a few months, Donk was in a bad way and Lucy tried unsuccessfully to manage the situation from England. Eventually she wrote about Donk's plight to the London-based World Society for the Protection of Animals (WSPA).

Officials there were touched by Donk's story and resolved to turn it into a publicity campaign. Donk was flown to England by jumbo jet, arriving at Heathrow on his way to a donkey sanctuary in Cambridge. The publicity was huge. "There was this crate with two ears sticking out of the top," recalls Lucy, "and a lot of media outlets were there."

Lucy resolved to extend her activities beyond solving the problem of one donkey and set up a charitable trust for dealing with the donkeys of Israel and the Palestinian territories. A feature article on the subject in the *Mail on Sunday* drew a remarkable response. Sorting through the contents of several large mailbags, Lucy and her mother discovered letters containing checks for £1,000 alongside others with one-pound coins taped to pieces of cardboard and everything in between. All in all, the article attracted donations totaling about £100,000.

Lucy returned to Israel, rented a room at Kibbutz Gezer near Jerusalem, and went to work. The kibbutz had a dairy that had been evacuated because of winter flooding and Lucy used it as her first sanctuary in Israel. Unfortunately, the kibbutz was divided over the establishment of the Donkey Haven, with some members resolutely opposed to the idea. The matter was finally resolved by Stevenson, a donkey brought in by Lucy who kept the entire kibbutz awake at night with his loud braying. The kibbutz manager informed Lucy that Stevenson would have to go.

Meanwhile Lucy had met her future husband Adi, on whom she called for protection when a bunch of moshav children threatened her for "stealing" their donkeys. Adi was born in Israel to parents who emigrated from Libya. He was raised in the Tel Aviv suburb of Bat Yam and had no experience with animals or country life before meeting Lucy.

"I was being threatened by these kids and I asked the kibbutz security officer what to do," relates Lucy. "He told me to return the donkeys to the kids, but there was no way I was going to agree to that. So he gave me Adi's phone number. It was eleven at night, but I called him, and we have been together ever since."

"I married a project," observes Adi with a rueful smile. "After leaving the army I worked in a number of security jobs, but now my future career is set."

The couple chose a farm in Gan Yoshiya located between two avocado orchards, which form a dark green protective wall for the donkey haven. They have been there for five years. Lucy flies back to England several times a year for board meetings and to visit her ailing mother.

The fame of the haven gets around mainly by word of mouth. Police, municipal officials, and individual citizens are liable to call Lucy at all hours of the day and night to report an animal in distress. A woman in the port city of Ashdod recently phoned to tell Lucy about a gang of children who were tormenting a couple of donkeys. "I went to Ashdod and there were these tough looking kids with metal bars," relates Lucy. "I did my 'mad Englishwoman act,' screaming and waving my arms, and they backed off."

Another donkey, with its eyes cut out, was reported by international observers in the Palestinian town of Hebron. "Mabel" had to be put down after a few months, but she lived out her life in peace and contentment.

Walking around the ranch, I am introduced to a variety of creatures: a mule with a horrendous wound on his back, a donkey badly mauled by a fierce dog, several beasts whose legs have had to be amputated (they manage quite well with three legs). Every animal has a name. Adi and Lucy recognize each one, but, just in case, they have all been microchipped.

The outreach program, explains Lucy, is in partnership with Brooke, a worldwide organization dedicated to caring for working animals. Founded in 1934 by Dorothy Brooke, another "eccentric Englishwoman," it provides much of the funding for the mobile clinic. Brooke discovered on a visit to Egypt that there were hundreds of starving horses, which had been left behind by the allied armies after World War I. She set up a fund to purchase the animals from their Egyptian owners. "The Brooke people don't really approve of our sanctuary," notes Lucy. "They would like us to put the donkeys back to work in the Palestinian territories, but we'll never do this. Still we agree about the outreach program and so we can cooperate on that."

Pierre Sharvit, an Israeli who arrived from France at the age of ten, is the vet of both the sanctuary and the outreach program. After his army service, Sharvit studied veterinary medicine in Belgium before returning to Israel. He conducts research at the Weizmann Institute and has a private practice, mainly for small animals. After being called by Adi and Lucy to an emergency, he became their regular employee, visiting the Donkey Haven every day and going out with them to the outreach locations.

"What we are doing is a drop in the ocean," he admits. "The Middle East is not short of problems, but you have to start somewhere. I feel we are getting through to the Palestinians. I don't relate to them paternalistically. I stress that a healthy animal is a good working animal, and therefore it should be properly treated. This is entirely pragmatic."

In 2006, Lucy was awarded the Genesis prize by the Humane Society of the United States. At the Los Angeles ceremony, she said: "My work in Palestine and Israel can be very difficult, because the people we are trying to help and the local authorities often do not think our work is very important. It is wonderful to know that somebody values our work and is willing to give us credit for what we do."

Many miles further south, about a dozen donkeys crop the weeds under the tall date palms of Kibbutz Ketura in the desert. These donkeys have no need of the ministrations of Lucy and her team. Well treated and as contented as the creatures at Gan Yoshiya, they are part of the agricultural environmental enterprise that is the subject of our next chapter.

12

Academy for the Environment

I came to Israel as a Zionist, and the greatest Zionist challenge today is learning to live in peace with our Palestinian citizens and our Palestinian and Jordanian neighbors. We have to learn how to compromise between our different visions, beliefs, and values, and how to preserve and share our joint environment. The Arava Institute is in the forefront of that challenge. The environment is the thing that holds us together.

This declaration by David Lerner, executive director of the Arava Institute for Environmental Studies, is delivered with quiet conviction. An immigrant from the United States and a doctoral student, he was the manager, secretary, and treasurer of his kibbutz and also a Zionist emissary to North America before taking up his present post in 1999.

We are sitting in the office of the institute, a scholarly campus where Israelis, Palestinians, Jordanians, and others from around the world study desert agriculture and environmental preservation. The office is situated in a long, low building constructed from ecologically sound and aesthetically pleasing mud. Through the window, we can see the spectacular backdrop of the towering mauve mountains of Edom, today the Kingdom of Jordan.

The location, at Kibbutz Ketura in the southern sector of Israel's Arava valley some twenty-five miles north of Eilat, is magical: the stark wilderness, the clear dry air, the almost tangible quiet, and the perpetually blue sky combine to create an ambience that is far removed from the bloody reality of Israel and Palestine. Yet this jewel in the desert has the greatest possible relevance to the problems of our two nations. "It is the most satisfying and exciting job I have ever had," emphasizes Lerner. "The institute is fulfilling all the things I think we should be doing."

He breaks off momentarily to make us coffee, first picking up a garbage bag and walking over to a nearby compost heap to deposit the used grounds. As we stroll back to his office, he explains why the Arava Institute has flourished during the violence of the past six years whereas so many other Israeli-Palestinian initiatives have foundered.

"Whether or not you agree or disagree about history, narratives, religion, or politics, you cannot disagree about the environment," he observes. "We drink the same water, breathe the same air, and share the same natural resources. If we don't work together to protect them, we are going to destroy these things. They don't disappear just because we start lobbing missiles at each other. At the end of the day the missiles stop and the environment is still here."

Like many cooperative projects, the institute was established during the Oslo years. It was the initiative of Allon Tal, a member of Kibbutz Ketura and a prominent environmental attorney. Dealing with the environment encouraged him to tackle cross-border issues and it soon became clear that the institute would create an international program dedicated to training Middle Easterners to be environmental leaders and activists. Today it offers a one-year course in environmental studies leading to a master's degree at Ben-Gurion University. It is developing an undergraduate stream and also promotes an ambitious research program.

The institute has six Jordanian students and one member of staff from Jordan, four Americans, two Europeans, and thirteen Israelis in its current semester. Sadly, there is only one Palestinian. Many more Palestinians have applied to study here, but the security authorities have refused to grant them visas. The institute has appealed to Israel's Supreme Court, challenging this policy. "It's a self-defeating policy," states Lehrer. "If we prevent Palestinians from studying here we are just creating hatreds and misunderstandings."

Ideally, he would like to see ten Israelis, ten Palestinians and Jordanians, and ten from the rest of the world taking each course. In the past, the institute has hosted students from Egypt, Tunisia, and Turkey, but since the second Intifada, it has become more difficult to attract Arab and Muslim candidates. Lehrer would like to have students from all the Arab countries, but his initial aim is to secure more visas for Palestinians.

The Jordanians seem to feel very much at home. Osama Suleiman can be regarded as a veteran. After completing the 2005 course, he returned in 2006 to serve as one of the two program assistants (PAs). Dressed in jeans and a bright green T-shirt, his earnest manner frequently interrupted with smiles, he explains that he acts as a link between the staff and the students. He and the Israeli PA assist the lecturers—sometimes even substituting for absent teachers—handle the students' problems, and organize day-to-day activities, including social events and field trips. "We even bring them toilet paper," he remarks with a laugh.

He describes his first semester at the institute as "a 180-degree shift." Born in Kuwait, he graduated in economics from the University of Jordan and worked at his family's restaurant in the Jordanian capital. He had never met Israelis before, but he soon found that there were more similarities than differences between Israelis and Jordanians.

"If somebody had told me two years ago that I would be studying with Israelis, I would have said they are crazy," he remarks. "Now my best friends are Israelis. They have visited my family in Amman, so my family members have also changed their preconceived views. Today I always try to see things from all angles, including from the Jewish point of view. We don't have to agree, but we should understand each other and respect the different opinions."

During his first year, his favorite course was Genesis and the Environment. An observant Muslim familiar with the Koran, he found the combination of Bible and ecological studies fascinating. He says that when he tells Israelis that he is a Muslim, they always think he is an extremist—particularly with the name Osama. This is a misconception, he insists. Islam is not an extremist religion. It is not about killing, but about the message from God.

Next year, he hopes to study for an MBA at Ben-Gurion University. As an economist, he feels that the way to promote the ecological message is through economic self-interest. It is not enough to tell someone that it is good to preserve the environment, he suggests, it is essential to explain why conservation makes good business sense. He also sees the environment as a way to peace. "The environment doesn't recognize political boundaries," he points out. "If anything happens to this region, it will sweep the area. It won't stop at the Jordanian border. If we want to preserve the environment we must work together and from this we can learn to make peace. For me peace is about people—not governments. This place puts my dream on track."

Amer Sweity's parents were born in Hebron on the West Bank, but he considers himself a Jordanian rather than a Palestinian. A graduate in land and water management from the Hashemite University in Zarka, he hopes to complete a master's degree in desert research at Ben-Gurion University following his year in the Arava. Because of his family ties with Hebron, he found it difficult to obtain a visa and he missed the start of the semester.

His Hebron relatives, who have recently had some of their land confiscated to build the separation fence, were doubtful about his studying in Israel, but he convinced them that not all Israelis are the same and they now approve of his studies. His special interest is climate, and he is working with a leading Israeli researcher on "Extreme Tropical Rainstorm Events in the Hyper Arid Middle East," a NATO Science for Peace project. He hopes to complete his own special project on this topic.

Water is basic for life, he points out. There are problems of water in Jordan, Israel, Syria, Lebanon, and Egypt. He has great hopes for the proposed Israeli-Jordanian canal project that would bring water from the Red Sea to the Dead Sea, with desalinated water being supplied to his country.

He admits that he found it very hard at the outset. He did not talk to his Jewish roommate for the first week, then they started hesitantly with jokes. "I suddenly saw that he is a human being, like me," he recalls. "Now we are good friends and we have a lot in common."

Amer learned Hebrew at the Hashemite University, choosing it because of its similarity to Arabic. After completing his master's degree in water studies, he hopes to pursue doctoral studies abroad, but he intends to return to work in cooperative water projects.

"The region needs people like us," he concludes.

Suleiman Halasah is the only Christian Jordanian on the course. The son of a geologist, he comes from Karak in the south of the country. His first degree in electrical engineering was from the University of Jordan, and his special interest is in alternative energy sources: solar power and wind energy. He thinks that the southern deserts of Israel and Jordan are suitable locations for such a project and aims to earn a master's degree before working in the field. Meeting Israelis was not a new experience for Suleiman, who had attended joint youth projects with them in Europe.

Samer Eid, the lone Palestinian on the course, is also a Christian. Brought up in Ramallah, north of Jerusalem, he had some contact with Israelis before coming to the institute, but not very much. His first two weeks were not easy: he discovered that his views on the Israeli-Palestinian conflict were diametrically opposed to those of his fellow Israeli students. Now he tends to keep away from politics, and he says that the reason coexistence succeeds at the institute is because of its location.

One of the projects that he has taken on himself is teaching Arabic to his fellow Israeli students. He has also offered to teach at the local regional high school. Samer graduated in chemistry from Birzeit University, near his hometown of Ramallah. After completing university, he worked for a pharmaceutical company and for his father's cosmetics business. Later he became a high school chemistry teacher. It was while he was surfing the Internet in search of an environmental studies course that a fellow teacher told him about the Arava Institute. The teacher, who had attended a course there, suggested to Samer that he apply.

Samer's special interest is in air pollution, and he has just received a sensitive piece of equipment to test the pollution levels in the Arava. If all goes well, he hopes to start testing for air pollution in East and West Jerusalem in the next semester. After completing his year at the institute, he plans to study for an MSc at Ben-Gurion, after which he intends to work in the field of air pollution.

Unlike his colleagues, Manar Alrifai has no plans for further academic studies after he completes his year at the institute. His family lives near Ir-bid in the northern part of Jordan, where they have extensive fruit orchards. He hopes to work there utilizing the knowledge gained at the institute. "I'm not an academic really," he says. "I love working outside. I'm a farmer like my father."

Manar studied international relations in Morocco, where he met Jewish students. Because of this, he thinks it was easier for him to make contact with the Israelis than for his fellow Jordanians. He says that he always wondered about Israel and could not understand how he and his friends did not visit the country that was so close by. When he heard about the institute, he jumped at the chance to spend a year "not as a tourist, but really living with Israelis."

Manar says that his favorite course is Sustainable Desert Agriculture with Dr. Elaine Solowey, a member of Kibbutz Ketura and a world famous expert in the subject. He likes the course, he stresses, and he admires the lecturer. Meeting her, it is easy to understand why. Dressed in a parka, with cropped gray hair framing a sunburned face, Elaine Solowey projects self-confidence. She conveys the feeling that she knows what she is talking about and does not suffer fools gladly. As we walk to her plantations, across the road toward the Jordan border, she briefly recounts her story.

She was raised in a family of Jewish farmers in California, immigrants from Sicily. Her grandfather owned orchards of cherries, peaches, almonds, and olives. When she was still young, she had doubts about the farming methods in California, "the pesticide capital of the world." For her thirteenth birthday, she demanded Rachel Carson's *The Silent Spring*, the classic denunciation of DDT and other toxins, and she still has the copy that she was given. After studying agriculture at Duke University, she came to Israel in 1971. At first, she lived on a kibbutz in the north, but she suffered from asthma and was advised to move to the desert. In 1975 she came to Ketura, married, and has been there ever since. In between giving birth to six sons, she continued her work in the orchards, but in 1985 she went to work with a Ben-Gurion University researcher who was experimenting with the introduction of trees from deserts outside Israel.

We walk past the extensive date orchards, where the donkeys control the weeds, to the area of her experimentation. She is more worried about deforestation than carbon emissions, she states. "Stand here," she orders me. "Under the tree it is ten degrees cooler: do it a million times and you change the climate."

She points to a mesquite tree that she introduced from the southwest of the United States. It only needs ten to twelve cubic meters of water a year; a citrus tree needs six times as much. The mesquite can be grown in areas where the rainfall is only two hundred millimeters annually. Its pods are full of protein and sugar, which can be human or animal food. The pods can be ground down for flour. The leaves and branches can be grazed by sheep and goats. The leaf litter enriches the soil and the roots stabilize dunes. Because of the thorns, which become longer around the trunk, the grazing animals will not harm the tree—"merely give it a haircut."

Solowey is involved in joint projects with both Jordan and Morocco. South of Marrakesh, the peasants farm for four months in the year and have to look for other work in the remaining eight months. If enough trees are introduced, they can support animal husbandry all year long. The trees can be domesticated to produce more fruit and give pasture to cows, camels, and donkeys as well as sheep and goats.

The argania tree, native to Morocco, was abandoned in favor of citrus cultivation, but recent drought years have made it unprofitable to grow citrus in the semi-arid area of the Atlas Mountains. Even after the neglect, there are still twenty million argania trees in Morocco. The Berber women gather up the nuts, grind them up, and sell the oil. An average tree gives seven kilograms of nuts, which produce half a bottle of oil, but Solowey has domesticated trees in her orchard that produce one hundred kilograms.

Another experiment is taking place further north in Israel, where the rainfall is sufficient. Under Solowey's guidance, a Bedouin farmer has planted trees to stop the erosion of a wadi, a dry riverbed, on his land. She is hopeful about his experiment because she thinks his neighbors will imitate him.

"The mesquite and the argania are only two examples," she points out enthusiastically. "There are dozens of varieties that can be brought in and domesticated. Peoples fight over resources, but it makes much more sense to broaden the resource base. If you enhance the agriculture, you also improve the political situation."

Jordanians, Palestinians, Jews, and Bedouin are all involved in her various research projects, she notes, while pointing to a "green blob," the Sinai creeper. The fruit of the creeper, the caper, can be used for jam and mustard. It grows with almost no water. The *marula*, introduced from Botswana in Africa, is rather larger with a mango-like fruit, and the *pitaya* from South America, a sort of cactus, produces a succulent mauve fruit that Solowey picks and cuts open, offering me a slice. Another shrub, the Jericho balm, is native. It is mentioned in Genesis.

Solowey has written a book called *Supping at God's Table* in which she describes the potential of desert agriculture. She is convinced that crops like the ones she grows can transform the economies of the Middle East and Africa. On a recent visit to Zimbabwe, she was appalled at the deterioration of the once flourishing agriculture. "It can be restored and made even better than before," she insists. "There is nothing as good as trees. Are you following me?"

Apart from Solowey's projects, the Arava Institute is cooperating with Jordanians and Palestinians in stream restoration, air pollution research, environmental education, and a host of other projects. Clive Liphkin, an immigrant from South Africa, is director of research at the institute. Tall and broad-shouldered with thick, closely cropped black hair, Liphkin describes the institute as "a living laboratory of the potential of the region."

Echoing the sentiments of his colleague David Lehrer, Liphkin points out that there is no difference between Arab and Jew—or right wing and left wing—when it comes to environmental problems. There is no point in the blame game. Everyone suffers if they get it wrong, and everyone benefits if they get it right. The comparative isolation of Ketura is a benefit, as it enables them to sit back and think away from the tensions and clashes further north.

Liphkin feels almost as much at home in the West Bank and in Jordan as he does in Israel. He is working together with Jordanians and Palestinians monitoring air pollution in four urban centers and renewing two streams that originate in the West Bank and flow into Israel on their way to the sea. "At the present time I can get to the West Bank more easily than my Palestinian colleagues can come here," he notes. "We work together and trust each other professionally. We have requested a grant to work in Gaza also, and I hope it will come through."

There may be political differences regarding the separation fence, for example, concedes Liphkin, but everyone agrees about the ecological harm caused by the barrier. Each individual has his own view, but they all have to deal with the environment. "There is cooperation every day," he emphasizes. "Peel away the superficial layer, and you have the reality of joint work. Israel may refuse to have dealings with the Palestinian Hamas government, and Hamas may refuse to recognize Israel, but we all breathe the same air, drink the same water, and use the same electricity."

That evening most of the students, Jewish and Arab, leave the balmy air of the Arava valley to drive up into the cool Negev hills where a Bedouin tent has been hired for an evening with Jewish and Arab high schoolchildren. The hundred or so students are working together on creating an ecological garden at Kibbutz Lotan a couple of miles to the north. The project is organized by Rina Kedem, a Jewish student at the Arava Institute specializing in environmental education.

Rina was born in the United States, but has lived most of her life in Israel. Working as a youth leader, she found herself taking teenagers on nature hikes both in Israel and in the U.S. She soon became aware of the powerful effect that the countryside had on the kids, and this was reinforced by travel in Asia and Australia, where she visited a number of eco villages. When she arrived at Ketura, she determined to investigate the state of ecological education at Jewish and Arab schools in Israel.

Rina took over a project that had been going on for five years in which Arab students from a high school near Nazareth come down to the Arava to meet with Jewish students in the regional high school. She suggested to both schools that they adopt an environmental project and the teachers responded enthusiastically. The children themselves came up with the idea of an ecological garden, and they designed and built it together.

In the crowded tent, the Arava Institute students all pitch in, assisting the teachers to organize the evening. The noise level is phenomenal as the fifteen- and sixteen-year-old Jewish and Arab boys and girls sit and talk. The only thing that interrupts the continuous conversation is the hypnotic rhythm beaten out by Samer and Osama on traditional clay Arab drums, which stimulates all those present to lively hand clapping and chanting. The Jewish and Arab children seem to be familiar with the same chants, and some even stand up and gyrate to the rhythm.

Following supper, eaten cross-legged in Bedouin style around low tables, the children form five mixed circles and hear about various projects. Ilana Meallem, a Jewish immigrant from England and a former student at the institute, tells one group about her "environmental justice" project with the Bedouin of the Negev. Having just completed her second degree on the subject of solid waste management, Ilana explains her work with the Bedouin women in an unrecognized township where there is no sewerage and no organized waste disposal. One of her projects is the introduction of a bio-digester to deal with at least some of the waste. There is also a program for producing gas from animal and human feces. "When I came to the Arava, my main interest was marine biology," she explains, "but after studying at the institute, I was determined to work with the Bedouin—specially the women, who carry the main burden of the problems of waste and pollution."

The Arava Institute is a multitasking facility that is involved in teaching, research, cross-border cooperation, and ecological projects. It also acts as a watchdog for the whole Negev desert, monitoring such programs as the army's activities and the reopening of the nearby Timna copper mines. The mines were forced out of the market many years ago, but today, with the huge demand for copper from China, it will be profitable to operate them again. This means that poisonous waste will be leaking into the desert and poisons will again be transported along the desert roads. The institute intends to keep a close eye on this.

The Arava Institute also fosters activities by its alumni so that Israeli, Palestinian, Jordanian, and other environmental activists who have studied together and become friends keep in touch as colleagues. Rabbi Michael Cohen, the director for special projects, was just back from a reunion of alumni in Akaba, across the bay from Eilat. More than 70 percent of the graduates work in the field of ecology, and most of them are members of the Arava Peace and Environmental Network (APEN), through which they maintain contacts after their time at Ketura.

He was enthusiastic about the reunion, where forty-five alumni from Israel, Palestine, Jordan, the U.S., and several other countries swapped memories and also talked about current environmental projects. "It was amazing to see what we had accomplished in ten years," he exclaims. "They keep in touch, share information, visit each other's homes, and often meet at conferences." A Reconstructionist rabbi from the United States, Cohen was a founding member of the institute, which, in his words, "brought together all the things I believe in: Judaism, Zionism, Israeli-Palestinian-Jordanian cooperation, and environmental preservation."

Cohen, who is rabbi emeritus of an American Jewish congregation, has spent much of his life living in Israel. Now he divides his time between lecturing at the institute and working for it in the United States. He is due to return to the U.S. for a couple of years, where he will spend his time on fundraising, student recruitment, and PR. Rabbi Michael, as everyone calls him, is also active in campaigning for Palestinian students to come to the institute. He is one of the organizers of the petition to the Supreme Court on this. "It's quite ridiculous that they are not allowed to study at our institute," he declares. "It is as if we Israelis are telling them not to cooperate with us, not to live together with us, and to become our enemies."

The Arava Institute is certainly one of the most hopeful projects in the field of cooperation and coexistence. The staff members are gratified that many of the region's environmental leaders are alumni, and they look forward to a time when the environment ministers of Israel, Palestine, and Jordan will all be graduates of the institute. Whether that day ever comes or not, the institute has already made a notable contribution to conciliation between the peoples of the region and to their ecological awareness.

Amer Sweity, one of the Jordanian students specializing in water management, observed in our conversation that King Hussein, the late Jordanian monarch, once warned that the next Middle Eastern war could be over water resources. Water, emphasized Sweity, was a vital need for all the countries of the region.

It was natural, therefore, that when the Israeli/Palestine Center for Research and information (IPCRI) organized a Water for Life conference, it should turn to the Arava Institute for organizational assistance. Two of the institute's graduate students, Israeli Ro'i Elisha of Ben-Gurion University and Palestinian Dima Halawani of Al-Kuds University, helped organize the international conference that took place in Antalya, Turkey, with the participation of some two hundred water experts—several of them from the institute, economists, and environmental activists from Israel, Palestine, and fourteen other countries.

This important meeting, which took place despite the bad political climate, was only one of the high-profile events promoted recently by IPCRI, an Israeli-Palestinian think tank dealing with politics, economics, security, borders, education, and Jerusalem, as well as environmental matters. IPCRI is the subject of our next chapter.

13

Thinking Together

Gershon Baskin, founder and codirector of IPCRI, was putting me off. No, he said, I should not come to see him yet. He asked me to wait until next week. I was trying to fix an appointment at the offices of the Israel-Palestine Center for Research and Information, a think tank with which I was familiar, having attended meetings regularly in the early 1990s. I had also been responsible for writing up *Peace Pays*, published by IPCRI, the coproduction of an Israeli economist and a Palestinian business executive who used forecasting to argue the economic benefits of a peace accord between the two peoples.

Baskin agreed to an interview, but made it conditional on the presence of Hana Siniora, his codirector, who was presently abroad. When Siniora returned, he promised, they would see me together. This emphasis on partnership is significant. Baskin confesses that it took him more than three years to learn to work together with his first Palestinian codirector, Zakariya al-Qaq. "We mirrored the general Israeli-Palestinian scene," he recalls. "We argued about everything all the time. Somehow we found ourselves presenting positions to each other that were more extreme than our actual opinions."

It was only after a "therapy session" in London with two British supporters of IPCRI who told them that they were a bad example of Israelis and Palestinians who were supposed to be working together that they found the correct modus operandi. Today Baskin admits that he saw IPCRI as his own brainchild and he found it difficult to share it with somebody else. In time, he came to realize that there was no alternative if he wanted a genuine joint project. Furthermore, he discovered that he and Zakariya were perfectly capable of agreeing to disagree.

The American-born Baskin first visited Israel at the age of thirteen, having requested a trip to Israel as a Bar Mitzvah present. Back in Long Island, he was an enthusiastic member of a Zionist youth movement and after graduating from high school, he spent a gap year at a kibbutz in Israel. Subsequently it occurred to him that in the entire year he had never spoken to an Arab.

He began to read more widely about the complexity of the situation, and the next time he came to Israel, it was to participate in the Interns for Peace program, spending two years in the Israeli Arab village of Kafr Kara helping to train community leaders. After leaving the village, he got a job at the Ministry of Education working to improve relations between Jews and Arabs in Israel and he was involved in the establishment of the ministry's Department for Democracy and Coexistence.

On the outbreak of the first Intifada in 1987, he went to Bethlehem and spent several hours at the Dehaishe Refugee Camp discussing the situation with young Palestinian Arabs. He was impressed that, although they talked incessantly about "ending the occupation," the matter of the Right of Return never came up. This convinced him that there was a genuine chance for mutual recognition between Israelis and Palestinians. He placed an advertisement in three East Jerusalem newspapers inviting anyone favoring a two-state solution and believing that Israelis and Palestinians could work together for peace to contact him. He received more than forty phone calls and arranged to meet many of the callers in the courtyard of the American Colony Hotel.

This was the birth of IPCRI. Baskin resigned his government job and started to plan the new organization. He received encouragement from the late Faisal Husseini, who was the most influential local Palestinian leader at that time. Husseini warned him, however, not to institutionalize the organization unless all four groups leading the Intifada agreed. This delayed the formal establishment of the NGO, but in 1989, Baskin read in a paper that Hana Siniora, editor-in-chief of the East Jerusalem paper *Al-Fajr*, was planning to set up a Jerusalem forum with Moshe Amirav, a member of the central committee of the ruling Likud party. He persuaded them to join forces with him and the two men became the first cochairmen of IPCRI, with Zakariya al-Qaq and Baskin himself as codirectors.

Years later, when Zakariya resigned, Siniora stepped down from the chairmanship and assumed the executive position of codirector. Hana Siniora was one of the first Palestinians to make contact with Israelis after the end of the Six Day War. A Christian from a well-established Jerusalem family, he was always ready to adopt unpopular ideas. On one occasion, after he went on record as proposing Palestinian participation in the Jerusalem municipal elections, his car was set on fire. Siniora stresses that today he does not support joining the municipality. He favors two separate municipalities in

Jerusalem—one Israeli, one Palestinian—with a special residents' committee for the Old City.

During the Oslo years, IPCRI flourished, with numerous workshops, study groups, publications, and regular meetings at the Notre Dame Hotel, just outside the Old City walls. It became one of the most important forums for discussions between Israelis and Palestinians. The think tank attracted Israeli Knesset members, senior government and municipal officials, security personnel, and businesspersons as well as intellectuals and academics. On the Palestinian side, participants were of an equivalent level, although in those days there was no Palestinian Authority and consequently no officials. At the same time, junior American and European diplomats often participated in the proceedings.

As the peace process developed, IPCRI was increasingly involved in the so-called Track II discussions, which often prepared and supplemented the official negotiations. In the early stages, the meetings were confidential, which meant that participants knew that reports of the discussions would not appear in the media. IPCRI did, however, publish a quarterly newsletter and reports on the various policy forums. Peacemaking, economics, education, and the environment were among the issues thrashed out in the think tank's activities.

IPCRI liked to tackle the most intractable problems, and in 1993, it organized the Israeli-Palestinian International Academic Seminar on the Future of Jerusalem. Jerusalem mayor Teddy Kollek and several of his officials participated, along with leading Jerusalem personalities from the Palestinian side and a host of international experts. The latter often brought their own special insights, including, notably, the minister for external relations from the Brussels region, who presented the multicultural reality of his town, "where different communities living together is a daily effort."

At the end of the seminar, IPCRI presented its own plan, including the "Charter for Jerusalem," which had been worked out by an Israeli-Palestinian panel. It proposed alternative models for either a unified municipality or two separate but cooperating municipalities. It envisioned a high level of decentralization, neighborhood self-administration, a joint mayor's forum, joint planning commissions, and a joint police force. At the time a daring concept, it is remarkable how well the ideas stand up more than a decade later.

More recently, Jerusalem was the subject of a public meeting sponsored by IPCRI, with a Palestinian cartographer and an Israeli attorney surveying the latest developments in the town. Both men, Hallil Toufakji and Danny Seideman, cautioned that recent events were making a rational solution to the problem of Jerusalem less likely. Seideman was particularly scornful of the separation fence in Jerusalem, which, while ostensibly separating Jews and Arabs, in fact often cut off Palestinians from other Palestinians. He compared it to a camel, "a horse designed by a committee."

Although the motive for the wall was demographic, it was in fact increasing the Palestinian population of Jerusalem as Palestinians flocked into what were previously Jewish areas in order to avoid being shut out from their places of employment, education, and commerce by the barrier.

"We are clinging on to the two-state solution by the tips of our fingers," warned Seideman, noting that only American pressure had prevented the construction of the so-called E-1 plan, which, by linking Jerusalem with the large urban settlement of Maale Adumim to the east, would have effectively split the West Bank in two. "The situation in Jerusalem is messy and sometimes liable to be violent, but it is manageable," he stated. "It is important to prevent the extremist Jews, assisted by evangelical Christians from promoting a clash with fundamentalist Muslims."

Toukakji and Seideman think that Jerusalem is a relatively stable city, with the three faiths coexisting more or less successfully, but it can easily be destabilized by challenging the legitimacy of one side or the other. The government has given control of many of the archeological sites to the Jewish settlers, whose aim is to gain control of the Temple Mount and its environs. Even some of the archeological excavations are nationally motivated and disapproved of by the Israeli Department of Antiquities. For example, the current rebuilding of the approaches to the Mughrabi Gate, which has sparked off Muslim protests, is unnecessary. Minimal repairs can be carried out without upsetting the Muslims. Both men called for the maintenance of the status quo as the best way to preserve stability.

The meeting attracted more than a hundred people to East Jerusalem's Ambassador Hotel. Following the presentations of the two men, there was a lively discussion of the possibility of involving outside bodies such as UNESCO in any future plans. Toufakji pointed out that the UN body had declared Jerusalem a heritage site. "Jerusalem doesn't just belong to us," he concluded. "It is part of the heritage of the whole world."

The outbreak of the second Intifada in the fall of 2000 initially hampered IPCRI's activities, forcing it to hold meetings abroad. Often it was even difficult to meet abroad, as it was impossible to get permits for Palestinians to travel to Turkey via Ben-Gurion Airport. Because of the violence, the think tank's office, which had moved from East Jerusalem to Bethlehem, had to move again to Tantur, a rambling stone building near the Bethlehem checkpoint on the outskirts of Jerusalem that houses a Christian ecumenical institute.

In addition, because of the explosive situation in Israel and Palestine, financial support from abroad declined. Despite all these difficulties, the activities continued. "Our work has expanded and contracted according to our budget," explains Siniora. "The situation has been terribly difficult. We have experienced horrific violence with people dying almost every day, but we have never stopped cooperating."

"At our peak," observes Baskin, "we had an annual budget of $1.6 million and a staff of twenty-six. We've.had to retrench since then. There are terrible social and economic problems in the Palestinian territories right now, so foreign donors, if they give at all, tend to favor humanitarian organizations."

With all the difficulties, points out Siniora, IPCRI managed to bring together more than two hundred Israelis, Palestinians, and experts from other nations to its Water for Life conference. It is true that it had to be in Turkey, he concedes. Baskin remarks that it was a good idea to have the conference abroad. He would have preferred a foreign location even if it had been possible to organize it locally. Having all the delegates in the same hotel is beneficial. Casual chats in the bar or at the dinner table are no less important than the formal session, he suggests. The sixty-four papers presented covered such topics as pollution control, climate change, water resources management, Israeli-Palestinian water issues and conflict resolution, transborder regional issues, recycling, and alternative water sources.

Another recent conference, also held in Antalya, was Education for Peace and Democracy. Representatives from universities in Israel and the Palestinian territories presented papers on cooperation in higher education, the effectiveness of education for peace and democracy, educating for peace in a reality of conflict, and many other related topics. Guests from countries like South Africa made special contributions. Many of the talks were given jointly by Israelis and Palestinians. The final plenary session on "Constructive Conversations in the Classroom on the Sensitive Issues of the Conflict" was presented by Ghassan Abdullah and Joni Orbach of MECA, the Middle East Children's Association

Among the presentations at the conference were several papers dealing with Israeli and Palestinian textbooks. Propaganda was found in the books used by schoolchildren on both sides, in some cases subtle, in others less so. IPCRI has also issued a series of reports on the vexed question of Palestinian school textbooks. Complaints about the textbooks are regularly raised by Israeli spokespersons, and IPCRI decided to tackle the matter. The procedure was fairly complex. An Arabic-speaking Israeli, a former headmaster, went through all the books, highlighting any passages he found objectionable. His reservations were then considered by a team of Palestinian teachers and reports were prepared under the supervision of Professor Salem Aweiss of Stanford University.

A detailed analysis of the textbooks found that, while open incitement against Israel does not exist, there are passages that could be seen as glorifying violent resistance. Possibly more serious, the topics of Israel, Jewish history, and the Jewish link to the region are almost completely ignored. The reports are moderately worded, and there are specific suggestions for improvements. Baskin notes that the reports could have been harsher, but IPCRI aims to influence the Palestinian side rather than to score points. The reports are posted on the PLO website and have been used in Palestinian reports to the European Union, so apparently they are having some influence.

Toward the end of 2006, the Israeli security authorities became more liberal about granting permits, making it possible for Palestinians to cross into Israel and also to travel abroad via Ben-Gurion Airport. In contrast to the past, most Palestinians receive permits, says Baskin, unless they are on a special "security list."

Noting that many of those prevented from traveling are members of Hamas, Siniora points out that the Hamas government has only been in power for one year. The PLO and Israel took many years to move toward mutual recognition, he recalls. Hamas has moved much faster in the right direction. "Enemies have to talk," he insists. "Our work is to make enemies talk to one another. Without that we are not going to achieve a two-state solution."

A series of demonstrations in favor of the two-state solution is the next big thing on the IPCRI agenda. June 5, 2007, was the fortieth anniversary of the Six Day War, and on that date marches were planned in one hundred cities around the world with a positive message of "Two States for Two Peoples—Peace and Justice."

"We want to be constructive," comments Siniora. "We are not only protesting about the occupation, but pointing the way forward. For example, I would like to see tree planting ceremonies. Recently, on the Jewish New Year of the Trees, a group of Jews and Palestinians (including rabbis) planted trees. We should follow their example."

"We can definitely have tree planting as part of the events," agrees Baskin. "We can do it near Salfit on the West Bank, where trees were destroyed by settlers, and also in Galilee."

Baskin and Siniora emphasize that although IPCRI is initiating the June 5 events, it wants to bring in as wide a coalition as possible to participate. They have brought the idea before the Israel-Palestine Peace NGOs Forum, a coalition of 114 organizations.

Worldwide demonstrations are all very well, I observe, but is the two-state solution still realistic? Baskin thinks that the opportunity will be lost only when the majority support for it on both sides disappears. This has not happened so far, he states. Siniora warns that the time for achieving two states is not unlimited, but stresses the fact that the Saudi peace initiative, which has been adopted by the Arab League, is still supported by all the Arab nations. The basis of this plan is the existence of two states living side by side.

IPCRI occupies both men more than full time, but they are also involved in joint media projects. Hana Siniora's Biladi media company continues to publish an online version of the *Jerusalem Times*, a continuation of *Al-Fajr*. Biladi is also a partner in All for Peace, an Israeli-Palestinian radio station that broadcasts out of Jerusalem and Ramallah in Hebrew and Arabic. His daughter in law, Maysa Baransi-Siniora, is the Palestinian codirector of the station. Gershon Baskin is a member of the editorial board of *Palestine-Israel Journal*, a joint quarterly that is now in its thirteenth year. Media cooperation between Israelis and Palestinians is the subject of our next chapter.

14

Joint Media Initiatives

The problems were mainly technical. That is how I remember it, looking back from the perspective of a dozen years to the first edition of a new joint magazine of Israelis and Palestinians. I was co–managing editor with Khuloud Totah, a Palestinian lady who had been living in Jordan. Both of us had been recruited by Ziad Abu-Zayyad and the late Victor Cygielman, the founding editors of the journal.

The name, by the way, was entirely fortuitous. We were sitting around putting forward ideas at random, and tending toward *Israeli-Palestinian Magazine*, or something of the sort, when Doreen, the South African-born wife of Dr. Simcha Bahiri, one of the founding team, who happened to be present, interrupted us: "Why does Israel always have to be first?" she demanded. "Give the Palestinians a chance."

When Abu-Zayyad heard this, he fastened on to the idea with great determination. The rest of us were prepared to go along, and so it became *Palestine-Israel Journal*. I was quite keen on "quarterly," but the two editors, who had started their venture with a very modest budget, did not want to commit themselves to four times a year at that point. They were not quite sure how things would work out.

Cygielman had been a leading member of the editorial board of the recently defunct *New Outlook*, a dovish Israeli monthly; Abu-Zayyad, an attorney, for a time had edited a biweekly Hebrew magazine for Palestinians and Israelis called *Gesher* [bridge]. They got together and conceived the idea of an English-language joint project. Cygielman had some difficulty in making the transition. In his special article for the first edition, he quoted his Palestinian friend the late Rashid Hussein to explain how the establishment of Israel, a triumph for the Jews, had been a tragedy for the Palestinians Arabs.

"Victor," I protested. "You are no longer at *New Outlook*. You don't have to explain the Palestinian side to an Israeli audience. This is a joint magazine: let the Palestinians explain their version—your job is to put over an Israeli point of view."

My next task was to propose to Manuel Hassassian, a Palestinian academic from Bethlehem (who is currently the PLO representative in London) that he should forgo some of his more extreme language when describing the Israeli occupation of the Palestinian territories. Khuloud, my Palestinian colleague, had to deal with similar problems, but my abiding memory is of the two of us struggling with an impossible computer system in Abu-Zayyad's East Jerusalem office.

I could only blame my own side, because the system had been installed by Israeli technicians. Often we lost whole passages of text. Frequently we swore and gnashed our teeth as the computer refused to indent paragraphs, change fonts, or excise words. We were often on the verge of despair—not about the content, but because of the frustration of putting words on the page.

In the end, we managed it somehow, and in January 1994, the first edition of the new magazine appeared. Khuloud and I were physically and mentally exhausted. It was not because of the contents and style of the journal, about which we sometimes argued, but on which we always reached consensus. It was because of that terrible computer program, which almost prevented the emergence of any content at all, whatever the style. The second edition was produced on a modern computer, but neither of us stayed around to enjoy the relative ease of production. Khuloud decamped back to Amman; I left to write a book.

New managing editors Leila Dabdoub and Dan Leon were to take the journal forward and set it on strong foundations. It has been going for a dozen years and some forty editions. The latest, volume 13, number 3, is technically vastly superior to that first production, but I still think that Khuloud and I deserve some credit. Without our Herculean efforts, the first edition would not have appeared, and maybe the subsequent achievements would not have been possible. I continued to serve on the editorial board, but after a few more editions, I dropped out of that also, so I can relate to it with detachment. The forgoing paragraphs, then, are in the nature of a declaration of interest.

A perusal of the articles in *Palestine-Israel Journal* enables one to follow Middle East developments of the past decade or so. In these years, the journal has published articles by Israelis, Palestinians, Europeans, Americans, and others. It has held regular roundtable discussions covering every crisis and each problem. It has discussed politics, security, religion, culture, borders, refugees, terror, occupation, trauma, human rights, and rival narratives.

The first edition in the winter of 1994 dealt with such subjects as "Time for Reconciliation," "The Road to Mutual Recognition," and "From Armed Struggle to Negotiation." These were appropriate matters in the optimistic Oslo years. The latest edition in the winter of 2006 considers "Conflict Management, Not Overall Solution" by Moshe Amirav and "The Concept of Hudna [Truce] in Islamic Sources" by Mustafa Abu-Sway, reflecting the more modest expectations that the past six years of violence have wrought.

Amirav, a member of the new centrist Kadima Party in Israel, states that conditions are not ripe for a solution of the Israeli-Palestinian conflict. He proposes an Israeli withdrawal from most of the West Bank and a cessation of hostilities for a defined period of ten years. In other words, he is suggesting an Islamic-style *hudna*, or truce. In his article, Mustafa Abu-Sway, the director of Islamic Research Center at Al-Kuds University, asserts that the traditional Muslim concept of *hudna*, a ten-year truce, allows the parties to reconsider its terms, but mutual respect for its terms can lead to a renewal, equivalent to a permanent treaty.

From the above it is clear that the journal is not negative or pessimistic, but, like everyone else, its idealism has been battered by current reality. The editorial board has grown from ten to twenty-five; the sponsors from fifteen to twenty-six. The budget, boosted by a big grant from the European Union, has increased at least tenfold. Ziad Abu-Zayyad remains the Palestinian editor; the current Israeli editor is Hillel Schenker, a former American who has lived in Israel since 1963.

Abu-Zayyad, an attorney and journalist, was one of the first Palestinians to reach out to Israelis after the Six Day War of 1967. His father had been an employee of the Jerusalem Municipality during British Mandate times and he immediately made contact with one of his father's former Jewish colleagues. "I called him at the office and nobody there spoke Arabic or English," he recalls. "I thought to myself that it was absurd that we couldn't communicate, when we lived so close to each other."

Before the end of 1967, Abu-Zayyad was studying Hebrew at the Beit Ha'am Community Center in West Jerusalem, and shortly afterwards he began addressing a variety of Israeli audiences in halls, private homes, kibbutzim, and other venues. He became an early supporter of the two-state solution, but was firmly opposed to participating in the Jerusalem Municipal Council. He felt (and still feels) that participation in a joint council would be tantamount to recognizing the Israeli occupation of East Jerusalem.

Despite this, he rejects an often-heard Palestinian argument that any cooperation with Israelis signifies recognition of the Israeli occupation of the West Bank and East Jerusalem. "Any Israeli, who is against the occupation and sees me as a partner and recognizes my rights, is my ally," he declares. "Peace is a shared interest of Israelis and Palestinians—nobody is doing anybody a favor."

In 1986, he left the Palestinian newspaper *Al-Fajr* to found *Gesher*, a Hebrew biweekly, which aimed to carry the Palestinian point of view to Israelis, including a section on local culture, literature, and folklore. It never made a profit, but he kept it going for five years. He had returned to practicing law when Victor Cygielman approached him with the idea of a new journal in English. It was established during the Oslo years when everyone was optimistic about peace, but it has survived successfully during the violent confrontation of the past six years.

When the second Intifada erupted in the fall of 2000, the Palestinian minister in charge of NGOs gave an order that all joint activities with Israelis be frozen, but Abu-Zayyad stood firm. The purpose of *Palestine-Israel Journal*, Abu-Zayyad notes, is to oppose the occupation and bring it to an end. The Israelis and Palestinians working there are on the same track. "I continue to work with Israelis," he explains, "because I believe that it is *not* normalizing the occupation. Our line is clear."

In 1996, Abu-Zayyad was elected as an independent member of the parliament of the Palestinian Authority, but he recently lost his seat to the Hamas Islamic Party. He is a practicing Muslim who prays five times a day and attends mosque on Friday, but he is not close to Hamas politically.

The journal gives a platform to anyone except those who deny either side's right to independence and freedom. The editors work together amicably, he says. They argue, but they don't fight. They find shared points of view and sometimes manage to convince each other. Ziad draws the line at Jewish settlers. He cannot envisage giving them a platform, as they are the instruments of occupation. Apart from that, the journal wants to reach as wide an audience as possible on both sides of the Israeli-Palestinian divide.

This is confirmed by Israeli editor Hillel Schenker, who says that Abu-Zayyad is just as concerned as he is to maintain contacts with the Israeli mainstream. He has even expressed concern that one of the more radical Israeli staff members should not drag the journal "too far to the left."

"There are mutual examples of concessions," notes Schenker. "We agreed not to have settlers contributing, and Ziad agreed to include the topic of Holocaust denial, although he thought it was not a topic for the journal. We explained that it was important to Israelis and he accepted that."

Schenker was a member of the left-wing Hashomer Hatzair youth movement in the United States and a kibbutznik before joining *New Outlook*, an Israeli magazine founded jointly by Israeli Jews and Arabs in 1957. For two decades, the magazine struggled to present a dovish view to the Israeli public. After the 1967 war, *New Outlook* was in the forefront of contacts between Israelis and Palestinians. The first meetings of Peace Now were held in its editorial offices.

Representing the magazine in New York, Schenker linked up with the Palestinian paper *Al-Fajr* to organize a high-level meeting of Israelis and

Palestinians at Columbia University in the days when Israelis were forbidden to meet with members of the PLO, although its "academic" sponsorship made it "legal." Later, Nabil Shaath, who served as foreign minister of the Palestinian Authority, would say that it was the first time that he realized that the Palestinians had "real partners" on the Israeli side.

Schenker, who became managing editor of *Palestine-Israel Journal* in 2003 and editor the following year, is intrigued by the internal disputes among the Palestinians. He thinks that since Hamas won the PA elections in 2006, pro-peace Palestinians have been less ambivalent about working with Israelis. There are still Palestinians who say, "No normalization until the end of occupation," but their voice has become weaker.

Despite the violence of the past six years and the ongoing deadlock, Ziad Abu-Zayyad remains hopeful. Palestinians have invested in their children's education, he says. "Once we invested in land and the Israelis took away our land," he remarks. "Nobody can take away education. For example, so many of the doctors in the Arab countries are Palestinians—and not just in the Arab world: look at your Israeli hospitals! The occupation is not natural. It won't last, and then we will live together in mutual respect and cooperation."

Taking its title from the memoir of Cyprus by Lawrence Durrel, www.bitterlemons.org, a joint Israeli-Palestinian website, represents a rather different approach from that of *Palestine-Israel Journal*. The journal, while offering a range of opinion, strives toward reaching reasonable consensus, whereas Bitterlemons is predicated on the idea of confrontation.

"I can always rely on Ghassan to disagree with me," states Yossi Alpher, one of the two founders of the website, speaking about the other. "When we first started planning the project, during the Oslo years, we assumed the peace process was going ahead, but even then we thought that there would be enough to disagree about."

Alpher is a former official of the Mossad, Israel's external intelligence service; Ghassan Khatib is a former prisoner of the Israeli security authorities. They don't represent opposing extremes, but they are definitely from opposite sides of the Israeli-Palestinian divide. "No pigs and monkeys," explains Alpher, outlining the principles of the website, "but also no warm, fuzzy, consensus!"

"I have always believed in engaging Israelis," notes Khatib. "It doesn't mean that I agree with them."

Subscribers can join the website for free on the basis of their e-mail address only. Once they have signed up, they will receive by e-mail four essays on Israeli-Palestinian topics every Monday and three to five articles on wider Middle East issues every Thursday. The service is only suspended for Jewish, Muslim, and Christian holidays. Alpher and Khatib always write on the Israeli-Palestinian question, together with another writer from each side. The Middle East articles, which come out under the banner of Bitter-lemons International, are written by a variety of contributors from around the world.

All the articles are commissioned by Alpher and Khatib, who also edit them, although Khatib, who unlike Alpher is not a native English speaker, employs an English language editor. All shades of opinion are permitted, but insults such as "pig," "monkey," or "Nazi" are ruthlessly blue-penciled out. Bitterlemons aims to offer subscribers vigorous but civilized discussion of the issues.

Khatib, who was born in a small West Bank village near Nablus, spent five years in Israeli prisons for membership in "illegal organizations." After studying at Birzeit, the leading Palestinian university, he earned an MA and a PhD in Britain before returning to lecture at his alma mater. In 1988, he established the Jerusalem Media and Communications Center (JMCC), an organization he still directs. The JMCC provides services to researchers, media people, and international agencies. It also organizes conferences and workshops and conducts opinion polls in the Palestinian territories.

Active in contacts with Israelis, Khatib was a member of the Palestinian-Jordanian delegation to the American-sponsored Madrid Peace Conference in 1991 and to subsequent bilateral negotiations in Washington. Later he was the minister of labor in the Palestinian Authority administration.

Alpher immigrated to Israel from the United States in 1962, serving in the Israel Defense Forces, IDF Intelligence, and the Mossad. After twelve years in the latter, he joined Tel Aviv University's Jaffee Center for Strategic Studies, becoming director and then going on to serve as the American Jewish Committee representative in Israel. He first met Khatib when the two of them were involved in so-called Track II meetings, in which Israelis and Palestinians met unofficially and informally. "We never agreed about anything," recalls Alpher, "but we liked and respected each other."

"I was already running the JMCC," says Khatib, "but I thought that Yossi's idea was very interesting."

Alpher, who describes Bitterlemons as a "sort of virtual Track II," concedes that he and Khatib actually do agree on two matters: a two-state solution and civilized discourse between the two peoples. It took them some eighteen months to establish the project. After they had worked out what they wanted, they established a division of labor that still exists: Khatib provides the technical infrastructure through the JMCC; Alpher is the fundraiser. Everything else is based on mutuality. Their main support comes from the European Union, although they also receive money from American sources.

An early attempt to produce the weekly essays in Arabic and Hebrew was abandoned when it was found that only a few dozen people on both sides became subscribers. Today they have more than twelve thousand signed up to the English network. "We are openly elitist," proclaims Alpher. "The people who read us can read English."

There is no way of knowing how many people read their weekly offerings, but they estimate it at some one hundred thousand people all over the world. There are university lecturers who recommend it to their students, rabbis who post it to the members of their congregations, and many who send it on to friends and colleagues.

In five years, the weekly essays have dealt with every imaginable topic, but it is instructive to pinpoint some of the major controversies. Nothing has stirred emotions more than the Israeli separation fence or wall, and here we can witness the different approaches.

Alpher: "The West Bank separation fence works. It keeps out terrorists, and for that matter illegal Palestinian immigrants and car thieves too. It has made a major contribution to a radical reduction in suicide bombings over recent months."

Khatib: "This wall is only about further injustice. It is accompanied by seizing, closing, or confiscating more Palestinian land and expanding illegal Jewish settlements. It also increases the humiliation and suffering of the Palestinian people, whose standard of living is deteriorating as a result."

On the other hand, the matter of the so-called Geneva Accord, reached by unofficial Israeli and Palestinian representatives in the fall of 2003, produced a less contentious exchange between the two editors:

Khatib: "There is no doubt that, when the two official governments sit for final status negotiations, they will benefit greatly from the ideas embodied in the Geneva Accord."

Alpher: "The Geneva Accord signals the public on both sides that peace is possible. It is a courageous act, and a positive major event in the annals of the Israeli-Palestinian peace process."

They differ again when it comes to "demography," the population balance between Arabs and Jews in Israel and the Palestinian territories. Alpher's article is headlined "It's Demographic Security, Stupid" whereas Khatib's is headed "Demography Negates Democracy."

Sadly, it must be recognized that Alpher and Khatib agree on one other thing: both men are pessimistic about the future. Alpher does not see a Palestinian leader who can deliver on any kind of viable peace process, nor does he see a capable Israeli leader on the horizon. Khatib supports the two-state solution as the only existing alternative to the continuing Israeli occupation of the West Bank, but he goes on to say that this alternative is becoming increasingly impossible day by day as Israel continues with its settlement policy.

Another joint Israeli-Palestinian media project, which has already been mentioned, is the All for Peace radio station, which was established in

2005. Starting out as a purely Internet operation broadcasting mainly music, it now sends out a full program of news and current events on FM and the Internet in Hebrew and Arabic. It has a staff of twenty-two, half of them Israelis, half Palestinians.

Among the radio's scoops was a conversation, mediated by Ziad Darwish, one of the station's Arab broadcasters who also knows good Hebrew, between Noam Shalit, the father of a kidnapped Israeli soldier, Gilad Shalit, and Abu Mujahad, spokesman of the Popular Resistance Committees, one of the groups holding Shalit. Negotiations for releasing the soldier in return for Palestinian prisoners in Israel jails had been dragging on for months.

Clearly the radio exchange between the two men was not any sort of negotiation for Shalit's release, but they did discuss openly the question of whether the Palestinians had passed on a list of prisoners they were hoping to exchange for the Israeli soldier and Noam Shalit offered to travel to Gaza and remain in Hamas captivity until an agreement was reached.

In an interesting development, the station agreed to give up a considerable sum of USAID funds because it refused to ban Hamas from the airwaves. "We could not say we were only interested in half the Palestinian population," Palestinian codirector Maysa Baransi-Siniora explained. "It's not about agreeing or disagreeing with Hamas. The movement represents large numbers of Palestinians."

All for Peace is an initiative of Hana Siniora's Biladi company in partnership with the Jewish-Arab Center for Peace of Givat Haviva, the educational institution of the former Kibbutz Artzi movement. The Givat Haviva campus is situated in the coastal plain southeast of Hadera. Easily accessible to numerous Jewish and Arab communities, it has been active for many years in bringing Jews and Arabs together.

Dating as it does to before the Six Day War, Givat Haviva is one of the two veteran Jewish-Arab coexistence organizations operating today. The other is Beit Hagefen [House of the Vine] the Arab-Jewish center in Haifa. These veteran institutions are the subject of our next chapter.

15

The Veterans in the Field

Imagine that you turn on the television to hear that Netzarim settlement is being bombed by Palestinian Apaches (attack helicopters). Twenty people have been killed and a hundred injured. Ambulances can't even reach the place where people are bleeding (some to death) because of the Palestinian checkpoints and the curfew. Imagine that the next item on the news is a massacre at the Western Wall. Two armed Palestinians succeeded in penetrating security, entered the place, and shot people without mercy. The news reveals that, according to medical tests taken later, they had mental complexes, so no legal procedure can be taken to punish them.

Thus opens an article in the bimonthly English language magazine *Crossing Borders*, published at Givat Haviva. It is the contribution of Palestinian high school student, Ala Maaytah, who explains that his idea is "to get you to imagine for a minute suffering yourselves in the inverted ways I have described." He goes on to concede that Israelis are also victims. He imagines himself as an Israeli Jew having lunch at a restaurant or traveling on a bus and being bombed. He visualizes going abroad and being afraid of wearing a Star of David. He concludes by proposing "to leave the world of imagination and think about solutions to our own problems, which would seriously help stop others' suffering."

Crossing Borders is a cooperative venture of Israeli Jews and Arabs, Jordanians, and Palestinians. A project of Denmark's International People's College, supported by the European Union and the Danish Foreign Ministry, its Israeli office is at the Jewish-Arab Center in the green, kibbutzlike campus of Givat Haviva.

Although, as its name suggests, the magazine is a transborder project and Givat Haviva chiefly concentrates on the internal Israeli situation, there is something characteristic of Givat Haviva in Maaytah's article. The irreverence, the direct, blunt, no-holds-barred style, the way it genuinely tries to see all sides is very much the way the center operates. "Our agenda is to put the conflict on the table," states Ferhat Agbariya, the codirector of the center's Face-to-Face project, which sets up encounters of Jewish and Arab high school students. "We don't run away from the problems, we meet them head-on."

Agbariya, a trim fifty-eight year-old with flecks of gray in his thick hair, was born and raised in the village of Musmus in Wadi Ara, an area of Arab towns and villages east of Hadera. After high school in Nazareth and political science studies at Tel Aviv University, he worked for a time in the Haifa office of the Ministry of Welfare, but he was interested in making contact with his Jewish fellow citizens and went to work for Interns for Peace training community workers to work in Israeli Arab villages and in the Palestinian territories. He has also been involved in Seeds of Peace, which takes Israeli, Palestinian, Egyptian, and Jordanian children to a summer camp every year in the Maine woods. His main work, however, has been at Givat Haviva. "It is my life's project," he says simply. "It is for my children's future."

The Face-to-Face workshop is almost always the first time the Jewish and Arab students meet each other, he notes. They start out by getting to know each other in a positive atmosphere. If they become friends at a personal level, that is a good thing, but that is not the primary aim. The most important things are that the students learn about each other's cultures and become aware of their own identity and the identity of the other side. They study the Israeli-Palestinian conflict and the Jewish-Arab situation inside Israel. They discuss political differences.

Usually about 120 students show up. They are divided into smaller groups of up to twenty children. Each group has an Arab and a Jewish facilitator who have been trained to manage the encounter. "We talk about the occupation and the actions of the IDF," explains Agbariya. "We deal with the suffering of the Palestinians, the discrimination endured by Israeli Arabs. We don't hold back anything. I see our work as a point of light in the dark reality."

"I serve in the IDF," notes Shachar Yannai, the Jewish codirector of Face-to-Face. "I know that it is very difficult for my Arab colleagues to accept this. I fought in Lebanon in the war this summer. It was really odd. There I was in combat against Arabs, and I was talking on the phone with my Arab friends from Givat Haviva, who called me to ask how I was. The other soldiers were very aware that I was talking on my mobile phone in Arabic, and were curious."

His fellow soldiers reacted very positively when they heard that his civilian job was bringing groups of Jewish and Arab kids together for dialogue. Regardless of their political views, they felt that he was engaged in a praiseworthy endeavor. They were impressed with the fact that he was dealing with values and not just making money. "Israel is a confused society," opines the tall, gangling Yannai. "You can hear a soldier saying something and its opposite in the same conversation."

He did not feel ambivalent about going to war in Lebanon after the Hezbollah kidnapped two soldiers and killed another eight, but he is more doubtful about serving in the territories. He thinks it might be much more difficult for him, but so far, he hasn't faced that situation. As someone who has grown up as a Zionist, he sometimes finds it uncomfortable to work with Arabs, who see Zionism as a swear word. He is not prepared to give up on his Zionism. "Rather than viewing the conflict as an Israeli-Palestinian, or Jewish-Arab, or even Muslim-Jewish, it is really a confrontation between Zionism and Palestinian nationalism," he suggests.

Yannai grew up in Ein Hashofet, one of the earliest settlements of the left-wing Kibbutz Artzi movement. He was educated there before serving in the IDF for five years, two of them in the professional army. Philosophy studies at Ben-Gurion University and a stint as headmaster of a boarding school followed before he ended up at Givat Haviva.

"We don't actually use the word *peace* in our workshops," he points out. "Our emphasis is on communication, dialogue, and coexistence." The first stage is to make contact with the schools, he explains. After the initial meeting with the school director, he and Agbariya meet with the class teachers to prepare the children. The teachers present the information and facilitators are dispatched to prepare them from a psychological point of view. The two-day workshop follows, including discussions, cultural events, a party, and overnight accommodation.

The basic assumption is that every participant talks in the language easiest for him or her, with the facilitators translating where necessary. Sometimes the Arabs talk Hebrew, sometimes they talk Arabic on principle, and sometimes the discussions take place in a mixture of languages, including English, but Hebrew tends to predominate. The fact is that most Israeli Arabs speak Hebrew, the majority language, whereas very few Jews know Arabic.

Givat Haviva sometimes feels it is "swimming against the stream," and therefore it has been encouraged recently by renewed sympathetic interest from the Ministry of Education. The ministry's current director-general has expressed personal support for the Face-to-Face project, which means it should be easier to recruit more schools to the scheme. Some two thousand students from thirty schools participated in 2006, and the plan is to recruit double that number in 2007. The eventual aim is to reach a third of all high school students. "We're not going to get to all of them," admits Yannai. "I want a situation where we are less marginal. I want young soldiers who reminisce about their school days and recall meetings with Arab students, to find that at least some of their fellows have also attended one of our workshops."

Agbariya and Yannai admit that only very few schools repeat the program two years running. Yannai explains that two days, plus the preparation and follow-up, are a large chunk out of the school timetable. Most schools, he thinks, want to achieve impressive matriculation results, and the Givat Ha-viva program uses up valuable time that could be spent on raising standards. There are, however, follow-up programs at the individual schools, in which both men participate. In addition they have observed a completely unanticipated "e-mail aftereffect."

"Even our generation doesn't appreciate the computer revolution," states Yannai. "These kids all have computers and they remain in touch via the Internet. They exchange e-mails, establish chat rooms, and make use of the various encounter forums on the web, like ICQ. Globalization is proving a huge asset in our work. For example, I found out that some kids who had participated in one of our less successful encounters were subsequently in touch with each other on a regular basis. They have their own computer language, you know."

Fifty-eight-year-old Agbariya is a veteran in the business of conciliation, whereas Yannai, twenty years younger, has only been directly involved for two years. He admits to admiring people who can keep it up for decades, but he is not sure how long he can keep going. "It forces you to deal with the problem all the time," he points out. "Every moment of the day you are dealing with the Jewish-Arab confrontation. It is natural that you ask yourself whether you want this constant friction. What keeps me going is the knowledge that the alternative is worse. If there is no dialogue then there is conflict."

Eighteen teenagers, boys and girls, Jews, Arabs and Druze sit on the sunny lawn under the pines and poplars. They are dressed in jeans and T-shirts and are shod in the latest style of sneakers. Some of the girls wear earrings, as does one of the boys. All of them—yes, all!—have cell phones. Yasmine, Baruch, Nissim, Ahab, Noga, Ahmad, Adam, Netta, Hava, and the others sit in a circle, divide into smaller groups, go inside to continue the discussion, break for refreshments, smile, scowl, talk, listen, think, communicate. They talk in Hebrew and Arabic. Until they open their mouths, it is impossible to tell who is Jewish and who Arab. Even the body language is indistinguishable. Fadi, the Arab facilitator, translates the Arabic. The Hebrew doesn't need translation. They talk about everything, switch subjects abruptly, react unexpectedly. The control of the two facilitators, Fadi and Yanna, is light. Only rarely do they intervene to try to guide the discussion.

This is their second day. They talked all yesterday afternoon, ate supper together, and spent the evening together. On a personal level, they have become friendly. They intermingle, giggle a bit, and smile at each other, but they haven't reached the nitty-gritty yet. Attempts by the facilitators to stimulate discussion on majority-minority relations, cultural identity, or civil rights fall flat.

Then—suddenly—they are arguing bitterly. It is the issue of terror, Palestinian suicide bombings, and IDF actions in the territories that has them going, although these are not issues that directly affect them. In a couple of years, the Jews and Druze will be recruited into the army and then they may be in the thick of it, but they aren't there yet. As for these Israeli Arabs, they won't be directly involved. Nevertheless, this is the topic that stimulates an animated dispute.

"The difference between us is that we don't glorify killing," cries one of the Jewish girls.

"How many virgins in heaven do you get as a reward for a suicide bombing?" asks a muscular boy with long, curly hair.

"What about the Palestinians who are killed by your soldiers?" retorts a tall, broad-shouldered youngster, just sprouting a small beard.

"That's different," claims the girl, brushing her thick hair from her forehead. "Our army kills terrorists—they are defending you Israeli Arabs as well."

"What about all the Palestinian *civilians* who are shot?"

"That is by accident. We don't do it on purpose!"

"So a five-year-old kid shoots himself?"

"No, they put their five-year-olds in the front line, they sacrifice them."

"Why do you think a suicide bomber blows himself up?"

"It's your education—you believe in sacrifice."

"Nonsense, it's because his mother and father have been killed by soldiers."

"Look, it's just as tragic for a Palestinian mother of a kid who is killed, as it is for an Israeli mother—I admit that."

As the argument continues, the anger, which has never threatened to become extreme, slowly burns itself out. After another break, the facilitators take more direct control, handing out pieces of paper and pencils and asking the participants to write down what they consider the most important events in recent history.

Every single Jew writes down the Holocaust as number one. After that, they propose the Israeli Declaration of Independence, the War of Independence, the two Intifadas. Most Arabs rate the Nakba, the catastrophe of Israel's creation, as the most important happening, even though it happened long before their birth. One of the boys, who has family in Lebanon, puts forward a much more recent example: Kafr Kana, a Lebanese village, which suffered dozens of casualties from Israeli shelling on two separate occasions. A Druze girl cites her community's 1950s decision to serve in the Israeli army as significant.

Breaking up into smaller groups, they discuss the various historical events. The facilitators try to get the Jews to describe the Nakba through Arab and Druze eyes and the Arabs to view the creation of Israel through Jewish spectacles. This attempt at role reversal is only partly successful. It is clearly very difficult for all the teenagers to imagine themselves on the other side.

In a final session, Yanna, the Jewish facilitator, places a flower and a thorny branch on the floor in the center of the circle and asks the participants to present each other with flowers or thorns to symbolize what they have come to feel about each other. A smiling Jewish girl presents the flower to the bearded Arab youth. "We argued," she tells him, "and we still disagree about lots of things, but it was really fun being with you."

An Arab boy presents the thorn branch to his Jewish counterpart and invites him to close his hand tightly around it, "so you can understand what the Nakba was like for us."

One of the Jewish girls, who had adopted a notably self-righteous tone earlier, now admits that she has learned a lot about the Arab point of view and presents the flower to one of the Arab girls. "We don't learn enough about this in school," she tells her teacher, who has come in for the final session.

"You have learned it here," replies the teacher. "You are now an ambassador. All of you are: you have both responsibility and a measure of authority. Make sure you communicate what you have learned here to your friends."

"A twenty-five hour workshop cannot change minds or alter the world," sums up Yanna, a relatively recent immigrant, whose Hebrew still has traces of a Russian accent. "If one of you has acquired one question mark about the relations between Jews and Arabs in Israel, this will not have been in vain."

"We have to recognize that Hebrew has been dominant," adds Fadi. "That is the reality, but if I have helped to balance things up slightly, at least to give Arabic some status here, or at least symbolic equality, that is worthwhile."

Face-to-Face is only one of the programs at Givat Haviva. In addition to the All for Peace radio station and the English language magazine *Crossing Borders*, Children Teaching Children, a two-year program for elementary school children in which some three thousand kids have participated, has been a notable success. The center also organizes training programs for young leaders in Israel's Arab community, including a student councils program, leadership groups in schools, and special courses for teachers and employees of local councils. It has established a Galilee regional center for this purpose in the Arab town of Sakhnin.

Givat Haviva is also heavily engaged in teaching Arabic—particularly spoken Arabic—and offering courses in Arabic culture, including enrichment courses in schools. Dozens of books and research papers are published annually by Givat Haviva's Institute for Peace Research and the center also maintains a large reference facility, the Peace Library, with seventy thousand titles and an impressive archive.

Among the newer coexistence projects are sports programs, notably soccer games, and art workshops. A special project called Sailing Together is organized in conjunction with the Jewish Maritime League. After the training, a small group of Arab and Jewish youngsters spends twelve days sailing off the coast of Cape Town. "The point about sailing," notes one participant, "is that you can't manage on your own. You have to work together."

The art project includes photography, with the young photographers visiting each other's communities to take pictures. The latest idea, planned for the fall, is a Children's March for Peace in conjunction with other peace groups, schools, and youth movements.

Some thirty miles to the north of Givat Haviva, the city of Haifa sprawls over the green Mount Carmel above a beautiful bay. Israel's third largest city and its main port, Haifa is also one of the few Israeli communities where Jews and Arabs have always lived together amicably. Although there was savage fighting in the town before and during the 1948 war, and as a result, the vast majority of the Arab inhabitants fled to Syria and Lebanon, Haifa was one of the few places where the Jewish mayor and other civic leaders publicly called on their Arab neighbors not to leave. Sadly, in the bitter atmosphere of the time, the plea was ineffective, and less than 10 percent remained.

Today some forty thousand of Haifa's 275,000 inhabitants are Arabs, two-thirds of them Christians, and the town prides itself on the good relations between its different communities. In the monthlong Lebanon war in the summer of 2006, Hezbollah rockets killed Arabs as well as Jews. In contrast to what happened in 1948, Haifa's Arab citizens did not leave even when urged to do so by Hezbollah leader Hassan Nasrallah. Immediately after the war, Beit Hagefen's Arab director Hani Elfar declared: "Arabs and Jews in Haifa are more determined than ever to continue the path of coexistence, and we have actually expanded the scope of our joint activities."

Beit Hagefen [House of the Vine] operates out of three buildings in downtown Haifa, between the German Colony, a neighborhood built by the German Templar sect at the end of the nineteenth century, and Wadi Nisnas, a picturesque quarter where many of the city's Christian Arab inhabitants live. Founded in 1963, the same year that Givat Haviva's Jewish-Arab Center started its activities, Beit Hagefen is supported by the Haifa Municipality and Israel's Ministry of Education. The center has an equal number of Jewish and Arab board members and an Arab director, Hani Elfar.

A Star of David, a cross, and a crescent, representing Judaism, Christianity, and Islam, greet the visitor at the main entrance to Beit Hagefen. Inside hangs a "carpet of peace," one panel embroidered with a peace symbol against a background of Israeli and Palestinian flags, another with three doves representing the three religions. A third panel has a pistol with its barrel tied in a knot; the word peace in Hebrew and Arabic is the central motif of another panel.

Posted on the notice board is a timetable of classes and groups for ceramics and pottery, sculpture, modeling, children's karate, gymnastics, ballet, belly dancing, and spoken Arabic. An art gallery displays paintings by Farid Abu-Shukra, Gideon Sela, Wafa Yassin, David Riv, and Assad Azi side by side.

Outside in the street, a large notice advertises coexistence walks. Led by director Hani Elfar and other guides from Beit Hagefen, these walks pass through Wadi Nisnas, the German Colony, and other parts of the city. There is an Art Works route leading past galleries where Arab and Jewish artists exhibit and sculptures by artists from all the communities. Plaques with poetry in Hebrew and Arabic line the Poetry Path route, and other sites visited in the walks include the Ahmadim Mosque, the Stella Maris Monastery, and the cave of the Prophet Elijah on Mount Carmel.

There are also walks through the Bahai Gardens, emphasizing the warm relations with the Bahai, a sect founded in Iran in the nineteenth century, which has its world headquarters in the rose-domed Universal House of Justice, set in spectacular gardens on Mount Carmel above Beit Hagefen. A new branch of the center, called the Abbas Community Center, is named after Abdel-Baha Abbas, one of the founders of the Bahai faith.

The Festival of Festivals, which marks Christmas, Hanukkah, and Ramadan and which draws more than one hundred thousand visitors to Wadi Nisnas, is another event promoted by the center. This year, says the director, the festival was more than a religious celebration; it was a tribute to Haifa's healing in the wake of the recent conflict.

Beit Hagefen also operates on a national level, introducing Israelis to Arab literature, folklore, and crafts by means of an Arab Culture Month in the spring. The center's Elkarma Arab Theater puts on some four hundred performances for children and adults all over the country, including plays in Hebrew for presentation to Jewish audiences. It has also performed in the Palestinian Authority, Morocco, and a number of European countries.

Every two years, Beit Hagefen organizes an international conference of religious leaders. Jewish, Muslim, Druze and Bahai leaders, Christians from all the churches, and other religious leaders come from sixty countries, including the Palestinian Authority, Jordan, Turkey, Morocco, the Americas, and several European and Asian countries. The religious personalities also hold meetings with young people from the local youth movements.

Beit Hagefen promotes a range of outreach activities, including visits between Jewish and Arab schools. On a blustery spring day, a bus full of ten-year-old Arab Christians from the Carmelite School in Wadi Nisnas comes to visit the Nofim School on Mount Carmel, where they meet with a class of their Jewish counterparts.

They start off by sitting in a large circle in the Nofim gymnasium. One of the Nofim children greets the guests and a Carmelite student replies in excellent Hebrew. The Jewish and Arab facilitators distribute labels marked peace, welcome, coexistence, meeting, and Jews and Arabs, which the children pin on their sweatshirts. The children are invited to get up and look for their own groups, which they do quickly and noisily. They now sit in five smaller circles, some of them on the floor. Although the Jews and Arabs have become mixed up into smaller groups, they maintain a clear segregation into sexes, with girls and boys facing each other on either side of the circles.

Zehava, one of the Jewish facilitators, calls out the names of the different groups, upon which the children have to give two loud synchronized claps. She is less than satisfied with the first round, but the children improve as the game progresses, and the claps come loud and clear. Within each group, the facilitators get the kids to introduce themselves.

Wassam, the Druze facilitator of the peace group, introduces himself and says he likes tennis. Ardash, a boy from the Carmelite School, proclaims that he likes football, followed by Mario, who says that he likes eating (loud laughter). Nardine, a girl, likes a local ball game called *mahanayim*, Sharon likes playing with her friends, John prefers computer games, Katie also likes *mahanayim*, but Yannai is one of the football enthusiasts. As each child must repeat the names of all those who have gone before, they are learning each other's names.

In an attempt to counter the dominance of Hebrew, the children are divided into three groups, each named after a vegetable (tomato, potato, and cucumber) in Arabic. A chair is removed from the circle, and Wassam starts off the game by telling a story. When he says "tomato," all the "tomatoes" have to change places. They rush around enthusiastically. Each time one of them ends up without a chair. That is the one who has to tell the next story. Sometimes, the kids just shout, "Salad!" and then all the children have to change places. After some ten minutes, the children are warmed up physically and mentally, and they also know each other's names.

The next game involves writing their names on bits of paper in Hebrew and Arabic, mixing up the papers, distributing them, and then finding them again, after which the large circle is resumed and refreshments distributed: pita with humus, potato chips, nuts, sweets, and Coca-Cola.

The time has come to go outside into the yard, where again the sexes automatically segregate. The boys play football; the girls participate in a circle dance involving a clapping rhythmic song and an individual girl dancing around the circle, performing opposite another girl; then the girls change places. Zehava asks whether there is a name for this game, which both Jewish and Arab girls know well. Apparently there isn't.

The next activity is joint classes for math, nature, English, and music. In the music class, the local teacher teaches the children a Hebrew song. She compliments the Arab girls on the speed with which they learn the melody, but berates the boys. Slightly ashamed, the boys make an effort and actually sing quite well.

She then plays an Arab song on a CD machine. One of the Arab facilitators says that her children learned this song last week. As the tune plays, all the children dance in their seats, moving their bodies, arms, and shoulders in time with the music. Another Hebrew song follows. It turns out that the Arab children know "Bim-Bam-Bom," a popular ditty from the 1960s, just as well as their Jewish counterparts. They all sing at the tops of their voices.

Finally, it's back to the gymnasium for the summing up. The children are by now uninhibited. The Jewish and Arab kids wrestle energetically within their own groups, but are far gentler when wrestling each other. The Arabs manifestly take care not to hurt their Jewish opponents and vice versa.

In another month, it will be the turn of the Jewish children to come down the hill to visit their Arab guests, but they are not waiting for the next get-together. They are all on the floor with their pens, pencils, and pieces of paper, exchanging e-mail addresses and mobile phone numbers, just like their older counterparts did at Givat Haviva. The electronic revolution is clearly something to be reckoned with.

In their multifaceted activities, Beit Hagefen and Givat Haviva, the veteran Jewish-Arab centers, continue to prove that the two peoples can live together amicably in Israel and cooperate in numerous fields. The former has won awards from UNESCO and the Albert Schweitzer Foundation. The latter has won admiration and recognition from around the world. Both have been in business for more than four decades and show no signs of slowing up—still less giving up.

Although Givat Haviva, in the tradition of its left-wing kibbutz founders, has remained resolutely secular, Beit Hagefen does, as we have seen, include religious elements in its activities, notably in its Festival of Festivals and its meetings between religious leaders.

The last meeting between the religious leaders issued a declaration including an appeal for tolerance, a condemnation of violence, a call to political leaders to work for a just peace in the Middle East, and a request to teachers to design an educational program for peace.

There is a distinct message here that religion does not have to be a divisive force. In our next chapter, we will visit some of the interfaith organizations that seek to place religion in the forefront of the Jewish-Arab-Israeli-Palestinian encounter. Many religious leaders insist that, far from being the root cause of the problem, religion can be an integral part of the solution. They maintain that engagement between the different religions offers a valid path toward mutual acceptance, if not agreement.

16

Religious Faith:
Problem or Solution?

It was a riveting moment, unscripted and unexpected: the two hundred or so people in the auditorium—Jews, Muslims, Christians, and Druze—burst into spontaneous applause at the Hebrew interjection by Sheikh Kamal Riyan of the Israeli Islamic Movement. "When we started *Kedem*, we were afraid, weren't we? We turned our backs on each other and hesitated to speak, but since then we have made progress, haven't we? We have become brothers, Rabbi Brin, haven't we? Even when we disagree, we are friends. Don't let us be afraid to talk about anything and everything!"

It was not that the previous two hours had been free of controversy or that the speakers had been particularly moderate in their language. Some extremely outspoken remarks had been made by the Jewish, Muslim, and Christian participants, but the proceedings had been formal, with each participant expressing himself in his own language—Hebrew, Arabic, or English—simultaneously translated. At this point, however, laying his hand affectionately on the shoulder of his Jewish opposite number, Sheikh Riyan crashed through the language barrier to express his gut feelings.

Although it was Rabbi Brin whom he addressed directly, Riyan was reacting to earlier remarks by another speaker, Yitzhak Levy, a rabbi and Knesset member of the extreme right-wing National Union Party. Levy had suggested that, as it was impossible to agree on political issues such as the establishment of a Palestinian state, the assembled religious leaders should limit themselves to social matters, such as fostering family values, curbing violence, and combating corruption.

"Please don't ask me not to talk about Palestine," continued Riyan. "It is my life. We and the Palestinians possess the same blood! What would you have said if somebody had told you to forget a Jewish state in 1948 and concentrate on family values?"

The very fact that Levy, Brin, and Riyan could sit down together was in itself remarkable. Levy and Brin are convinced that the whole land of Israel belongs to the Jews, and Brin is a West Bank settler. Riyan, of the Islamic Movement, believes that the area between the Mediterranean and the Jordan River should be a Palestinian Muslim state.

The three of them were participating with three others in a public symposium, "Cooperation between Religious and Political Leaders," part of a three-day conference of Jewish, Muslim, Christian, and Druze leaders in Jerusalem organized by Kedem: Voices for Religious Conciliation. At the end of the conference, sheikhs of the Islamic Movement condemned the Holocaust denial meeting in Tehran, which had just taken place, and a group of National Religious Party rabbis protested against the damage caused to a Muslim cemetery in Jerusalem by the construction of a museum. Despite their diametrically opposing views, the leaders of the three monotheistic religions found themselves able to agree on a host of issues and to remain on friendly terms when they disagreed.

"It enriches us to live together with Jews, Muslims, and Druze," declared Father Nadim Shakour, a Maronite priest. "But my love for my Jewish friends does not permit me to forget—or to let others forget—our village of Birim." Birim, a Christian Arab village on Israel's northern border, was evacuated during the 1948 fighting. The villagers were assured that their departure was temporary and that they would be allowed to return, but in the intervening years successive Israeli governments have cited reasons of "security" to prevent the former villagers from living there. Shakour was deliberately raising this controversial matter.

Knesset member Menachem Ben-Sasson of the centrist Kadima Party recalled the Golden Age in Spain, when Jews and Muslims conferred together. He suggested that it was possible to learn from the past, when Muslims, Jews, and others had sat together in a Majlis [assembly]. Although compromise might seem like a rude word in today's religion-dominated Middle East, Ben-Sasson allowed, in the past Islam had found a formula for religious coexistence that lasted more than four centuries

Muhammad was a religious and a political leader, observed Abbas Zekoor, a Muslim Arab Knesset member. He opposed idol worship, and the members of all three religions agree with his stand. Religion cannot stop hatred, but hatred should be directed against Satan, the common enemy. Zekoor, who is also a preacher at his local mosque, lauded the recent cooperation between Jews, Muslims, and Christians in opposing a planned Gay Pride Parade in Jerusalem.

Shlomo Brin, a rabbi and a resident of the Jewish settlement of Alon Shvut near Bethlehem, insisted that it was impossible to ignore a complex reality in which Israeli Arabs supported Israel's enemies. Nevertheless, Jews and Arabs could cooperate based on ethical and religious obligations. "We believe in the God of Abraham, who brought morality and ethics to the world," he proclaimed. "Muslims fast for thirty days during Ramadan; Jews observe *kashrut* dietary laws. We both know that we must learn to control ourselves, and cannot do everything we want to do."

The conference fully vindicated the principles of Kedem, which was formed in 2002 to bring the members of the three religions together. In the past, the movement denounced the caricatures of the Prophet Muhammad published in the European media, but it also criticized police violence against right-wing Jewish settlers on the West Bank during the evacuation of a settlement. The movement espouses the belief that Muslims, Jews, and Christians do have a basis for dialogue, and the Jerusalem assembly proved that this is the case.

This view is shared by Dr. Yehuda Stolov, founder and codirector of the Interfaith Encounter Association (IEA), another of the many religious groups seeking communication and dialogue. Religion, he believes, is not the great divider that many people think it is; faith can be a positive force for mutual understanding and respect. "Politics needs agreement, which is difficult to attain," he points out. "The religious model, on the other hand, allows you to live harmoniously with disagreements."

Citing an example of this, Stolov talks about the Mishnah, the great Jewish work of commentary composed between 200 BCE and 200 CE, in which the rabbis argue incessantly over the meaning of the Bible. He notes that Islam also has various alternative streams. Interreligious dialogue, he maintains, is an effective channel toward greater understanding between Jews, Muslims, and Christians. "We of the IEA have no political agenda," he explains. "We are aiming to ensure that life is tolerable no matter what political settlement is reached. To take this principle to its extreme: life should be reasonable for everyone, even if Israel-Palestine were to become an ultra-Orthodox Jewish state, or a Hamas state."

Stolov is an unlikely campaigner for religious dialogue and understanding. Growing up in a traditional home, he attended a religious school, joined the National Religious youth movement, and became fully observant while still in his teens. After studying at the famous Mercaz HaRav Yeshiva in Jerusalem, which has served as the ideological hothouse of the Jewish settlement movement in the occupied territories, Stolov was part of the settlement group of one of the movement's most controversial colonizing projects: Joseph's Tomb Yeshiva in the heart of Nablus, the largest Palestinian city on the West Bank.

"Back in 1984, relations with the locals were still quite good," he recalls. "But even then I believed there should be more contact with the Palestinians, although I had not yet developed my current approach."

I remark that his settler friends would never identify the "Arabs of Judea and Samaria" as "Palestinians."

"I call them what they call themselves," he replies. "I have no problem with that, but I never refer to the land itself as 'Palestine.'"

Stolov doesn't see anything contradictory in his identity as a former settler and his role as a proponent of interfaith dialogue. He admits that his Palestinian interlocutors often don't know how to relate to his past, but he has not found them hostile. It certainly does not put a stop to the dialogue.

It was several years after his time at Joseph's Tomb, when he was studying at the Hartman Institute in Jerusalem, that Stolov met a fellow student who was in contact with interreligious groups and found himself intrigued. He had already completed a doctorate in physics at the Hebrew University.

His initial interfaith discussions were with Christians living in Jerusalem, most of them European. He studied the origins of Christianity and then moved on to Islam, becoming increasingly convinced that discussion and joint study could help to prevent hatred and increase understanding. In 2001, he got together with a group of Muslims and Christians and formed the Interfaith Encounter Association. As time went on, he felt that it was more important to forge links with local Arab Muslims than with Christians from abroad. Although three-way contacts continue, the main focus is on the Jewish-Muslim encounter.

Most of the seventeen IEA encounter groups are in Israel, although the six Jerusalem groups include Palestinians who are not Israeli citizens. Since the second Intifada, it has been more difficult to make contacts with Palestinians, but IEA still manages to organize meetings in Israel and those parts of the Palestinian territories where Israelis are allowed to go. They have also held meetings in Amman, the capital of Jordan, and plan encounters in Europe and North America.

During the recent month of Ramadan, when Muslims fast from dawn to dusk, two meetings were held at the Hope Flowers School in Al-Khader, a suburb of Bethlehem, on the subjects of forgiveness and reward, which are two of the concepts dealt with by Muslims during the monthlong fast. The two ideas were considered from the Islamic and Jewish points of view.

Although Hope Flowers School is situated in so-called Area C, which is under Israeli security control, it is not easy to reach it. We had to clamber over high earth ramparts of the type that the Israeli security forces have erected around the West Bank towns and villages as a security measure. After the separation fence is completed, it will become even more difficult to reach Hope Flowers.

The school was founded by Hussein Issa, a Palestinian educator who had grown up in a refugee camp. He instituted a unique educational system with the children learning the conventional subjects in morning classes and receiving special peace and democracy classes in the afternoons. He also organized psychological counseling for both children and adults. The school claims that not one of its graduates has been involved in suicide bombings or other acts of violence.

Hope Flowers started out in 1984 as a kindergarten for twenty children in a rented room. Within a decade, the school was licensed in its new building and educating some 250 Muslim and Christian students up to grade twelve. The school conducted exchange programs with Israeli schools and all the students learned Hebrew. Plans for further expansion have been stymied by the network of Israeli check points, roadblocks, and barriers, which make it impossible for many of the students to reach Al-Khader. As a result, the number of pupils has actually declined.

We are welcomed to the school by Ibrahim Issa, son of the founder and current coprincipal, who tells us that Hope Flowers believes in coexistence and mutual respect between "the three Abrahamic religions." We divide into two circular groups to discuss the question of forgiveness: Philip, a Jewish Israeli, originally from England; Ilana, a manifestly religious American Israeli with a round hat of the type favored by Orthodox women; Hind, the Muslim codirector of the school, a solid Muslim woman in traditional caftan and kaffiyeh head covering; Hitham, a very modern-looking young lady in jeans, who is a sports instructor at Hope Flowers; Muhammad, local director of the Palestinian Red Crescent; Hala, his wife; Meg, an American Christian volunteer teacher from Bethlehem; and Rachel, a teacher from Jerusalem, in addition to Yehuda Stolov and myself.

Rachel, gray-haired, intense, and patently sincere, tells us the story of her mother, who hurt her deeply, but whom she felt unable to forgive until her death. It was only later, after she had a child of her own, that she found forgiveness in her heart. Hala suggests that a person has to empty himself or herself of hatred before he or she can forgive. There can be no reconciliation between Jews and Arabs, she feels, as long as the separation wall exists. Her husband, Muhammad, confesses to a feeling that his hard work for the Red Crescent is not always appreciated, and this sometimes angers him, but he says that he is able to forgive.

Hind, the coprincipal, speaks of a child who has been taught to hate. He is frightened. His father has been imprisoned and he has witnessed his uncle being beaten by Israeli soldiers. The most difficult thing to forgive is injustice. Nevertheless, when conditions improve, people will forget their fear and hatred and learn to cooperate. Hitham points out that those present do not represent the Palestinian majority. She herself finds it difficult to forgive. If you don't liberate yourself and forgive with a full heart, God will not accept this. Ibrahim and Yehuda both explain that human forgiveness precedes divine forgiveness in Islam and Judaism.

For a few minutes, we lighten the tone, exchanging experiences about different types of fasting. The Muslims describe what it is like to fast every day from sunrise to sundown. The morning, says Hala, is no big deal, but toward the afternoon, you feel increasingly hungry. The Jews talk about their Yom Kippur fast. This lasts for only one day, but that day is more than twenty-five hours. The Muslims express amazement at such a long time without food and drink. It is then time to break for the special *Iftar* dinner, which breaks the fast for the Muslim participants but is simply a pleasant meal for the Jewish guests.

At supper, I sit next to Ibrahim, the coprincipal, a good natured-man whose wire-rimmed spectacles constantly slip down his nose to be pushed back from time to time. His diabetes prevents him from fasting the whole month, but he fasts as long as he can. Formally, he is a Muslim, he explains, like his father who founded the school, but he really regards himself as "interfaith."

The school building is now large enough for more than eight hundred students, he tells me. At their peak, they had some five hundred, including the high school, but because of the situation, they are down to two hundred fifty elementary school pupils, who are all from the immediate vicinity. "Neither side likes us because we are a school of peace," he asserts. "The Palestinians have withdrawn our license and the Israelis blockade us and prevent our kids from getting here."

He recalls a conversation with an official of the Israeli Shin Bet security service. He has had many meetings with Israeli soldiers and security men, he notes, but this time the two really hit it off. "He asked me what he could do to help," he relates. "I told him, three things: one, let our children come to the school from all over the West Bank; two, help me to renew my contacts with the Jewish schools, which have been disrupted by the barricades; and three, stop arresting me. Of course he couldn't help with my first two requests, but I have to say that, since that conversation, I have not been arrested."

Unlike most Palestinians, Ibrahim does not blame the Israelis entirely for the current situation. He acknowledges that the Palestinians side did not have a peace strategy. They did not reassure the Israelis, but on the contrary scared them with suicide bombings, which made them put up the separation wall.

The farewell greetings were extremely warm with strong embraces and mutual hopes for more meetings in the future. At the subsequent meeting, on the subject of reward, once of the participants was so struck by the similarities between Jewish and Muslim concepts that he was moved to declare: "The striking closeness of Islam to Judaism proves that Abraham taught Isaac and Ismail the same message!"

The most high-profile interfaith meeting to date was the 2002 conference in Alexandria. Hosted by Sheikh Muhammad Sayyed Tantawi, head of Egypt's

Al-Azhar University, and attended by George Carey, the Archbishop of Canterbury; Israeli Chief Rabbi Eliahu Bakshi-Doron; and Sheikh Taysir Tamimi, the head of the religious courts of the Palestinian Authority, it attracted worldwide attention. An impressive number of Jewish, Muslim, and Christian leaders from Israel, Egypt, and the Palestinian Authority were present. At the end of the conference, the religious leaders issued a joint declaration:

> According to our faith and traditions, killing innocents in the name of God is a desecration of His holy name and defames religion in the world. The violence in the Holy Land is an evil, which must be opposed by all people of good faith. We seek to live together as neighbors, respecting the integrity of each other's historical and religious inheritance. We call upon all to oppose incitement, hatred, and the misrepresentation of the other.

The range of interfaith meetings and encounters, while admittedly only involving a few hundred people, is remarkable, ranging from the meeting in Alexandria, to conferences such as that organized by Kedem in Jerusalem, to an assembly of fifty students in a university lecture room or half a dozen ordinary citizens of different faiths meeting over a cup of coffee.

The search for religious understanding is impressive, but occasionally a get-together can be less successful. A meeting that I attended in Jerusalem, devoted to a consideration of the festivals of Hanukkah, Christmas, and Eid al-Adha, turned out to be an earnest search for understanding that sometimes descended into farce.

Several sincere enthusiasts were joined on this occasion by a few manifest eccentrics, and for the most part, it was entertaining rather than enlightening. The Christian coordinator, a stocky, crop-haired lady with a severe expression, started off rather badly by interrogating a sweet lady in traditional *hijab* head covering who had come all the way to Jerusalem from the Arab village of Fureidis near Haifa to wish her Jewish friends Happy Hanukkah and her Christian friends Merry Christmas. "You were not invited," she told her. The Jewish woman who had brought her, a religiously observant person with her hair covered by a woolen hat, was bitterly insulted. She left the meeting, taking her Arab friend with her.

An explanation of the Jewish festival of Hanukkah, the "Festival of Lights," concentrated on this aspect rather than on the second century BCE Jewish revolt against the Syrian Greeks. A tiny flame, said the Jewish coordinator, can banish a roomful of darkness. As it is the fourth night of Hanukkah, and we light four candles, she suggested, let us meditate four times.

A massive blond Christian, with a full flowing beard and a giant crucifix dangling on his chest, then presented the story of Christmas, comparing the stable where Jesus was born, to a stable that he had seen under a house in the Arab village of Taiba. He also pointedly suggested that Jesus "resisted the Roman occupation." The parallel was rather obvious.

There followed a song in Esperanto, with the singer accompanying himself on a homemade guitar. He said he was Swedish but also seemed to be Jewish as evidenced by the skullcap on his unruly hair. His song over, he continued with a story about Rabbi Akiva, which the Christian coordinator pronounced "irrelevant." I tried to relieve the atmosphere with a mild joke about the real international language today being "broken English," but he reproved me in severe tones: "I am prepared for a serious discussion on Esperanto—not for foolish jokes!"

Another of those present was a Japanese-speaking Italian who gave a lengthy explanation of the various languages inscribed on his sweatshirt. An American Jew, a recent arrival apparently, talked about his experiences in Vietnam, where he had frequently met with Buddhists.

There followed a serious lecture about the Muslim festival of Id al-Adha, the festival of the sacrifice, by an Arab teacher from the Jerusalem suburb of Shu'afat. She informed us that this festival, which always falls around the time of Hanukkah and Christmas, commemorated the story in the Koran when Ibrahim forbore to sacrifice his son, Ismail, and sacrificed a ram instead. During the four-day festival, rams were sacrificed, roasted, and distributed to the needy. The celebration was often combined with the hajj, the pilgrimage to Mecca that all Muslims endeavor to carry out at least once in their lifetimes. It was a quiet, interesting presentation that contrasted somewhat with the rather abrasive exchanges that preceded it.

In the ensuing discussion, it was noted that in the biblical story it was Isaac, not Ismail, who was the sacrificial victim. The tall blond Christian observed that Jesus was also traditionally the "sacrificial lamb."

"Except that Jesus was in fact sacrificed, whereas Isaac/Ismail was not," I offered.

"Please, we are in an interfaith meeting," the Christian coordinator snapped at me. "We must call him Joshua. Jesus means 'his name will be blotted out' in the Talmud!"

This was news to the rest of us, and several people pointed out that "Jesus" was a universally accepted appellation. The coordinator would not be placated. "If you come here to our meeting," she declared in iron tones, "you newcomers must abide by the rules that we have laid down."

At this point, the plainly embarrassed Jewish and Muslim coordinators suggested that we break for food, which we all helped to prepare. The Arabs had brought pita and hummus; the Jews offered donuts, which have become traditionally associated with Hanukkah. The group broke up to chat informally during the meal, and even the Christian coordinator thawed out somewhat, but on that occasion I did not feel there was much profit in remaining. As this meeting showed, interfaith activities definitely tend to attract eccentrics, but most of the encounters are serious and constructive.

In this chapter, we have only uncovered the tip of the interfaith iceberg. Founded in 1991, the Interreligious Coordinating Council in Israel (ICCI) is an umbrella organization of more than seventy Jewish, Muslim, and Christian institutions actively working toward understanding between the different faiths. Meetings are going on up and down the country all the time. Furthermore, they include Jews and Muslims, Israelis and Palestinians who are far removed from the well-meaning leftists who usually are found at conciliation and coexistence programs.

Sheikh Kamal Riyan has observed that he feels more at home with National Religious rabbis than he does with Israeli secular peace activists. He points out that the rabbis are prepared to compromise over everything except halacha, religious law. Some of them are even prepared to accept the concept of Palestinian statehood. Rabbi Menachem Froman, a Jewish settler, told me long ago that the Arabs of Hebron, many of them devout Muslims, were more upset by the bikini-clad Jews on Israel's beaches than they were by his nearby settlement of Tekoa.

One does not have to be religious to find the interfaith exchanges fascinating and thought-provoking. They raise all sorts of new ideas. Is it possible that, despite the obvious dissonance, religion can be part of the solution, rather than the heart of the problem?

Our final chapter deals with the preeminent cooperation and coexistence operation on the scene: the Peres Center for Peace. It is not involved in interfaith matters, nor does it cover environmental topics. Both these subjects are adequately addressed by other groups, and the Peres Center aims to avoid duplication, assisting and plugging gaps where necessary. As we will see, it promotes a remarkably wide range of programs ranging from medical cooperation to peace education, and from economic partnership to sports.

17

First among Equals

Considering that there are so many organizations working for peace, cooperation, and coexistence between Israelis and Palestinians, how come the overall situation is so bad? This question has been puzzling me throughout the research and writing of this book, so I put it to Ron Pundak, director of the Peres Center for Peace, who also serves as cochairman of the Palestinian-Israeli Peace NGOs Forum, which has a membership of more than 100 groups.

"That is the paradox that we come across every day," he replies. "All my experience indicates that, despite the deteriorating situation, most Israelis and Palestinians want reconciliation and peace. This is reflected both in the range of our activities, and in all the public opinion polls. In my opinion, the political leadership is ten to fifteen years behind the public—on both sides."

He cites polls that show 50 percent of Israelis and Palestinians in favor of compromising for peace, even when the violence is raging, and 70 percent when the situation is relatively tranquil. He estimates that if a concrete peace agreement is on the table the approval rate will be nearer 80 percent.

Pundak heads the biggest, richest, and most visible organization working for reconciliation and cooperation between Israelis and Palestinians, with an international board that includes Jimmy Carter, Henry Kissinger, Mustafa Khalil, John Major, Valery Giscard d'Estaing, Mikhail Gorbachev, Nadine Gordimer, Amoz Oz, and many other well-known personalities. A panel like that enables the center to mobilize financial support for its various projects from American, European, and other international sources on a scale that other NGOs can only dream about. Despite this, Pundak emphatically repudiates any claim to leadership of the movement by the Peres Center: "We are simply one of the organizations," he observes, "a big one admittedly, but we have no imperialistic pretensions. There is a great deal of work to be done and there is room for everyone. We assist when we can and fill in where we should."

The Peres Center is not active in environmental cooperation or interfaith dialogue, as there are many other groups dealing with these matters, and it made a "strategic decision" not to deal with internal Israeli Arab matters. It plays an active role in almost very other type of activity involving Israelis and Palestinians.

With his black-rimmed glasses, earnest expression, and quiet, systematic style of speech, Ron Pundak suggests, more than anything else, a university lecturer. He does in fact have an academic background, but over the years, he has been intimately involved in contacts between Israelis and Palestinians at the highest levels. After serving in the IDF Intelligence Corps, he studied Middle East history at the Hebrew University, subsequently completing a doctorate at London's School of Oriental and African Studies. After service in the Mossad intelligence service, he worked as a journalist on *Haaretz* before being recruited by Deputy Foreign Minister Yossi Beilin to promote so-called Track II discussions with important Palestinian personalities.

Together with fellow academic Yair Hirshfeld, Pundak opened in 1992 the Oslo channel that led to the Oslo Agreement between Israel and the Palestinians, the establishment of the Palestinian Authority, and the peace process of the 1990s. The Israeli-Palestinian Economic Cooperation Forum (ECF) was also established, and he and Hirshfeld did the groundwork for a permanent accord framework that became known as the Beilin-Abu-Mazen document of 1995.

Pundak continued with his diplomatic activity beyond the unsuccessful Camp David summit of 2000, but the eruption of the second Intifada that fall effectively brought it to a stop. The following year Shimon Peres asked him to take over the Peres Center for Peace, which the former prime minister had established in 1996. Like many peace projects, the center was going through a difficult period because of the continuing violence between Israelis and Palestinians. Today, despite the problematic security situation, the center is thriving and actually expanding its activities in partnership with Palestinian institutions.

We have already come across one of the center's projects at Jerusalem's Hadassah Hospital, where it participated in the financing of a variety of training and enrichment programs for Palestinian doctors, nurses, and technicians.

Health, explains Pundak, is one of the four "pillars" on which the work of the center rests. Cooperation in all fields, but particularly joint economic and business ventures, is the second pillar; education for peace is the third pillar, and people-to-people contact is the fourth pillar.

The health services in the Palestinian territories, which were inadequate before the outbreak of the second Intifada, have deteriorated even more in the past six years. Today there is a huge humanitarian crisis in the West Bank and Gaza with the result that Palestinian population only has access to minimal health, education, and social services—and sometimes not even to those.

In response to the deteriorating public health situation, the Peres Center has created the Saving Children program, whereby Palestinian doctors have an option to apply to the center in cases where sickness cannot be diagnosed or has been diagnosed but cannot be treated in the Palestinian territories. In consultation with the Palestinian doctors, the sick children are transported to alternative Palestinian locations or, where necessary, to Israel. The center provides ambulances, which take the children to Israeli hospitals with their parents, and arranges entry permits with the security forces. The program pays for their hospitalization and aftercare and facilitates contacts between the Israeli hospitals and the local Palestinian doctors.

Some three thousand children have received medical care, including brain surgery, open-heart surgery, and cancer treatment, through this program in the past three years. In line with its policy of seeking cooperation with other bodies, the center has enlisted the help of a number of Italian regional authorities for the Saving Children project, and seventy Palestinian, Israeli, and Italian doctors attended a pediatric conference in Caesarea.

The Peres Center regards itself as "almost an Israeli-Palestinian Chamber of Commerce," fostering cooperation between exporters, information technology enterprises, textile plants, farmers, and others. Together with PalTrade, the Palestine Trade Center, which represents over 200 leading businesses in the Palestinian territories, the center has mapped out a program of economic and business cooperation between Israel and Palestine that would triple the Palestinian GDP within five to ten years and also benefit the Israeli economy.

Obviously, this scenario depends on political and security stability, which would be best achieved by a peace agreement, but the two organizations believe a start can already be made. Furthermore, business cooperation and trade will improve the economic situation and thus make a peace accord more likely.

Their impressive joint publication *The Untapped Potential* utilizes the work of researchers on both sides. The study carried out by PalTrade and the Peres Center reviews the recent past and makes recommendations for the future. Noting that the two Intifadas have had an extremely negative effect on trade between Israel and the Palestinian territories, the paper goes on to propose two "strategic decisions." The first is to work toward a final status agreement based on two states living side by side. The second proposes "friendly economic separation," which will involve a quasi-customs union with border-crossing arrangements to facilitate trade. "Hostile separation," involving economic disengagement with each side hunkering down behind the separation fence, will cause severe damage to both economies, states the publication.

The study is not merely theoretical. It deals with concrete issues, stating forcefully that the current situation at the crossing points between Israel and the Palestinian Authority territory is having a devastating impact on the Palestinian economy and is also harming Israel's economic situation.

In particular, the disastrous situation at the Karni crossing between Israel and Gaza is pinpointed. A continuous fence separates Israel and the Gaza Strip, with Karni as the only venue for transferring materials. The transport of goods has been constantly disrupted there, leading to the collapse of agriculture and industry in the Gaza Strip. Israeli factories, which used to operate in the Karni Industrial Park on the border, have fled the scene. With the completion of the separation fence between Israel and the West Bank, the Gaza situation could be replicated on that front also. The study demands the creation of a "business and trade-friendly border crossing regime."

The growth of inter-Arab trade in recent years, which benefited the other countries of the region, is recorded. Whereas Palestinian and Jordanian exports were similar in the mid 1990s, by 2005 Jordan was exporting ten times as much as the Palestinian territories. This dramatizes the harm caused to the Palestinian economy by the violence of recent years.

The study also points out that if it establishes good trading relations with its Palestinian neighbor, Israel will also benefit regionally, opening trading outlets all over the Middle East. An obvious branch that will improve in an environment of peace and cooperation is tourism, with huge potential benefits for both Israel and Palestine. Agriculture, textiles, handicrafts, and jewelry are other fields where cooperation and coordination can make these sectors complementary rather than competitive.

Lavishly illustrated with graphs and tables, *The Untapped Potential* makes specific recommendations for increasing the volume of trade and stepping up cooperation in many fields. The resulting increase in both the Israeli and Palestinian GDPs would result in the creation of hundreds of thousands of new jobs and transform the situation on the ground, improving the quality of life for both peoples.

Not content to wait for the improvement of the political situation, Pal-Trade and the Peres Center have embarked on a series of cooperation projects in agriculture, tourism, handicrafts, textiles, and information technology. Businesspersons meet regularly despite the difficulties of crossing over into each other's territory.

One of those working closely with the Peres Center is Saad Khatib, Pal-Trade's director of trade policy. The Jerusalem-born Khatib is a genial, stocky man, with a closely cut goatee beard and mustache. Not himself a businessman, he has a doctorate in International Trade Law from Ohio State. He worked for a Palestinian program on trade policy sponsored by the London School of Economics and has researched Israeli-Palestinian-European trade relations for the European Union. As a PalTrade official, he has been working with the Peres Center for four years and has found a common language with the center's economic team.

Over the past year, there have been fifteen face-to-face business meetings between Palestinians and Israelis, he notes. This resulted in establishing—or in some cases reestablishing—useful business relationships, which has been a useful stimulus, but much more needs to be done. "Frankly the atmosphere is scary," he observes, "because the Israeli government is talking about separation all the time. If this separation takes place, we are both going to lose a lot of potential benefits."

Right now, the situation does not encourage trade because Palestinians cannot enter Israel and Israelis cannot enter the Palestinian territories. If business partners don't meet, it is hard for them to do business. In addition, Palestinian businesses that do manage to maintain links with Israelis cannot guarantee deliveries, because they don't know whether the border is going to be open or not.

For example, if Karni, between the Gaza Strip and Israel, is closed for three or four days, the Palestinian side cannot meet its commitments and the Israeli business partner will switch to a Jordanian or Egyptian company. Five or six Palestinian factories have in fact moved out of Gaza into Egypt so that they can keep their promises to their Israeli partners. As they have hired Egyptian workers, this has resulted in a loss of jobs for the Palestinians. "It is ironic," notes Khatib. "We are so near to each other, and yet so far away. I even know of companies who have shipped goods to Israel from Gaza via Sinai, Alexandria, and Ashdod port! That's no way to do business!"

PalTrade and the Peres Center are preparing a specific list of proposals to facilitate cross-border operations. Hopefully it will influence decision makers on both sides. Despite the illogical situation, business relations continue. There is a lot of trade in stone and marble. Gaza furniture is still popular in Israel. Palestinian designers design furniture specifically for the Israeli market.

Processed food used to be a good export for the Palestinians, but today they cannot ensure that the food is kosher, because rabbis can no longer come across to supervise. This used to happen. Before the second Intifada, rabbis used to come to Nablus, Hebron, and Ramallah to inspect the factories and give kashrut certificates.

Agriculture is also a very promising field: Palestinian farmers export vegetables to Israel and Israeli farmers sell fruit to the Palestinians, but this produce is particularly vulnerable to delays at crossing points. "The situation is driving us apart," says Khatib sadly. "Both sides are looking for alternative outlets."

The small businesses on the Israeli side are specifically harmed, he says, because larger companies have more influence with the security forces and can get permits. For example, an Israeli *moshav* farmer selling milk products to the Palestinians is the one who suffers. The large Tnuva Company can exercise influence to get its produce through.

"When we had a meeting of textile manufacturers a few months ago, the Israelis suggested that we lobby their authorities jointly," he recalls. A particularly successful relationship existed in the past in the realm of high tech and computers, notes Khatib. However, Palestinian software producers, who used to work with Israeli companies, have started dealing with German, French, and Austrian companies because they find it easier to travel to Europe than to Tel Aviv. Last month representatives of some forty Israeli and Palestinian IT companies got together under the auspices of the Peres Center and PalTrade and reestablished contacts, but if they cannot meet regularly, it won't lead anywhere.

When the separation wall is completed, there are supposed to be five crossing points, notes Khatib, but unless they are run efficiently, it won't help. Karni is run based on quotas, but it ought to be run based on demand. The officials say how many trucks they can handle, but it is impossible to do business that way. The market should regulate the volume of trade, otherwise prices shoot up.

Khatib notes that after 9/11, the border between Canada and the United States was closed for a couple of weeks. Considering that a billion dollars worth of trade crosses that border every day it was clearly in everybody's interest to find a solution, so they worked out a system of prescheduling, risk assessment, and management, which now limits delays to only an hour or so. A similar system should be applied at the border between Israel and Palestine.

"We understand that security must be handled very carefully," concedes Khatib, "but with scanners, sniffing dogs, and efficient inspection procedures you can facilitate trade. At the moment, this is not happening.

"Despite all this, we have no choice but to be optimistic. We have to go on working together. I am a member of a think tank including Israeli, Palestinian, European, and American economists and businessmen. We are looking for ways to improve the situation. We are not going to give up."

Apart from businessmen, the Peres Center has brought together psychiatrists, psychologists, and social workers from both sides. Professionals from the Bethlehem Guidance and Training Center met recently with Israeli counterparts of the Geha Mental Health Center to discuss the treatment of children and adolescents. Two seminars for young political leaders in Cyprus and Jordan respectively were organized by the center together with the Palestinian Panorama NGO. The center has also financed the establishment of five new computer peace centers in four West Bank towns and Gaza. Even Israeli and Palestinian historians, who disagree about almost everything, have met under the auspices of the Arab Thought Forum and the Peres Center.

The center is also involved in education for peace projects in both Israeli and Palestinian schools and exchange visits between students on both sides, including football matches and other sporting activities. Distinguished athletes from abroad, such as Brazilian soccer star Ronaldo, have visited the twinned soccer schools project. There is also a twinned kindergarten program.

One of the more ambitious projects of the center is the construction of Peace House in Jaffa. The center deliberately chose the multicultural community adjoining Tel Aviv. Situated in a peace park, where large gatherings can take place, Peace House will include an exhibition hall, auditorium, computerized information center, and reference library.

At the start of this chapter, Ron Pundak, director of the Peres center for Peace, noted the paradox of the enormous scope of peace and cooperation activities currently taking place despite the situation of deadlock and confrontation the exists in the current reality. It is impossible not to query another paradox: the name of the center. Shimon Peres a Nobel peace laureate, who this year became President of Israel, is revered all over the world and hailed as a champion of peace, but many Israelis remember that as Defense Minister in the 1970s, Peres was a champion of the settlements. Indeed the major settlement enterprise in Samaria, the northern West Bank, was initiated and carried out under his auspices and with his support. More recently, Peres sat contentedly in the government of Ariel Sharon, which after being elected in 2001, pursued a policy of disproportionately strong military response to the second Intifada, effectively destroying the Oslo peace process.

Challenged on this, Ron Pundak phrases his answer carefully: "Shimon Peres is a man of vision, the architect of peace, who brought us the Oslo Agreement. In addition to that, of course, he is an energetic actor on Israel's political scene, and in that role, he might sometimes support—or at least go along with—problematic policies. The center that bears his name represents Peres the statesman, the tireless campaigner for peace and cooperation, the visionary of the new Middle East."

Epilogue

In the foregoing pages, we have visited only some of the projects where Jews and Arabs, Israelis and Palestinians, endeavor to coexist and cooperate. In appendix B, I have listed 56 projects, groups, organizations, and NGOs carrying out joint projects, all of them in Israel and the Palestinian territories. Another recent book, *Bridging the Divide*, lists one hundred NGOs active in the field. The Palestinian-Israeli Peace NGOs Forum has 114 registered members; the Mid-East Peace Links website, compiled by Kimberly Walker, records 151.

There can be little doubt that our confrontation is the most talked-about and the most worked-on issue in the world today, and yet the situation remains grave and deadlocked. I cannot say why this is so. I can only say with the utmost emphasis that it does not have to be so. Thousands of people in hundreds of projects are proving this every day.

Let no one misunderstand the message of this book. I have *not* said in the preceding pages that Jews and Arabs are coexisting amicably inside Israel and across the Israeli-Palestinian divide. What I am saying—indeed shouting—is that they *can* coexist, as proved by the fact that *some* of them do.

That many continue to work together, even in the least favorable conditions, is an eloquent testimony to the faith, courage, and goodwill of those individuals who reject stereotypes and refuse to accept the given "wisdom" of the inevitability of conflict and confrontation. The remarkable people about whom I have been privileged to write—Jews and Arabs, Israelis and Palestinians—who spend most of their waking hours working together, cooperating, playing, talking, creating, performing, and building, demonstrate what can be achieved.

Sadly, over the years, it is a different set of people who have set the tone: the terrorists and the trigger-happy soldiers, the suicide bombers and the wall builders, the inciters and the home destroyers, the land thieves and the uprooters of orchards have swaggered across our joint landscape for the past six years, and in fact long before that.

The choice is very clear: on the one side—Jewish and Arab—suspicion, distrust, and fatalism, leading to violence and brutality; on the other side – Jewish and Arab—hope, optimism, and goodwill, leading to friendship, partnership, and understanding.

The miraculous reality of a renewed Jewish nation must not exist as a walled ghetto, cut off from its surroundings. It should become an integral, organic part of its environment. The Zionist movement, the movement for Jewish national revival, has chalked up incredible achievements in the past hundred years, but it has not managed to reach a comprehensive peace with its Arab cocitizens and neighbors. We Jews have marched a million miles, but we are faltering over the last few yards.

Shuli Dichter, the codirector of Sikkuy, is quoted in this book as saying that achieving equality for Israel's Arab citizens is a "Zionist mission." I also quote David Lerner, the director of the Arava Institute, as saying, "The task of Zionism today is learning to live in peace with our Palestinian citizens and our Palestinian and Jordanian neighbors." In the chapter on ICAHD, I quote a Christian who came to rebuild a Palestinian home as approving my self-definition as a "Zionist" despite the fact that (in my previous book) I proposed a single state for Jews and Arabs, to be called the "State of Jerusalem." I do consider myself a Zionist. Along with Dichter and Lerner, I firmly believe that the task of Zionism today is to secure the integration of the Zionist enterprise into the Middle East.

The separation fence (or wall) that is currently being constructed is a catastrophe. Geographically illogical, aesthetically revolting, environmentally harmful, politically idiotic, and economically disastrous, it does not even provide the military and demographic security for which it was ostensibly designed. Even if it ran along the 1967 border, it would be a mistake. Its current route facilitates a land grab that only benefits marginal Jewish groups while causing frustration and unnecessary hardship for thousands of Palestinians. At every step of my journey, I witnessed how the separation barrier—and the mentality that it represents—works against reconciliation and partnership.

Jews and Arabs are inextricably entangled in this land. We cannot be torn apart, and all attempts at disentangling us will damage both of us beyond repair. A realistic route for a fence or wall that will separate us does not exist. While I continue to think that the simplest and most logical solution is a multicultural state for all the communities of Israel and Palestine, I have been compelled to realize that it does not command significant support at this time. I contend, however, that this is not the central issue.

It does not matter whether my vision is implemented, or whether the so-called "two-state solution" is the final model. The difference between one state with autonomy for its various communities, and two states closely cooperating in security, economics, business, development, energy, transportation, labor, and the environment is not significant. The vital thing is to eschew violence, separation, and hostility, and to replace them with dialogue, coexistence, and cooperation.

Selected List of Organizations Currently Engaging in Coexistence, Cooperation, Partnership, and Dialogue between Jews and Arabs in Israel, Palestine, and the Region

(Does not include groups based in the United States and Europe.)

Abraham Fund: www.mpdn.org/abraham.htm
Adam Institute: www.adaminstitute.org.il
All for Peace Radio: www.allforpeace.org
All Nations Café: www.geocities.com/AllNationsCafe
Alternative Information Center (AIC): www.alternativenews.org
Alternative Palestinian Agenda: www.ap-agenda.org/initiative.htm
Anarchists against the Wall: www.awalls.org
Arabic-Hebrew Theater: www.arab-hebrew-theatre.org.il
Arava Institute for Environmental Studies: www.arava.org/new
Arik Institute for Reconciliation, Tolerance, and Peace: www.arikpeace.org
Association of Forty: www.assoc40.org
Bat Shalom: www.batshalom.org
Beit Hagefen: www.beit-hagefen.com
Betzelem: www.betselem.org
Bitterlemons: www.bitterlemons.org
Brit Shalom: www.britshalom.org
Bustan L'Shalom: www.bustan.org
Center for Jewish-Arab Economic Development (CJAED): www.cjaed.org.il
Challenge: www.challenge-mag.com
Crossing Borders: www.crossingborder.org
Families Forum/Parents Circle: www.theparentscircle.org
Freddie Krivine Foundation: www.freddiekrivinefoundation.com
Friends of the Earth Middle East (FoEME): www.foeme.org
Friendship Village: friendvill2.homestead.com/Projects.html

Givat Haviva: www.givathaviva.org.il
Hamoked for the Defense of the Individual: www.hamoked.org.il
Hand in Hand bilingual schools: www.handinhand12.org
Hope Flowers School: www.mideastweb.org/hopeflowers
Interfaith Encounter Association: www.interfaith-encounter.org
Interns for Peace: www.mpdn.org/interns.htm
Interreligious Coordinating Council: www.icci.org.il
Israel Committee against House Demolitions (ICAHD):
    www.icahd.org/eng
Israel-Palestine Center for Research and Information IPCRI:
    www.ipcri.org
Ir Shalem/Ir Amim: www.ir-amim.org.il
Just Vision: www.justvision.org
Middleway—Shvil Zahav: www.middleway.org
Negev Coexistence Forum: www.dukium.org
Neve Shalom/Wahat al-Salam: www.nswas.com
Olive Tree movement: www.o-t-m.org/drupal
One Voice: www.onevoicemovement.org/wps/portal
Open House, Ramle: www.openhouse.org.il
Palestinian Center for Conflict Resolution and Reconciliation:
    www.mideastweb.org
Palestinians and Israelis for Nonviolence: pinv.org
Palestine-Israel Journal: www.pij.org
Parents' Circle: see Families Forum
Peace Child Israel: www.mideastweb.org/peacechild
People's Voice: www.mifkad.org.il
Peres Center for Peace: www.peres-center.org
Re'ut Sadaka: www.bkluth.de/reut/MAIN.html
Seeds of Peace: www.seedsofpeace.org
Shemesh: www.shemesh.org
Sikkuy: www.sikkuy.org.il
Sulha: www.sulha.com
Ta'ayush: www.taayush.org
White Flag, Palestinian/Israeli band: www.salam/shalom.net/Whiteflag
    .html
Windows—Channels for Communication: www.win-peace.org

Selected Bibliography

Akawi, Yasser, ed. *From Communal Strife to Global Struggle*. Jerusalem: Alternative Information Center, 2004.

Alpher, Yossi. *And the Wolf Shall Dwell with the Wolf* [in Hebrew]. Tel Aviv: Kibbutz Meuchad, 2001.

Armstrong, Karen. *A History of God*. London: Heinmann, 1993.

———. *Islam: A Short History*. London: Weidenfeld & Nicholson, 2000.

Bar-On, Mordechai. *In Pursuit of Peace*. Washington: U.S. Institute of Peace, 1996.

Ben-Ami, Shlomo. *Scars of War, Wounds of Peace*. London: Weidenfeld, 2005.

Bentwich, Norman. *For Zion's Sake*. Philadelphia: Jewish Publication Society, 1954.

Ben-Gurion, David. *My Talks with Arab Leaders*. Jerusalem: Keter, 1973.

Brockelmann, Carl. *History of the Islamic Peoples*. New York: Putnam, 1947.

Carey Roane, ed. *The New Intifada*. London: Verso, 2001.

Chelouche, Yosef Eliahu. *Reminiscences of My Life* [in Hebrew]. Tel Aviv: Alexandrovich, 1933.

Cohen, Aharon. *Israel and the Arab World*. New York: Funk & Wagnals, 1970.

Eliachar, Eli. *Living with Jews*. London: Weidenfeld & Nicholson, 1983.

Eliav, Arie Lova. *Israel's Ladder* [in Hebrew]. Tel Aviv: Zmora Bitan, 1976.

———. *Land of the Hart*. Philadelphia: Jewish Publication Society, 1976.

Feuerverger, Grace. *Oasis of Dreams*. New York: RoutledgeFalmer, 2001.

Gavron, Assaf. *CrocAttack* [in Hebrew]. Tel Aviv: Zmora Bitan, 2006.

Gavron, Daniel. *Saul Adler*. Rehovot: Balaban, 1997.

———. *The Other Side of Despair*. Boulder: Rowman & Littlefield, 2004.

Halabi, Rabah, ed. *Israeli and Palestinian Identities in Dialogue*. New Brunswick, NJ: Rutgers University Press, 2004.

Halper, Jeff. *Obstacles to Peace*. Jerusalem: PalMap, 2005.

Hass, Amira. *Drinking the Sea in Gaza* [in Hebrew]. Tel Aviv: Kibbutz Meuhad, 1996.

Hirst, David. *The Gun and the Olive Branch*. London: Faber, 1977.

Hitti, Philip K. *The Arabs*. Chicago: Gateway, 1956.

Hussar, Bruno. *When the Cloud Lifted*. Dublin: Veritas, 1983.
Hroub, Khaled. *Hamas: A Beginner's Guide*. London: Pluto, 2006.
Kaufman, Edy et al., eds. *Bridging the Divide*. Boulder: Lynne Rienner, 2006.
Karabell, Zachary. *Peace Be Upon You*. New York: Alfred A. Knopf, 2007.
Kashua, Sayed. *Arabs Dancing* [in Hebrew]. Tel Aviv: Modan, 2002.
———. *Let It Be Morning* [in Hebrew]. Tel Aviv: Keter, 2004.
Lewis, Bernard. *The Arabs in History*. London: Hutchinson, 1950.
Marx, Emmanuel. *Bedouin of the Negev* Manchester: Manchester University Press, 1967.
Morris, Benny. *Righteous Victims*. New York: Random House, 1999.
Payes, Shany. *Palestinian NGOs in Israel*. London: Tauris Academic Studies, 2005.
Rosenblum, Doron. *Israeli Blues* [in Hebrew]. Tel Aviv: Am Oved, 1996.
Roth, Cecil. *Short History of the Jewish People*. London: East & West Library, 1948.
Shehadeh, Raja. *The Third Way*. London: Quartet Books, 1982.
———. *Strangers in the House*. Vermont: Steerforth Press, 2002.
———. *When the Bulbul Stopped Singing*. London: Profile Books, 2003.
Shepherd Naomi. *The Zealous Intruders*. London: Collins, 1987.
Shlaim, Avi. *Collusion Across the Jordan*. Oxford: Clarendon, 1988.
Shuval, Hillel, and Hassan Dwiek, eds. *Water for Life in the Middle East*. 2 vols. Jerusalem: IPCRI, 2006.
Storrs, Ronald. *Orientations*. London: Nicholson & Watson, 1939.
Vester, Bertha Spafford. *Our Jerusalem*. Jerusalem: Ariel, 1988.
Wallace, John and Janet. *Still Small Voices*. New York: Harcourt, 1989.
Warschawski, Michel. *On the Border*. London: Pluto, 2005.
Zeitlin, Rose. *Henrietta Szold*. New York: Dial Press, 1952.

Newspapers, Journals, and Websites

www.bitterlemons.org
Crossing Borders, Givat Haviva, Jerusalem, Masar
Haaretz, Tel Aviv
Ha'ayin Hashvi'i [in Hebrew], Tel Aviv
International Herald Tribune
www.justvision.org
Maariv [in Hebrew], Tel Aviv
News From Within, Jerusalem
Palestine-Israel Journal, Jerusalem
Windows [in Hebrew and Arabic], Tel Aviv
Yediot Aharonot [in Hebrew], Tel Aviv

Index

Abu-Rabiya, Safa, 103–104, 112–114
Al-Aksa Intifada, *See* Intifada 2000
Alami, Mussa, 93
Arab Israelis, *See* Israeli Arabs
    (Palestinians)
Arabic-Hebrew Theater, 117, 127–131
Arafat, Yasser, 96, 97, 100–102
Arava Institute for Environmental
    Studies, 139–148
Ashkenazi-Sephardi differences, 90–92
Association for Civil Rights in Israel
    (ACRI), 7, 10

Barenboim, Daniel, 117
Begin, Menachem, 98, 99
Beit Hagefen, 99, 164, 171–175
Ben-Gurion, David, 92–93
Ben-Gurion University, 112–114, 140,
    142, 143
Betzelem, 7, 10, 100
Bible, xvi, xvii, 40, 87, 141
bilingual schools, *See* Hand in Hand
Bitter Lemons, 161–164
Border Police (policeman), 7, 74, 79
British Mandate, xvi, 32, 92, 94

Civic Action Groups (Sikkuy), 108–110
civil rights, *See* human rights

coexistence, 12, 42, 52, 81, 102, 106,
    114, 195

Dayan, Moshe, 97
disengagement (unilateral withdrawal)
    from Gaza, xiii, xviii, 103, 106–107,
    111
donkeys, *See* SHADH

Eliav, Lova, 96–97
environment, xv, 137–148, 153, 188,
    See also Arava Institute
European Union (EU), 23, 31, 191

Geneva Accord, 163
Givat Haviva, 99, 164, 165–171, 174
Goldmann, Nahum, 97
Gush Emunim, 98

al-Haq, Law in the Service of Man, 10
Hadassah Hospital (Mount Scopus,
    Jerusalem), 73–85, 93, 188
Hamas, 44, 154, 160, 161, 164
Hand in Hand bilingual schools,
    47–55, 66
Hebrew University, 11, 32, 42, 49, 59,
    75, 80
Holocaust, xvi, 6, 93, 94, 160, 169

honor killings, 69, 80, 129
Hope Flowers School, 180–182
human rights, 1–13, 115
Hussar, Bruno, 58–61, 66
Husseini, Haj Amin, 93

Independence Day (Israeli), 48, 66,
     169, 178
interfaith, 172–173, 174–175,
     177–185, 188
Interfaith Encounter Association (IEA),
     179–185
Intifada 1987, xvii, 6, 7, 9, 43, 81, 100,
     101
Intifada 2000, 15, 19, 50, 57, 62, 103,
     106, 119, 152, 180
Islam, 87, 88
Islamic Jihad, 4
Israeli Arabs (Palestinians), 11, 16, 57,
     94–95, 112–114, 166
Israeli Committee Against House
     Demolitions (ICAHD), 25–34, 35, 47
Israel Defense Forces (IDF), xvii, 3, 4,
     5, 7, 8–11, 18, 20, 30, 37, 42, 57,
     73, 98, 169; Civil Administration of,
     27, 30; service in, 64, 71, 124, 162,
     166; refusal to serve in, 28, 99, 100
Israeli occupation, xvi, 13, 31, 44,
     159–160; settlements (settlers), xvii,
     xix, 38, 40, 73, 79, 96, 98–99,
     102–103, 160, 178–180
Israel-Palestine Center for Research and
     Information (IPCRI), 100–101,
     148–155

Jerusalem, xv, xix, 151–152

Kedem, 177–179, 183
Koran, 87, 141, 184

Moked for the Defense of the
     Individual, 3–13, 47, 100

Nakba, 48, 66, 169
Neve Shalom/Wahat al-Salam, 49–50,
     54–55, 57–71; School for Peace,
     66–71, 99
New Israel Fund, 6–7

occupation, *See* Israeli occupation
olive (trees, oil), xviii, 38–46, 47
Olive Tree Movement, 34, 36
Olmert, Ehud, 50, 110
Or Commission, 106–108, 114
Oslo Agreement (Accords, peace
     process, years), xv, xvii, xviii, 9, 18,
     81, 101, 102, 151, 159, 188
Ottoman Empire, xviii, 26, 88, 89,

Palestinian Authority (PA), xix, xx, 5,
     21, 190
Palestine-Israel Journal, 155, 157–161
Palestine Liberation Organization
     (PLO), xix, 9, 95–100, 101–103
Palestinian refugees (refugee camps),
     xvii, xviii, 1, 94–95, 150
Palestinian uprising, *See* Intifada 1987
PalTrade, 189–192
partition of Palestine, UN plan, xvi,
     xvii, 94, 100; British plan, xviii,
     93–94
Peace Now, 98–99, 100
Peres, Shimon, 188, 193
Peres Center for Peace, 185, 187–193

Rabbis for Human Rights, 32, 38
Rabin, Yitzhak, 100, 101–102
refugees *See* Palestinian refugees
Religion, *See* interfaith
roadblocks (check posts, checkpoints),
     1, 2, 9, 20, 45, 83, 129, 182, 190

Sadat, Anwar, xvii, 98
Safe Haven for Donkeys in the Holy
     Land (SHADH), 133–138
Sephardi Jews, 89, 99; differences with
     Ashkenazi Jews, *See* Ashkenazi-
     Sephardi differences
separation barrier (wall, fence), xvi, 21,
     25, 65, 83–84, 141, 151–152, 163,
     190, 196
settlements, *See* Israeli ocupation
Shamir, Shimon, 107–108
Sharon, Ariel, 16, 99, 103, 110, 124
Shin Bet security service, 3, 4, 182
Sikkuy, 104–117
Sinai Campaign, xvii

Six Day War, xvii, 58–59, 73, 95–96, 159, 164
suicide bombs (bombers), 17, 19, 53, 75, 169

Ta'ayush, 37, 47
Tantur, 20–21, 152
Tennis Coexistence Project, 117, 119–123
two-state solution, xv, xvi, 154, 163, 197

Weizmann, Chaim, 92–93
White Flag, 117, 124–127
Windows—Channels for Communication, 3, 5, 15–23, 125

Yom Kippur War, 97

Zionism (Zionist), xvi, 28, 30, 39, 84, 88–94, 106, 116, 139, 147, 167, 196